Herb Gardening in Five

Seasons

To Abigail

may herbs bring

joy in all seasons

Adelma Grenier Simmons

HERB GARDENING
in Five Seasons

ADELMA GRENIER SIMMONS

Drawings by Kathleen Bourke

HAWTHORN BOOKS
A division of E.P. Dutton
New York

Library of Congress Catalog Card Number: 75-130732

ISBN: 0-525-48448-5

22   21   20   19   18   17   16   15

Herbs are Forever—and For All

Happy is the herb gardener through all the seasons and the years. His is a life enriched with rare fragrances to be enjoyed at dawn and dusk and in the heat of noon. It is an esthetic experience to watch the patterns, textures, and shades of a gray-and-green garden develop through the changing seasons. Our latent instinct for design is aroused and we amuse ourselves by arranging these muted tones and pleasing textures in garden rows, swirls, and knots. The householder's pride and pleasure can be satisfied in the rich harvest of green leaves and savory seeds for seasoning and in the everlasting foliage and blossoms for dried bouquets.

Spring, summer, autumn, winter, and Christmas—all have added meaning now, for to each season the garden yields a special taste and presents a picture quite its own. From the bleakness of early spring, when the pointed leaves of sorrel and the green spears of Egyptian onion pierce the frozen ground, to the richness of October when gray artemisias are ghostly signs against the autumn tapestry— and far into the winter, your herb garden will continue. Long after the first frosts have destroyed your neighbors' floral borders, coral-leafed santolinas, the wrinkled rosettes of horehound, and the wooly-soft lamb's-ears will yield bouquets, wreaths, and swags to those who will walk in the cold of this melancholy season.

Fortunately the study of herbs touches all aspects of our lives, at all ages, under all conditions. What was a rigorous physical experience in youth and middle age may become an absorbing study for the armchair gardener who, halted in activities by age or physical handicap, can still enjoy a fascinating world of legend and history.

Without moving far from a sunny window-sill garden or a cozy seat by the fire, you may plant an herb garden that knows no size, but may be as large or as small as your imagination reaches. In reality, you can derive hours of study and pleasure from a small collection of herbs grown in a window box, or a garden can be made outdoors in miniature—green and growing in a 24-inch circle. In the active days of youth, plan and plant your gardens, sow your seeds, and employ your harvests. Make seasonings, vinegars, mustards, jellies, decorations, potpourri, sweet jars, and pomanders tied with herbs of meaning. In later years, open up herbals and old garden books to study with amusement, tolerance, and not a little awe the wonderful history of herbs. Trace their uses from pagan ritual to Christian ceremony, their inclusion in early medicines, in witchcraft, in song and story until their enchantment lays a gentle hold on your daily life.

For you, herbs will not be history only, but a living part of your daily life. They will be green medicines, fragrances, seasoning magic, soft tones and muted colors, textures pleasant to the touch and names that are good to hear and bear much repeating. In the many ways these plants touch our lives and enrich them, in their venerable past, exciting present, and useful future, they offer proof that truly, herbs are forever.

Many thanks are due Elvin McDonald, Editorial Director of McDonald-Bourke Associates, for his careful evaluation and coordination of my material; Kathleen Bourke for her exquisite drawings and fine interpretation of my quick garden sketches; Gloria Bamberger and Herman F. Marshall, photographers; Dorcas Brigham for help and inspiration in my early days with herbs and for the verification of botanical names and varieties in this book; Mrs. Dutton, of Garrison House Gardens, who furnished the very first herbs for my garden and was patient with my enthusiasm and ignorance; Mittie Arnold and Margaret Thomas, of Greene Herb Gardens, always generous with information and encouragement; Julian Eddy, landscape architect, who presented our herbs in charming gardens and displays at many flower shows and enticed us into larger fields; Caprilands' staff, Rose Roberts, once a nurse in our household, who now presides over the kitchen, Leona Havens who came to us long ago as a guest and stayed to become my valued shop assistant, Eddie Roberts and Micky Synal who help in house and garden; my friends in the Herb Society of America and the Coventry Garden Club; and the little group of earnest seekers of herbal knowledge who met here each week for many years. To all of these, and to many more I send my herbal gift of rosemary—for grateful remembrance.

Finally, my sincere appreciation to Helen Van Pelt Wilson for her persistent belief in our book—*HERB GARDENING IN FIVE SEASONS*—for her labors over my recipes and the final editing of all material.

ADELMA GRENIER SIMMONS

Caprilands
Coventry, Connecticut
January, 1964

This book is fondly dedicated to

My husband who designed my first herb garden and arranged my collection of herbs in order and in beauty;

and

Dr. and Mrs. Robert Cleverdon—Bob and Maggie—for their friendship, encouragement and work on the first little books which grew into HERB GARDENING IN FIVE SEASONS.

The Wide World of the Herbalist

Through the centuries in which man has explored and recorded his findings in the world of herbs, funds of information have widened and accumulated. Precious books are available for study in libraries, and some reprints of ancient volumes may be purchased at nominal prices.

Herb lore was collected by men and women in all walks of life—medicine men and sincere scholars can be contrasted with charlatans who snatched at every herbal straw to further their own fortunes; pious monks and monastic physicians, working with body as well as soul, opposed magicians and so-called witches who reveled in the dark world of ignorance and superstition.

Great poets like Virgil wrote about herbs, and peasants made memorable verses about them or told and retold tales that have become our folklore. Kings experimented with herbal medicines, and even the august Charlemagne gave orders for the planting of herbs and vegetables. His is probably the much-quoted definition of herbs, "The friend of the physician and the pride of cooks."

All of us who study, write, or talk about herbs, or grow them, owe a debt to the past, for herbal history invests even our most unprepossessing plants with an aura of romantic legend. Quotations from herbals form part of

mòst writers' material. The sayings of men like Dioscorides, Pliny the Elder, Nicholas Culpeper, and John
Gerard are our precious heritage. Though their words
are both fact and fancy, they give us a feeling of continuity and demonstrate the timelessness of herbal lore.

We do not stand alone in the wide world of herbs for
there are many great gardeners there to keep us company—men like Francis Bacon, essayist, planner and
planter of gardens for gentlemen, whose words I recall
while walking through the reddening strawberry borders
of my garden in fall, "Strawberry leaves dying yield a
most cordial smell." William Lawson, who lived in the
seventeenth century, took the country housewife's garden to heart, and today seems to whisper over our shoul-
der and advise, "Set slips in May and they grow aye."
He also gives us a vision of his ideal garden that carries
good advice and is charming to recall: "Large walks,
broad and long, close and open like the Tempe groves in
Thessaly, raised with gravel and sand, having seats and
banks of camomile."

From this world of herbal information great names
rise out of the mist of centuries. In days when there
was little knowledge, these men studied and became
sources of reference for their times. Brief notes about
some of them are included here. Such a short account
must leave out some important names, and I hope you
will forgive my omissions.

The history of herbs starts five thousand years before
the Christian era. The ancient Chaldeans, Chinese, Egyptians, and Assyrians had schools of herbalists. Their
learning came in precious scrolls and by word of mouth
through teachers, necromancers, and astrologers to the
Greeks who through their philosophers and historians,
particularly Aristotle and Plato, and their physicians
Theophrastus and Hippocrates, advanced the use of herbs
in literature, history, and medicine.

It was in the first century that Dioscorides became
famous in botany and medicine. A Greek from Asia
Minor, he traveled with the Roman legions, probably as

an army doctor. He studied the healing herbs of the world he knew and recorded his findings in *Materia Medica*, which dealt with more than five hundred plants. His original work was destroyed, but a Byzantine copy dated about 512 A.D. survived the years and has been studied in facsimile by many generations. In the sixteenth and seventeenth centuries Dioscorides was the most widely read of all authors. His popularity was due in part to the enlargement of his work by Pierandrea Mattioli who also embellished the text with magnificent woodcuts. A condensed edition is available today and makes fascinating reading.

Pliny the Elder, a contemporary of Dioscorides, wrote of many things in his *Natural History*—both the practical and the fabulous. Through his pages roam birds, animals, and plants that never were; there are cures that surely must have killed; and magic parades as science, accepted and practiced for generations. Pliny met his death in the destruction of Pompeii, refusing to leave his research, his books, and home. My volumes of Pliny are old, hard to read, and falling to pieces, but they are so filled with interest and discoveries that I feel time with them is well spent.

After Pliny the succeeding centuries brought us the period of monastery herbals. The cultivation of plants in the quiet world of the cloister produced many treatises on growing herbs and vegetables. The Benedictine Rule included daily work and gardening as important in the religious life. Plans of the monastery of St. Gall still present a graphic record of the period.

It is in the sixteenth and seventeenth centuries that we come to the English herbals that are best known and most frequently quoted. Here the names of Bancke (1525), *The grete herball* (1526), and Turner (1568) lead us to the most quoted herbal of all, John Gerard's *The Herball or Generall Historie of Plantes* published in 1597. Gerard was a barber-surgeon whose greatest interest was gardening. Fashionable Holborn in England was the place where he cultivated the long list of plants

that furnished subject matter for his pen and a garden
for the study, wonder, and admiration of his contempo-
raries. While the years and advance of science may have
taken some luster from Gerard's name (his tall tales of
"trees bearing geese" and the "Barnakle tree" can scarcely
be credited as scientific accounts), he is still read for
many truths that bear repeating. His book is richly illustrated. Much of its content was drawn from a manuscript left by a Dr. Priest whose work was not acknowl-
edged. For Gerard was condemned by a later publisher,
but his own abilities were so great that no ancient accu-
sation has been able to change his standing. Sometimes
to forget the awfulness of the atom, I follow his advice,
"Who would therefore looke dangerously up at Planets,
that might safely looke down at Plants?"

John Parkinson was Herbalist to Charles I and is remembered for a book published in 1629 called *Paradisi
in Sole Paradisus Terrestris*. Later he produced a much
larger work called the *Theatrum botanicum: the theatre
of plants, or, an herball of a large extent*.

Astrology and the herbalist have ever seemed to go
together, but in the seventeenth century the vogue of
tying each herb to a star was at its height and Nicholas
Culpeper (1616-1654) made the most of the fad. He
established a practice as astrologer and physician at
Spitalfields and caused great indignation among medical
men of his day by publishing *A Physicall Directory*, an
unauthorized translation of the *Pharmacopoeia* issued
by the College of Physicians. In spite of, or perhaps
because of, the controversies that Culpeper caused, he
became the most popular writer of his day and still finds
enthusiastic readers. His herbals went into many edi-
tions and often appear in old bookshops.

*   *   *   *   *

Is it "urb" or "herb"? Do we drop the *h* or pronounce
it? This is a question which can part close friends and
tear societies asunder. New Englanders tend to follow

the old pronunciation that came from the early settlers' word, "yarb," while from New York state on west, you may be accused of being cockney if the *h* is dropped. Your choice is open to either (or *eye*ther) pronunciation. What is important is to use these plants, to grow them, and to learn about them, however you pronounce "herb."

My book is divided into five seasons because herbs are cultivated largely in areas where the five seasons are evident and guide gardening practice. Here at Caprilands, we emphasize the changes of the year by festivals, using the seasonal plants in decoration and serving traditional, seasonal foods at the table. It has been our pleasure to revive many early European customs and add them to our New England ones. In each season, we tell the stories connected with its special observances, serve the foods of that turn of the year, and decorate the house accordingly. We change rugs, draperies, pictures, and accessories five times a year, for we make a separate season of Christmas. In this way, we have a setting appropriate in texture, symbols, and color to the time of the year. I have always been a collector and have found it difficult to part with anything. The older, the more worn my possessions are, the greater their value to me. To use this accumulation all at once is impossible, so changes of season fit my life perfectly.

Many years of herb gardening at Caprilands have made hundreds of herbs important to me. It was a difficult task to limit the plants in the Dictionary. All seemed vital. To make an intelligent selection has caused much sifting of values. Herbs of greatest usefulness here at Caprilands have been placed in separate chapters— scented geraniums, thymes, mints, and artemisias. Sweet woodruff is such an integral part of spring that I felt you would rather find it in its special place than in the Dictionary. *Alchemilla vulgaris*, beautiful Lady's Mantle, is a part of the Summer Diary. The botanical and common names of the herbs are cross-referenced in the Index to guide you in finding plants for which you seek information.

Contents

Preface: HERBS ARE FOREVER—AND FOR ALL   v

Introduction: THE WIDE WORLD OF THE
             HERBALIST   ix

List of Illustrations   xvii

PART I   WINTER DIARY
1. Plans for an Herb Garden   3
2. How to Grow Herbs Indoors   18
3. The Scented Geraniums   27
4. Herb Teas and Tea Parties   43

PART II   SPRING DIARY
5. Planting the Herb Garden   54
6. The Versatile Thymes   64
7. May Day Party   78

PART III   SUMMER DIARY
8. Herb Gardens in Summer   95
9. The Mighty Mints   101
10. Plans for an Herb Show   114
11. Harvesting and Drying Herbs   120
12. Midsummer Party   135

PART IV   AUTUMN DIARY
13. Winter Protection for Herbs   147
14. The Artemisias   152
15. Harvest Party   168

PART V   CHRISTMAS DIARY
            16. Capturing the World of Fragrance   179
            17. Wreaths from the Herb Garden   193
            18. How to Make Pomander Balls   201
            19. Christmas at Caprilands—Legends
                and Recipes   207

PART VI   DICTIONARY OF FIFTY SELECTED HERBS
            Appendix A   LISTS OF HERBS FOR READY
                         REFERENCE   325
            Appendix B   HOW TO PRONOUNCE HERB
                         NAMES   334
            Index   339

Illustrations

LINE DRAWINGS

NAME   PAGE

SCENTED GERANIUMS   30
Pelargonium crispum 'Prince Rubert'
Pelargonium scarboroviae 'Strawberry-scented'
Pelargonium capitatum 'Attar of Roses'
Pelargonium quercifolium 'Staghorn Oak'
Pelargonium tomentosum
Pelargonium 'Clorinda'
Pelargonium odoratissimum 'Apple'
Pelargonium 'Dr. Livingston'

THYMES   70
Thymus serpyllum vulgaris (lemon thyme)
Thymus serpyllum (mother-of-thyme)
Thymus serpyllum aureus ('Golden Lemon')
Thymus serpyllum argenteus ('Silver Lemon')
Thymus vulgaris 'Narrowleaf French'
Thymus lanicaulis (wooly-stemmed thyme)

SWEET WOODRUFF   79
Asperula odorata

LADY'S MANTLE   92
Alchemilla vulgaris

MINTS   107
Mentha spicata (spearmint)
Mentha citrata (orange mint)
Mentha rotundifolia variegata (pineapple mint)
Mentha piperita (peppermint)
Mentha rotundifolia (apple mint)
Mentha pulegium (pennyroyal)

ARTEMISIAS   155
  Artemisia dracunculus sativus (tarragon)
  Artemisia abrotanum (southernwood)
  Artemisia ludoviciana albula or 'Silver King'
  Artemisia vulgaris (mugwort)
  Artemisia absinthium (wormwood)
Achillea millefolium (common yarrow)   224
Aconitum napellus (aconite or monkshood)   226
Agrimonia eupatoria (agrimony)   228
Ajuga reptans (bugleweed)   230
Allium cepa ascalonicum (shallot)   232
Allium cepa viviparum (Egypt or top onion)   234
Allium sativum (garlic)   236
Allium schoenoprasum (chives)   238
Anethum graveolens (dill)   240
Angelica archangelica   242
Anthemis nobilis (English camomile)   244
Anthriscus cerefolium (chervil)   246
Borago officinalis (borage)   248
Carum carvi (caraway)   250
Chenopodium botrys (ambrosia)   252
Chrysanthemum balsamita var. *tanacetoides* (costmary)   254
Chrysanthemum parthenium (feverfew)   256
Coriandrum sativum (coriander)   258
Foeniculum vulgare (fennel)   260
Galium verum (Our Lady's bedstraw)   262
Hyssopus officinalis (hyssop)   264
Lamium maculatum (cobbler's bench)   266
Laurus nobilis (bay)   268
Lavandula officinalis (lavender)   270
  Leaf detail of *Lavandula multifida*
  Leaf detail of *Lavandula dentata*
Levisticum officinale (lovage)   272
Linum usitatissimum (flax)   274
Lippia citriodora (lemon verbena)   276
Majorana hortensis (sweet marjoram)   278
Marrubium vulgare (horehound)   280
Melissa officinalis (lemon balm)   282
Monarda didyma (beebalm)   284

Myrrhis odorata (sweet cicely)   286
Nepeta cataria (catnip)   288
Ocimum basilicum (sweet basil)   290
Origanum vulgare (oregano)   292
Petroselinum crispum (parsley)   294
Pimpinella anisum (anise)   296
Rosmarinus officinalis (rosemary)   298
Rumex scutatus (French sorrel)   300
Ruta graveolens (rue)   302
    Detail of seed cases
Salvia officinalis and variety 'Tricolor'   304
Sanguisorba minor (salad burnet)   306
Santolina chamaecyparissus (lavender-cotton)   308
Satureja hortensis (summer savory)   310
Satureja montana (winter savory)   312
Stachys olympica (lamb's-ears)   314
Tanacetum vulgare (tansy)   316
    Detail of *Tanacetum vulgare* flowers
    Leaf detail of *Tanacetum vulgare* var. *crispum* (fernleaf tansy)
Teucrium lucidum (germander)   318
Valeriana officinalis (garden heliotrope)   320
Viola tricolor (Johnny-jump-up or heart's-ease)   322

GARDEN PLANS

1   Butterfly Garden   5
2   Dooryard Garden   8
3   Garden of Herbs for Drying   10
4   Wheel Garden   12
5   Garden of Geraniums   14
6   Stained-Glass Window Garden   16

PHOTOGRAPHS

Lemon Verbena in a Tub   38
Entrance to Caprilands   55
Author's Dooryard Garden   57
Entryway Garden at Caprilands   59
Border at Caprilands   65
A Kitchen Garden   81
A Butterfly Garden   93
Garden of Esther Larson   98
Drying Herbs at Caprilands   122
Southernwood at Caprilands   161
Herb and Spice Wreath   195
Pomanders and Advent Wreath   197
Door Swag at Caprilands   208

Herb Gardening in Five Seasons

Winter Diary

A time to dream
A time to plan,
Time essential
To every man.
—A. G. S.

The quiet aloneness of winter has a special charm for the herb gardener, and I confess this season is my delight. Through the restless, rushing hours of spring, and the long days of summer that begin at dawn and end with weeding in the twilight, I find myself looking back at the peace of the past winter, and forward to the next one. The winter landscape, bare and stringent, reveals a beauty of form and line that is not visible in spring and summer.

Through the small-paned windows of my northwest writing room, the winter landscape stretches toward the surrounding woodland. Here and there are patches of seed herbs, brown and disorderly, but food for birds in the cold days ahead. Clumps of perilla stand red-brown against the snow. They have furnished seeds for some time now, and the birds' appreciation of them has increased this plant's value to me so that I excuse its prolific growth. In the fields there are seeding southernwoods and oreganos with brown blossoms still fragrant. Some were forgotten, others were left as food for small wild animals.

As I look over my typewriter and the herbals opened to the light of the north window, I see through the limbs

1

of a gnarled old elm the flashing blue-gray of a nuthatch in a corner of the Saints Garden. There, against a gray chestnut fence, mounted on a huge elm stump, a statue of Fiacre, the gardeners' patron saint, protects the frozen borders of rue, sage, germander, and santolina. To assist him we have covered the area with salt hay, a most effective blanket as it contains no seeds; just to make sure that roots are not exposed in thawing weather, we will cover them again with Christmas tree boughs after Twelfthnight. On the stove a pot of maté, a holly tea from South America which is as stimulating as coffee without its ill effects, adds to my pleasure in the winter's quietness.

It is in winter that gardens grow their best—on paper —while the snow drifts through plant rows, covers walks, and fills in stone walls. Garden books are in pleasant heaps by the fireside, and pencils trace black lines, guides for green hedges, fragrant borders, and clumps for emphasis. One garden plan begets another, the planning as fascinating as chess.

But there's much more to be done in winter. The sixth of January arrives and Epiphany sees the last lighting of the Christmas candles and the bustle of removing greens. Traditionally boxwood then appears in decorations, a green that lasts almost indefinitely. I turn now to the shed stored with dried materials. I am eager to use them in arrangements that will fill the void in rooms so recently made festive by Christmas greenery and glitter.

1. Plans for an Herb Garden

And all without were walkes and alleys dight
With divers trees enranged in even rankes
And here and there were pleasant arbours pight
And shadie seats, and sundry flowering bankes
To sit and rest the walkers' weary shankes.
                                    —Edmund Spenser

Winter is the time to enjoy the planning of an herb garden, and these plans become increasingly ambitious with the reading of books, magazines, and catalogs. As the snows melt and the first balmy days of spring draw the gardener out of doors, the task ahead is brought nearer. Obstacles unseen, or brushed aside in the fine enthusiasm of developing a perfect design on paper, suddenly become realities. Often the plan must be revised quickly to make it practical. But all is done with optimism, and the basic winter planning proves worthwhile.

Whether the herb garden is small or large, it needs to be exquisitely neat and weedless, with wide paths and compact borders, the same plant often repeated to make a good showing. A background is important, a hedge, wooden fence, or stone wall, perhaps with espaliered trees. For new gardens by modern houses a fence of cedar, redwood, or grape stake looks well. Here at Caprilands, I wanted a fence in keeping with our eighteenth-century Connecticut farmhouse, so I built a three-board fence of weathered gray chestnut. This encloses some of the garden areas, and also furnishes support for taller plants and vines.

In this country we are often faced with the problem of too much open space. Relatively few of us have old walls or the opportunity to develop secluded nooks, secret gardens, and exciting vistas. We suffer from a lack of mystery and surprise in our plantings. Everything can be seen at first glance. On the other hand, we have so little help that we must work simply and realistically, designing mainly do-it-yourself projects.

A good plan is all important, then, for a garden that is full of delights, but at the same time fairly undemanding. Certainly the most difficult garden to maintain is one that is unplanned. Such was the hit-or-miss type of the 1900's, really a revolt against the formality of the knot and parterre, the raised beds, and geometric designs that formerly characterized even kitchen gardens. Today, again, we often design with some formality, especially in the herb garden where we find balanced beds attractive and easier to care for.

Actually, there is no really easy way to have a good garden, although there are shortcuts. And there are plants that do take care of themselves, in fact so well that they often crowd other desirable, less vigorous kinds. I think of the "perfect" herb garden as about 12 by 18 feet. Well organized, it will not require back-breaking labor once soil has been prepared, walks laid, a center motif clearly stated, and borders planted with favorite but often miscellaneous plants set out in orderly beauty. Finally if a thick mulch of buckwheat or cocoa hulls is spread, weeding for such an area will take only an hour a week even in summer.

BUTTERFLY GARDEN

This garden (Plan 1) is approximately 12 by 18 feet, and my purpose was to have a good design that incorporated as many perennial herbs as possible with minimal maintenance. Here the focal point is a statue of St. Fiacre in an old wooden shrine which is mounted on a cedar post bleached with age. An armillary dial with

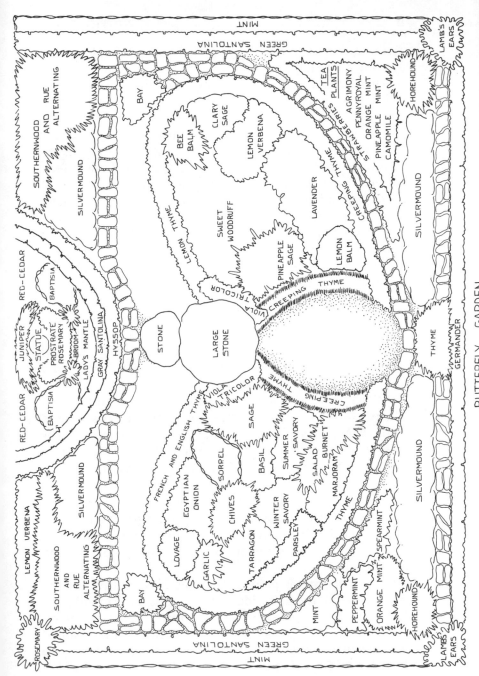

BUTTERFLY GARDEN

5

arrow compass and circle or a birdbath of simple design
are other possible features.

The butterfly plan provides two distinct sides or
"wings" with which to work, both with flowing lines in
pleasing contrast to the straight formality of the outer
form. The center walks form the body of the butterfly
and lead into small walks surrounding the wings. Even
in a little garden, walks need to be wide, at least 4 feet,
for comfort and ease in weeding, and to give a sense of
space around thickly planted areas. Old brick or fieldstone is the best material for the walks.

Borders that bind a design together need to be straight
and reasonably symmetrical. Keep curves and patterns
within straight exterior lines. At the sides, I have used
green santolinas and mint for their color and scent. For
the edge where a low, trim plant is needed, the hardy
germander (*Teucrium lucidum*) is a logical choice.
Trimmed, it looks like dwarf boxwood. The wall of a
building makes a background for this garden, an ideal
place for taller herbs like southernwood and rue, and
potted standards of lemon verbena.

Evergreens form a background for the statue of St.
Fiacre, with prostrate rosemary in front, Lady's mantle
in the center, and clumps of baptisia and broom on either
side. Gray santolina contrasting with the greener leaves
of hyssop runs in a parallel border to set off this important part of the garden.

The left wing of the butterfly, the culinary area, is
bordered by thymes and Johnny-jump-ups. It includes
lovage, garlic, Egyptian onion, chives, sorrel, basil, summer savory, sage, tarragon, winter savory, parsley and
marjoram.

The right wing is planted for fragrance, with the same
border as on the left side. It includes pineapple sage,
lemon balm, lavender, sweet woodruff, beebalm, lemon
verbena, and clary sage. Lemon verbena can be planted
directly in the soil and cut low enough to be attractive
in this position, or it can be grown in a large pot which

is sunk to the rim. This way it is easy to bring it inside before the autumn frosts.

The annuals in this garden include basil, summer savory, and marjoram. The biennial parsley is treated here as an annual. The tender perennials that need to winter indoors (as described in Chapter 2) include lemon verbena, pineapple sage, and rosemary.

In a section at the lower right, I have set out a small collection of tea plants—agrimony, camomile, orange mint, pineapple mint, and pennyroyal—and bordered them with the little French strawberry or *fraise des bois*.

This butterfly plan is offered simply as a base from which you can work out your own design. I know this plan is workable, for I have followed it for several years. Of course, variations are possible in the overall size, the design, and the choice of plants.

DOORYARD GARDEN

This garden (Plan 2) is planned to fit an ell-shape formed by two walls of a house. Once the beds for such a garden have been outlined with brick or fieldstone and the herbs are established, it takes relatively little maintenance, but yields a welcome harvest of fresh and dried herbs for cooking.

My plan is bordered at the front and right by creeping thymes. The background border includes apple mint, wormwood, angelica, tansy, lovage, and artemisia 'Silver King,' with a large terra-cotta pot of rosemary at the kitchen door.

The herbs I consider essential for such a garden include beebalm, chervil, garlic chives, Egyptian onion, French sorrel, winter and summer savories, basil, costmary, oregano, rue, tarragon, pineapple mint, spearmint, orange mint, peppermint, calendula, hyssop, anise, coriander, burnet, camomile, Italian curly parsley, chives, sage, and thyme.

Today's pleasure in terrace and patio living has brought a new interest in herbs for it is convenient to have a culinary garden close to the barbecue and outdoor living

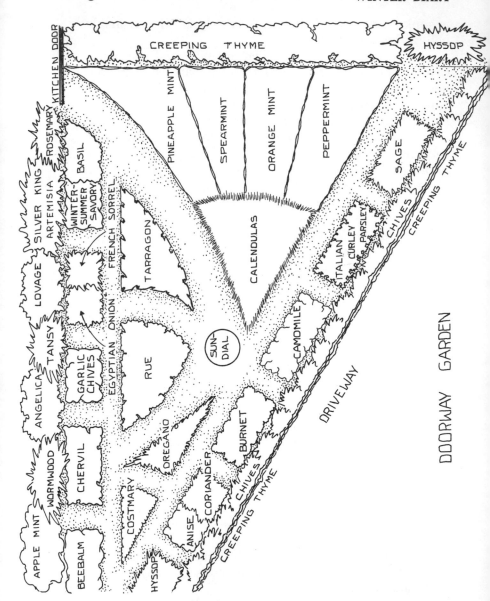

area. Some herbs, as spearmint, chives, and parsley,
might be grown in plant pockets made by removing some
stones or paving tiles from the floor of patio or terrace.

To have an ample supply of herbs near the barbecue, I suggest a planting of these:

PERENNIALS	ANNUALS AND BIENNIALS
6 bronze fennel	12 basil
2 chives	6 borage
3 chives, garlic	12 chicory
2 culinary thymes	12 Chinese cabbage
3 Egyptian onions	6 dill
4 French sorrel	36 lettuce, oakleaf
3 lemon balm	12 parsley, curly
2 lovage	3 parsley, plainleaf
3 orange mint	12 summer savory
3 peppermint	12 Swiss chard
2 rosemary	
4 sage	
6 salad burnet	
3 spearmint	
6 sweet marjoram	
2 tarragon	
1 winter savory	

GARDEN OF HERBS FOR DRYING

This simple and appealing plan (Plan 3) can be adapted to almost any size of garden or to any herbs. It is appropriate as a Mary or Biblical garden. It requires a space about 10 by 14 feet. Once plants are established, this garden will give lots of pleasure in summer, and a quantity of fragrant dried material for winter; yet it requires little maintenance and is especially good for a U-shaped area formed by two wings of a house or for a city garden where space is at a premium. It can be surrounded by a close-clipped lawn, but looks even better with an outline of old brick.

A sundial serves here as focal point in the center, but a statue could be given a beautiful setting at the back, perhaps with a small reflecting pool.

The important feature here is the four groupings of herbs: for medicine, for bees, for fragrance, and for

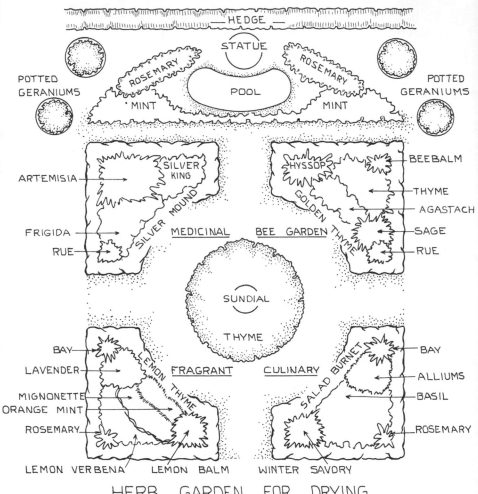

HERB GARDEN FOR DRYING

ADAPTABLE FOR A BIBLICAL GARDEN

cooking. In the medicinal corner a border of artemisia
'Silver Mound' surrounds other taller artemisias, with a
clump of rue for accent. The bee area has a border of
golden thyme around hyssop, the upright *Thymus vulgaris*, agastache, and sage, with another clump of rue
for accent directly opposite the clump in the medicinal
corner.

For fragrance, there is a border of lemon thyme with lavender, mignonette, and rosemary, with a large potted lemon verbena in one corner, a lemon balm at the entrance, and a large potted bay at the other. The culinary corner includes a border of burnet and chives, a large plant of rosemary at the corner, winter savory accenting the entrance, and a bay tree opposite the one in the fragrance corner.

WHEEL GARDEN

This is an elaboration, larger and more permanent, of the ever popular planting of herbs between the spokes of an old wagonwheel (Plan 4). Unless you are experienced in making gardens and growing herbs, you might want to start by planting a wagonwheel of herbs, then after a season or two you could enlarge it to the permanency of a plan like this.

If you use a wagonwheel, raise it on bricks or fieldstone to make a low wall the shape of the rim. Set the wheel on this and fill in with good soil up to the spokes. Plant clockwise, starting at the hub. Place some focal point there. I have a terra-cotta figure of St. Francis, but a vigorous trailing thyme might also be used.

In the first circle beyond the hub, plant rosemary of various sizes. Next have a circle of tarragon, then winter savory, chives, a circle of various types of basil, and low curly parsley alternating with chervil around the outside circle. Beyond the rim, plant creeping thymes between the bricks or stones. To keep this planting attractive, trim the tops of the herbs often enough to maintain the original design.

You will see that there are no mints in the wheel and no vegetable herbs; so, leading to it, make a walk with neat beds on either side, edged with stone and planted to spearmint, pineapple mint, peppermint, and orange mint. Add sorrel, chives, Egyptian onions, rue, hyssop, artemisias, lavenders, and edge the beds with low, decorative plants like germander or lamb's-ears. Your garden thus grows out from the radius of the wheel and can be expanded

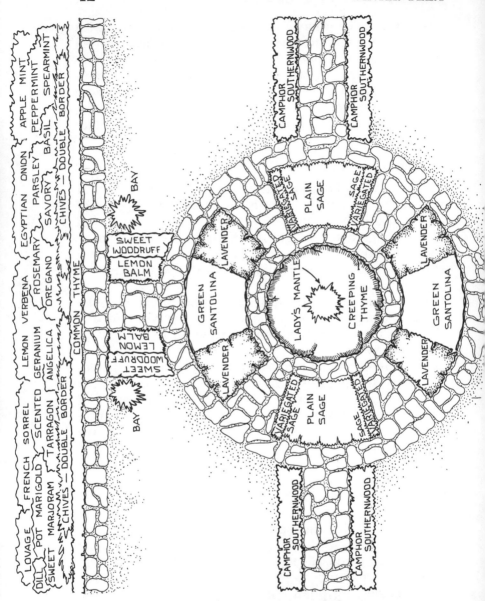

gradually as your interest and knowledge increase.

My design for Plan 4 requires a space about 20 by 24 feet. The pattern is set by fieldstone with a sundial in the

center, Lady's mantle and creeping thymes around it.
The circular planting is green and gray with green santolina, variegated and plain sage, and lavender. Camphor-scented southernwood borders the main walks leading to the wheel. Ideally there should be an edging plant
along this. Steps could lead up to it and a vantage point
be provided for enjoyment of the pattern of the wheel.
Combine the border plants in any way that pleases you.
I have selected some of my favorites for fragrance, culinary use, and for leaf texture and contrast.

Garden of Geraniums

This plan (Plan 5) is relatively simple to follow, but
requires a large number of plants. My geranium garden
has for background the mossy stones of an old wall.
Perennial geraniums, the cranesbills, grow against the
wall in a ground bed, and baskets of trailing geraniums
(*Pelargonium peltatum*) hang from the eaves of a nearby
shed. This garden is beautiful with flowers, rich in leaf
textures, shapes, and colors, and it yields some of the
most tantalizing fragrances in the world. It is especially
nice near an outdoor living area, as a retreat off a master
bedroom, or as a city garden that receives at least two to
three hours of direct sun in summer.

The walks may be of brick or fieldstone, and, depending on size of plants, the plan calls for from one hundred
to two hundred geraniums. If this is too many for you,
reduce the size (shown as about 20 by 24 feet), or select
some other herbs as fillers. The creeping 'Caprilands'
thyme, for example, would make a wonderful cover even
in partial shade. Or, one section could be devoted to
favorite mints, another to the sages.

Although my plan divides the geraniums into groups—
citrus-scented, oakleaf, fancy-leaved, and rose-scented—
any of the scented varieties described in Chapter 3, or
others you may find in greenhouses and the catalogs of
specialists, would be appropriate to such a garden. To
increase your pleasure, keep varieties correctly labeled.

There are many ways to manage a garden of gerani-

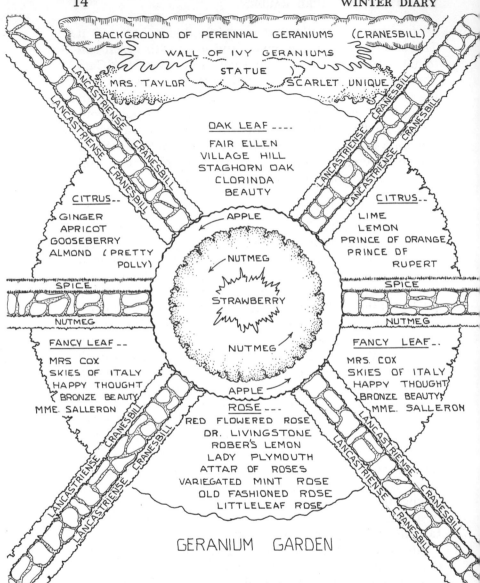

BACKGROUND OF PERENNIAL GERANIUMS (CRANESBILL)
WALL OF IVY GERANIUMS
STATUE
MRS. TAYLOR   SCARLET UNIQUE

LANCASTRIENSE CRANESBILL
LANCASTRIENSE CRANESBILL
LANCASTRIENSE CRANESBILL

OAK LEAF ----
FAIR ELLEN
VILLAGE HILL
STAGHORN OAK
CLORINDA
BEAUTY

CITRUS--
GINGER
APRICOT
GOOSEBERRY
ALMOND (PRETTY
POLLY)

CITRUS--
LIME
LEMON
PRINCE OF ORANGE
PRINCE OF
RUPERT

APPLE

NUTMEG

STRAWBERRY

SPICE
NUTMEG

SPICE
NUTMEG

NUTMEG

FANCY LEAF --
MRS. COX
SKIES OF ITALY
HAPPY THOUGHT
BRONZE BEAUTY
MME. SALLERON

FANCY LEAF --
MRS. COX
SKIES OF ITALY
HAPPY THOUGHT
BRONZE BEAUTY
MME. SALLERON

APPLE

ROSE ---
RED FLOWERED ROSE
DR. LIVINGSTONE
ROBER'S LEMON
LADY PLYMOUTH
ATTAR OF ROSES
VARIEGATED MINT ROSE
OLD FASHIONED ROSE
LITTLELEAF ROSE

LANCASTRIENSE CRANESBILL
LANCASTRIENSE CRANESBILL
LANCASTRIENSE CRANESBILL

GERANIUM GARDEN

ums. The first is to keep plants potted, sinking each pot
to the rim in soil for the summer, and lifting it to bring
indoors for the winter. The second is to unpot each

plant in spring and place it directly in the soil. Growth will be more luxuriant this way, but you will have a problem in fall when frost threatens. Then you will have to lift each plant carefully, trim away long straggly roots and top growth to about 4 inches, and repot. Or you can discard the old plants after taking cuttings of half-mature wood. Root these in moist sand and pot them later on to have plants ready to put out the next spring after danger of frost has past. If you have a greenhouse, this garden is a delight. In winter, the plants provide color, fragrance, and interest indoors; in summer, they offer all this outside yet require little care, thus leaving you free for other pursuits.

STAINED-GLASS WINDOW GARDEN

This elaborate plan (Plan 6) takes lots of space, time, plants, and ingenuity. Even when established, it requires considerable maintenance, but it will be a joy for the herb gardener who has the time to care for it. The center design of green and gray santolinas creates the beautiful effect of a Gothic stained-glass window. Actually a knot garden, it is set like a jewel in a border of neatly trimmed germander.

The plan shown is approximately 30 by 40 feet, but 15 by 15 feet would suffice to create the window of santolinas bordered by germander, and the surrounding beds of thyme, sage, and lavender. With a sundial in the center, this makes a wonderful little garden for a sunny city backyard, or for the middle of an expanse of green lawn with trees and hedges beyond, as on a suburban lot. This complete plan provides space for most of the plants the herb gardener wants to grow, annuals, perennials, biennials, and tender perennials that need to be wintered indoors.

THE YARB PATCH

This still has much to be said for it, and the gardener who loves plants and adventures in horticulture revels in it. Even though formal patterns work best for most

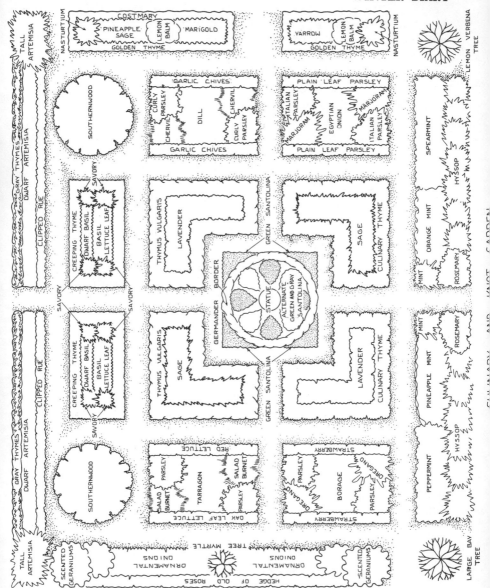

herb gardeners, if you have the space, do have a spot
where plants can run riot—where extra seeds can be
dumped, weeded-out plants set, chives allowed to run

their course, and oreganos and thymes can go wild. Such a garden delights the bouquet-maker in spring and summer and is an inspiration for dried arrangements and seed collecting in autumn. If you have such a wild, unmanageable mass of miscellaneous material, you will always have seeds and seedlings to fill in winter-killed areas in a border, and many big, awkward flowers of tansy, woad, mullein, wild bergamot, Jerusalem artichoke, helianthemum, hollyhock, and giant artemisia that are magnificent but unmanageable in formal gardens.

Such an herb patch is a lot of fun. A friend of mine who maintains one of the most beautiful of patterned gardens once said of a fellow horticulturist famous in the herb world, "Her garden was not neat. In fact, it was a mess, but there was everything there. Rare, unusual things, old and new, and she knew and had the time to tell you about them."

Finally, your herb garden is not complete until there is a place for you to sit comfortably with room for a companion or so. I like benches of well-weathered wood best. Antique washbenches can sometimes be found and they are in keeping with most herb gardens. Iron furniture, painted black or dark green, is practical and not too blatant, but wood really looks better. If your benches and other furniture look handmade, they will appear as a natural part of the garden. Save your aluminum chairs for the terrace. Let the herb garden throughout look old, peaceful, and nostalgic with quiet colors and soft textures.

As you make plans for an herb garden, you will quickly discover, if you have not done so already, that there are countless plants that have, or have had, herbal uses. Few of us have the ambition, space, or time to grow them all. The lists in the appendix offer a careful selection of herbs in categories.

2. How To Grow Herbs Indoors

Storms and winter weather
Bring plants and people close together;
—A. G. S.

I value the cold months of the year when I have time
to devote to growing herbs indoors. Potted herbs are very
convenient if the leaves are used frequently in the
kitchen. I enjoy their fragrance and winter color, too,
and the opportunity to observe them closely in a way
hardly possible outdoors. Of course, many tender perennial herbs must be wintered indoors.

Whether you grow herbs in a sunny window, under
fluorescent lights, or in a greenhouse, keep in mind that
they will probably not grow as luxuriantly inside as outdoors. Also, the best kinds for your window garden are
those that do not get too big. Select a well-lighted place
with at least five hours of direct sun. Provide fresh air
every day, not by a direct draft, but through a partly
opened window or door in an adjoining room. Adequate
humidity (about 30 to 50 per cent) and a fairly cool
atmosphere (never above 75 degrees, and that high only
for brief periods) are important, too. Try for a range
of 50 to 70 degrees. Failure with herbs indoors is usually
the result of too little light, too much heat, too dry an
atmosphere, or pots that are too small.

Potted herbs thrive in a mixture of equal parts garden
loam, sand, peat moss or leaf mold, and well-rotted, pulverized manure (the dry commercial product may be

18

used). Keep the soil evenly moist, never soggy wet and
never bone dry. Feel it before you water. Fertilize with
a soluble houseplant food about once a month. Group
pots in a tray of moist sand or pebbles, or set individual
pots in saucers, filling these with pebbles or sand kept
damp.

UNDER FLUORESCENT LIGHTS

If you do not have a window with sufficient sun, install
a fluorescent light fixture. A typical set-up includes two
40-watt tubes in a standard commercial reflector. Tubes
are suspended 12 to 18 inches above the surface on which
pots rest and are turned on for 14 to 16 hours out of 24,
never continuously, as this is damaging.

There are several kinds of fluorescent lamps on the
market, some of which have been engineered specifically
for growing plants. If your local dealer does not stock
these, you can buy them by mail, or use plain fluorescent
tubes marked "deluxe warm white," "daylight," "natural,"
or "cool white." These will have to be replaced with new
tubes every six to twelve months. Dust off the tubes and
the reflector about once a month to obtain maximum
illumination.

Good herbs to try under fluorescent lights include basil
(especially the decorative 'Dark Opal'), African baby's-
breath, sweet bay, cardamom, chives, lavender, lemon
balm, lemon verbena, sweet marjoram, mints, parsley,
rosemary, and sage. If you try this kind of herb gardening, you will want to experiment with most of the herbs
recommended later in this chapter for growing indoors.

IN A HOME GREENHOUSE

Herb gardening in a home greenhouse is delightful.
If you have this opportunity, you may want to devote
most of the greenhouse to herbs, allotting a large space
for scented geraniums, plus plenty of room for sizable
pots and tubs of other favorites. Since potted herbs do
well in the average greenhouse, that is, one with a night
temperature-range between 50 and 62 degrees in winter

and about 50 per cent relative humidity combined with fresh air, they make ideal companions for wax begonias, cinerarias, cyclamen, freesias, snapdragons, sweet peas, amaryllis, and coleus.

Several flowering herbs can be grown in a greenhouse although they do not normally thrive as house plants. These include *Calendula officinalis* (pot-marigold), *Centaurea cyanus* (bachelor's-button), *Centaurea gymnocarpa* (dusty miller), *Chrysanthemum parthenium* (feverfew), and nasturtium.

Borage can be one of the loveliest of greenhouse plants, as young seedlings potted from the garden, just before frost, come into bloom early in the year, and provide a showy display of starry blue flowers until late spring.

I know that every home greenhouse is a delight to step into on a snowy winter day, but the one that contains a collection of herbs is best of all, for its fragrance is beyond description. As a checklist, I think the home greenhouse needs some of these herbs: basil, borage, catnip, chives, fennel, lemon balm, lemon verbena, mint, parsley, sage, and sweet marjoram.

POTS, BOXES, AND TUBS FOR HERBS

One of the special pleasures of growing herbs indoors lies in selecting containers for them. These may vary from standard clay or plastic pots to wooden tubs and planter boxes. For the window garden, I recommend that potted herbs be grouped together in a redwood or cedar box of a size to fit your location; a box 12 inches wide, 36 inches long, and 8 to 12 inches deep is a good standard size.

To protect window sills and tables, use saucers or trays to catch excess moisture. These can be of clay, plastic, or galvanized metal made to fit any location. If you decide to have a window box indoors, either bury potted herbs in moist sphagnum moss contained by it, or plant the herbs directly in a good planting mix. Do this planting in August or September, outdoors if possible, so that plants can become established before being brought indoors just ahead of the frost.

Part of your success with herbs indoors depends on insect control. High temperatures, a dry atmosphere, and lack of fresh air create a breeding place for red-spider mites. To avoid this, provide plenty of fresh air, keep the temperature below 70 degrees most of the time, and wash the foliage once a week. If spraying becomes necessary, try a kind like rotenone, considered safe with foodstuffs.

Unless you keep potted herbs cut back for use in the kitchen, it will be necessary to prune and trim them periodically so that they look neat and do not outgrow the space you have allotted them. Repot each year in August or September.

In choosing pots or tubs for herbs, keep in mind that a container should have a diameter one-third to one-half the height of the plant. A basil that will grow about 18 inches tall, indoors, will look well-proportioned and should thrive in a pot or tub 6 to 10 inches in diameter. Remember, also, that small pots such as 2- and 3-inchers dry out quickly, and if not adequately watered, may hinder good growth.

IDEAS FOR HERB BOX PLANTINGS

To make a culinary box, border it with curly parsley (put small plants close together for an attractive, lacy edge), a pineapple mint at one end, and oregano at the other. Then add sweet marjoram, several young basils (before they have bloomed), and winter savory. Place in the same box one plant of tarragon, a large rosemary in the center, and one rose geranium along with it. Thymes can be used as fillers. Chives may be added, too, but I prefer to pot them separately, allowing them to freeze outdoors, then bringing them inside to force on a sunny window sill.

I have another favorite culinary box which calls for two sorrel plants (to be cut back frequently for soup),

one young salad burnet seedling (which does not yet
have a long taproot), one tarragon, one winter savory,
one clump of chives, one clump of garlic chives, two
sweet marjoram, one thyme, and two sages. This box
does not include basil, but if you want it, sow seeds in
a 10-inch bulb pan, and grow separately.

For a fragrant window box, plant peppermint geranium
(*Pelargonium tomentosum*) at the center edge to cascade over it, a 'Nutmeg' geranium at one end, and an
'Apple' geranium at the other. Place a rose geranium in
the center, and add one basil, one marjoram, and one
rosemary. Another favorite box of mine includes the
citrus scents, lemon balm, lemon verbena, lemon geraniums, and the three lemon thymes.

SELECTION OF HERBS TO GROW INDOORS

African Baby's-breath. Known botanically as *Chaenostoma fastigiatum*, this makes a neat clump of ascending branches to about 8 inches and often covered with
small white flowers. The foliage is fragrant when bruised.

Basil. A tender annual, this does reasonably well as a
house plant if it is not allowed to bloom or set seed. Cut
the seed heads off, and use the leaves in seasoning.
Basil thrives on feeding with liquid fertilizer in soil that
is humusy and well drained. The purple-leaved 'Dark
Opal' is especially attractive indoors and can be grown
by sowing a few seeds in a 6-inch pot in July or August.
To ward off red-spider mites, wash or spray the leaves
regularly (once a week unless badly infested) with soapy
water.

Borage. An annual herb easily cultivated at a sunny
window or in a greenhouse. Either pot a young seedling
in autumn, or sow a few seeds in a pot of moist, rich,
well-drained soil. Blooming will begin around the New
Year and continue until the plant becomes so large and
rangy that it is often necessary to discard it toward the
end of spring.

Camphor Tree (Cinnamomum camphora). The source
of the camphor of commerce, has cinnamon- or camphor-

scented leaves and makes an excellent shrub for pot culture.

Cardamom (Amomum cardamon). All parts of the plant are spicy. It has narrow lance-leaves to 12 inches long, and may grow to a height of 6 feet. True cardamon comes from the closely related *Elettaria cardamomum,* but a substitute is made from *Amomum.* As a house plant, it is of interest chiefly for its foliage of tropical appearance, and the herb gardener who wants to decorate with potted herbs will find it useful in a shady, moist, warm situation.

Catnip. If you have a cat, it will be blessed indeed if you grow this herb. Give the plant sun, a cool, airy place, and a soil nicely moist at all times. Cut back to keep in bounds.

Chives. As a potted plant, chives does especially well when allowed to freeze outdoors in the fall before being brought inside for the winter. This is one herb that can be found at most of today's supermarkets in a 2- or 3-inch pot; it has probably been trimmed back and needs but to be moved to a 4- or 5-inch pot of moist soil and into sunny warmth to produce succulent leaves for seasoning. Well-grown plants bear attractive heads of flowers off and on through the year.

Dill. An interesting pot plant for anyone who delights in the smell of the bruised foliage. Sow a few seeds in pot or planter box in late summr or early fall.

Dittany of Crete. Gray foliage makes this a useful pot plant. Start by digging a young plant from the garden or buy one already potted, in the fall. Grow in lean soil and keep on the dry side. Cut back to induce fresh, compact growth; then trim as necessary to keep in bounds.

Horehound. A good window plant, this needs only several sunny hours a day in winter. It can be started from seeds sown in spring, or from small plants dug from the garden in autumn. Keep cut back as blossoms are ugly and full of burrs.

Lavender. Several kinds make excellent house plants. Common lavender *(Lavandula officinalis)* can be a de-

lightful pot plant when provided with coolness, a few
hours of daily sun, and an evenly moist, porous soil.
The tender perennial lavenders, including *L. multifida*
(fernleaf), *L. stoechas* and *L. dentata* all have aromatic
foliage and interesting flower heads. My favorite is
L. heterophylla. Certainly all are worthy of a place in
the window garden or greenhouse.

Lemon Balm. This hardy perennial grows easily indoors from seeds sown at almost any season, or from a
young plant dug from the garden in spring or fall. Cut
back to keep it compact and use the leaves freely.

Lemon Verbena. A favorite for its clear, clean odor.
In Guatemala I have seen it grow as high as a young
apple tree. If it is to attain any size at all in the North,
grow it in a large wooden or terra-cotta tub with rich,
humusy soil and plenty of well-rotted manure. Feed with
liquid houseplant food from late winter through the
summer.

Lemon verbena does best summered outdoors, and
when brought back inside, all of the leaves are likely to
drop. Before this happens, collect them for potpourri
and tea. Store the plants moist, not dry and never wet,
in a cool, light place, as a frost-free cellar or basement
with windows, in a garage or deep coldframe. By February tiny leaves will appear; plants can then be brought
back to warmth and sun. Or grow your lemon verbena
at a window all year and prune back as necessary to keep
to convenient size. Red-spider mites and white flies may
be troublesome. Wash the foliage well every week with
tepid water and spray, weekly if necessary, with mala-
thion.

Mint. Many kinds make interesting house plants.
Red-spider mites may be troublesome if the air does not
circulate freely and if the atmosphere is hot and dry.
Good mints for potting include apple or wooly, Corsican,
curly, orange, peppermint, pineapple, silver, and spearmint. Start by rooting cuttings in spring or fall, by digging small plants from the garden, or by buying young
plants of the kinds you want.

Parsley. Start this hardy biennial from seeds sown at almost any time (first soaking them in water for 24 hours). Sunlight, coolness, an evenly moist, rich soil, and plenty of fresh air will make potted parsley yield an abundant crop of leaves for cutting.

Rosemary. An evergreen perennial too tender to winter outdoors in the North. I find it grows best in a cool, draughty window, and flourishes with good drainage, a roomy pot, and evenly moist soil. If you have a sunny basement window or deep coldframe that does not freeze severely in winter—these are good for rosemary.

Sage. This is easily grown in a pot. Start by digging from the garden or by sowing seeds at almost any time. Sage needs plenty of sun, fresh air, and an evenly moist soil in order to produce an abundant crop. The tender variety 'Tricolor' (gray leaves variegated with rosy pink and white) and *Salvia rutilans* (pineapple sage) are excellent plants to keep potted around the year or to put outdoors for summer with only cuttings or divisions brought inside every autumn.

Scented Geraniums. Numerous species in this group are discussed in Chapter 3.

Strawberry. The runnerless Alpine varieties make interesting pot plants in a sunny, cool window where there is fresh air. They are best kept potted from the time seeds or divisions are started. A 6-inch standard pot will hold one clump nicely. It takes six to ten plants to produce an appreciable quantity of berries. Keep pots buried to the rims outdoors in summer and leave them there in the fall to be frozen. Spread a mulch of hay or loose leaves at Thanksgiving time. After the New Year, bring the potted strawberries indoors to a sunny, moist, cool location and keep the soil evenly moist. Feed biweekly as soon as growth becomes apparent. If all goes well, white flowers will soon appear, followed by the long, slender berries.

Sweet Bay. Purchase as a young potted plant and provide morning or afternoon sun. As soon as a pot is filled with roots transplant to the next size. Watch out for scale

on the underside of leaves. I go over the small plants
with a soft-bristled brush. To remove the insects from
large plants use an oil spray. Bay trees are particularly
lovely in the autumn garden and will withstand the first
frosts, so they may be enjoyed outside until late fall.
Inside, keep them as cool as possible but always at a
temperature above freezing. A large bay is almost beyond
price.

Sweet Marjoram. This upright, tender perennial can
be started from seeds at almost any season, or you can
buy a young potted plant in the fall. It makes an attractive trailing specimen, and you will be able to enjoy it
while cutting judiciously for seasoning. Sweet marjoram
needs sun for part of the day and should have enough
water to keep the soil evenly moist. Spray the foliage
frequently with water to help discourage pests.

Thyme. The thymes are good for hanging baskets and
look well cascading from planter boxes. They need lots
of sun, coolness, and an evenly moist, well-drained soil.
Trim as often as necessary to keep them within bounds.
'Silver Lemon' (*Thymus serpyllum argenteus*), *T. vulgaris fragrantissimus*, and golden-edged thyme (*T. s.
aureus*) are tender and must be wintered inside.

Winter Savory. A hardy perennial with leaves useful
in seasoning. This can be grown in a pot, starting with
a young plant dug from the garden or with one purchased
in autumn from a grower.

3. The Scented Geraniums

As aromatic plants bestow
No spicy fragrance while they grow,
But crush'd or trodden to the ground,
Diffuse their balmy sweets around.
                    —Oliver Goldsmith

The sweet-leaved geraniums have a nostalgic charm. The scent of just one crushed lacy leaf of rose geranium brings back the past—tall Victorian houses with dormer windows, cupolas, porches like valentines, and big bay windows filled with plants. And these windows were cool and sunny. Fires banked at night did not radiate much heat, and in cold weather plants were protected from freezing by layers of newspaper slipped between them and the windows.

It was in this environment that the rose geranium grew to an astonishing size and provided slips for neighbors and friends as well as leaves for jelly and a sweet odor for the hands of visiting children. Other geraniums— the peppermint and the oakleaf—trailed over the sills, and the 'Apple' and 'Nutmeg' had green and gray masses of small leaves that were like bits of velvet in the sun. The lemon geranium grew so large that it looked like an exotic tree, with its tightly curled leaves growing in rings around the stalks. It was often set on the floor, planted in a butter tub. When you brushed against a plant, the lemon odor came so clean and fresh that you always went back again just to touch the vigorous, crisp leaf and to draw a long breath.

Children like to hear how, in the early days of the seventeenth century, the Dutch and English sailing ships brought the first sweet-smelling geraniums home from long voyages to the South African Cape. Sailors then, as now, looked for some gift to carry to those awaiting their return, and they found the geranium part of the strange world beyond Europe.

It was about 1632 that the first scented geranium arrived in Europe. Interest in them spread quickly, and at the end of the century they had attained much favor. By 1750 colonial America and the geranium had met, and by 1870 the plant gained such popularity that over one hundred fifty varieties were listed in catalogs. This is the period most remembered for geranium windows. They had now become readily available, and even those who lived in remote farmhouses had access to several kinds.

GERANIUM OR *Pelargonium*

While the scented geraniums are members of the vast geranium family, they are known specifically as species and varieties of *Pelargonium,* a word derived from the resemblance of the seedcase to a stork's bill. All of the geraniums commonly cultivated as pot plants—the zonals, Martha Washingtons, and scenteds—are in reality pelargoniums that came originally from the South African Cape. There they are perennials that grow into sizable shrubs and trees, just as they do in southern California.

Scented geraniums are not only nostalgic reminders of old gardens, plant windows, and grandmother's kitchen, but they are attractive enough to create interest even without their pleasant associations. Leaf forms may be laced, fanshaped, divided like a pheasant's foot, a crow's foot, an oak leaf, a maple leaf, a ruffle, a crisp ruff, a grape leaf, or a spreading umbrella. Texture may be velvety or sticky.

The scents in many varieties are as strong as those of the fruits and flowers from which they derive their

names. 'Rober's Lemon Rose' holds its scent longer than
the rose, and the peppermint geranium (*P. tomentosum*)
fairly makes your mouth water. One of the lemon geraniums (*P. crispum*) is so truly citrus-like that it suggests
a tinkling glass of lemonade on a hot summer day.

The scented geraniums give off a pleasing odor when
they are brushed, and yield a fragrant oil which may be
distilled. The fragrance comes from the back of the
leaves, and it is released by stroking or brushing them.
Our grandmothers soaked the leaves in vinegar or alcohol to make sweet waters to bathe an aching head. The
French, however, in their search for new sources of
essences for perfumes discovered, about 1800, that *P.
capitatum, P. roseum* and *P. odoratissimum* could substitute for the rare and extravagantly expensive attar of
roses. From that time on, fields of the scented geraniums
were grown in North Africa and southern France for
distillation. About one pound of leaves is required to
produce one gram of oil. Three ounces of oil is dissolved
in a gallon of alcohol to make the sweet extract with a
real rose odor that is one of the principal oils used in
soap and potpourri and perfume.

Classifying the vast number of scented geraniums is
a difficult task. Should they be grouped by odor, leaf
pattern, or habit of growth? No one method seems to
suffice. It is a common opinion that only one rose geranium exists, one lemon, and one mint. It comes as a
revelation to the budding collector to discover, to begin
with, that there are over fifty kinds of geraniums with
a rose odor, a dozen or more of which are readily available. I have listed alphabetically my favorite scented
geraniums, according to botanical names with a common name appended (if there is one), with notes on leaf
shape, color, fragrance, habit of growth, and color of
flowers.

FAVORITE SCENTED GERANIUMS

Pelargonium   abrotanifolium   'Southernwood-leaved.'
Pungent, finely cut leaves resemble those of southern-

SCENTED GERANIUMS. (Left above) Lemon *Pelargonium crispum* Prince Rupert; (center) Strawberry *P. scarboroviae*, (below) Clorinda, large-flowered and pungent. (Center above) Attar of Roses *P. capitatum*, (middle) Peppermint *P. tomentosum;* (below) Apple *P. odoratissimum.* (Left above) pungent Staghorn Oak *P. quercifolium,* (below) Lemon Rose Dr. Livingston or Skeleton Rose.

wood (*Artemisia abrotanum*); woody stems are shrubby. Tiny blooms are white, the two upper petals each marked by a carmine dot.

P. blandfordianum. A cross of *P. graveolens* × *P. echinatum* produced this tall gray-leaved plant bearing white flowers marked with carmine. Color and deeply cut seven-lobed leaves make this a nice contrast to the green geraniums. The scent is musky.

P. capitatum 'Attar of Roses.' The elusive rose scent of this geranium is one of the most treasured in the world. Attractive plant with light green, trilobate leaves: crenate, soft, and hairy; lavender blooms.

P. 'Clorinda.' A cross between a form of *P. domesticum* × *P. quercifolium* produced this vigorous plant of trailing growth and large crenate, trilobate leaves, rough-textured and dusty green. It is sometimes said to be eucalyptus-scented, but, to me, the fragrance is more like wild roses. Grown mainly for the brilliant pink blooms which appear in abundance over a long period. Grows well in big terra-cotta tubs, flourishing and trailing over the edge if watered and well fertilized. Neglected, or in very dry periods, leaves turn autumnal reds, and many branches become bare, but when given water the stalks fill out again.

P. crispum. A lemon geranium with a fragrance second only to that of the old-fashioned rose geranium (*P. graveolens*). Small ruffled and fluted leaves grow on stiffly upright stems like pyramidal evergreens, with orchid pink flowers in season. Good to grow as small tree in a tub.

P. crispum 'Gooseberry-leaved.' Ruffled leaves are mottled yellow so that it is useful in place of flowers in the foreground of a bed or window box. It yields an abundance of pale lavender flowers, the upper petals lined with cerise. Difficult to propagate, but worth the trouble.

P. crispum minor. The fingerbowl geranium, with sessile leaves smaller than those of the usual *P. crispum,* but blessed with the same lemon odor.

P. crispum 'Prince Rupert.' Like a stiff, upright little evergreen. During the span of one summer in the garden, under average conditions, it will become a small shrub. I plant it in decorative terra-cotta pots and allow stems to grow as large as they will. This can be one of the showiest of plants for the pot garden; sturdy and strongly lemon-scented.

P. crispum 'Prince Rupert Variegated.' A distinguished plant that lives up to its royal name. The leaf is ruffled, green, and variegated creamy white. Under most conditions it remains small, never large or unmanageable. Mildly lemon-scented.

P. denticulatum. The finely cut leaves form a dense, compact plant that bears small lavender flowers. Rose-scented.

P. 'Dr. Livingston.' The old-time favorite, skeleton-leaf rose geranium, vigorous with an odor sometimes described as lemon, sometimes as rose. Certainly it is fragrant, a handsome plant with light green foliage and tiny pale lavender flowers. The leaf presses well for bookmarks or letter enclosures. The shape is arresting, and the scent pleasing as it rises from a turned page.

P. filicifolium. Leaves are so finely cut that it is known commonly as "fernleaf geranium." The plant is desirable as a novelty for collectors. Leaves are sticky and have a pungent scent unpleasant to many. The tiny pink flowers have carmine marks on the two upper petals. A tall and spreading plant.

P. fragrans 'Nutmeg.' This highly scented plant does well where the small gray-green leaves can trail over the edge of a pot. I like to use a solid edging of it outdoors for beds of scented geraniums that bank the north side of my house and in the wheel center of the geranium garden. It conceals the stalks of taller varieties, and unifies outline of the border. Keep plants at low-border height by cutting back tops.

P. glutinosum 'Pheasant's Foot.' Deeply cut, brown-marked leaf shaped like a pheasant's foot. Vigorous, grows rapidly and makes a handsome background if used in bed or window box. Pungent.

P. graveolens. A large geranium with deeply cut gray-green foliage and lavender blooms. Grows 3 to 4 feet tall if not cut back frequently; leaves may be used in jellies or for tea. Rose-scented.

P. graveolens camphoratum or 'Camphor Rose.' This succeeds in being both camphorous and rosy at the same time. I keep a pot at my kitchen door where I can pinch the leaves at will. The leaf is velvety, pleasing to the touch and bewitching to the nose.

P. graveolens 'Gray Lady Plymouth.' I consider this the best of the variegated rose geraniums. Vigorous, excellent for pots or beds. Deeply cut gray-green leaf like *P. graveolens,* but with a border of white. Rose-scented.

P. graveolens 'Lady Plymouth.' Slow-growing, this makes an interesting center for a window box where it gives the appearance of a white flower. The leaf is similar to the other *graveolens* types, but much larger, a light green with strong rose odor. Grows to tremendous size, especially outdoors.

P. graveolens 'Little Gem.' This small version of the sweet old-fashioned rose geranium flowers freely and makes an interesting border plant in the garden. Pungent.

P. graveolens minor or 'Little Leaf Rose.' The very small leaves are cut like those of the old-fashioned rose geranium, and the plant stays compact with only a little trimming. Small orchid blooms cover the plant in the spring and early summer. Pungent.

P. graveolens 'Rober's Lemon Rose.' The sweetest of the rose scents. It has a long thick leaf cut like that of a tomato. A vigorous plant that yields hundreds of sweet leaves for use in potpourri or tea.

P. graveolens 'Variegated Mint-scented Rose.' Gray-green leaves, deeply lobed, and edged with creamy white. Excellent in a window box where the foliage variation can be seen well. The odor is a pleasant combination of rose and mint.

P. grossularioides 'Cocoanut.' A delicate looking plant that actually has a tenacious hold on life. It is one geranium that self-sows, and I find seedlings in my greenhouse every summer. The odor is pungent and delightful, to me at least—not everyone shares my admiration for it. A trailing plant with slender stems growing out of a crown of larger leaves. The tiny lavender blooms are interesting when observed closely.

P. 'Joy Lucille.' This favorite for window box plantings was developed at Logee's North Street Greenhouses, at Danielson, Connecticut, and resulted from a cross of *P. tomentosum* X *P. graveolens*. The deeply cut leaf is feltlike on trailing stems. Excellent for the edge of a window box, a large tub, or in a hanging basket. Officially, this has a peppermint scent, but it reminds me of lilacs.

P. limoneum 'Lemon.' Fan-shaped, toothed leaves strongly lemon-scented. The variety 'Lady Mary' has a more delicate lemon scent and attractive magenta blossoms.

P. melissinum 'Lemon Balm.' One of the most rapid-growing of scented geraniums, important where height is needed. It smells like lemon balm (*Melissa officinalis*) and has a light green leaf resembling that of a maple tree and small lavender flowers. I carry over a few of these plants at their full summer heights, storing them in the cellar where they get a little light and enough water to keep them from shriveling in winter. In the warm days of spring they leaf out, and after danger of frost is past, I set them outside. Before summer is over, they rise like great fragrant trees to the very roof of my kitchen.

P. 'Mrs. Kingsley.' A ruffled leaf and showy red blooms. The leaves, like those of curly parsley, are pungent with a tinge of mint.

P. nervosum 'Lime-scented.' One of the most fragrant and refreshing odors among geraniums: truly lime. No imagination needed. The small leaf is sharply dentate on a compact plant with lavender flowers.

P. odoratissimum 'Apple.' A light green oval leaf, crenate and velvety, on vinelike branches, with tiny white flowers in spring. I commend this to every gardener, whether for window sills or outdoors. I plant it every year, alternating it with the similar but grayer 'Nutmeg' as a border along a walk. There it maintains a trim look and is fragrant to brush against as I walk to and from the garden. Apple-scented.

P. 'Old Scarlet Unique.' Unusual with attractively cut leaves, very ruffled, and often with a red edge, wooly and grayish, a striking foil for the large scarlet flowers which appear over a long season. Pungent.

P. 'Old Spice.' Known also as 'Logee' and *P. logeei.* Originated by Ernest Logee, Danielson, Connecticut, about 1948, this is a sweetly scented, trailing plant with small white flowers.

P. 'Prince of Orange.' Compact and small-leaved with a refreshing orange odor and lots of fine pale orchid blooms; crenate leaves.

P. quercifolium 'Beauty.' Mint-scented, rough-textured, oak-type leaf marked brown. Excellent for hanging baskets or any planting where a large-leaved trailing plant is needed. Tiny rose-colored flowers touched with purple on the upper petals.

P. quercifolium 'Fair Ellen.' Round-lobed, rough leaves and stems of this trailing plant are sticky. Lavender flowers, of medium size, in abundance. Pungent.

P. quercifolium giganteum 'Giant Oak.' Three- to five-lobed leaves, large and coarse, marked in the veins with deep purple. Rangy growth with sticky stems and leaves; small rose flowers. Often trained to tree or standard form, and as a background; not useful in small quarters.

P. quercifolium pinnatifidum 'Sharp-toothed Oak.' Leaves are larger than those of 'Fair Ellen,' elongated, strikingly purple-marked, crinkled, five-lobed, and very pungent. Attractive pale pink flowers.

P. quercifolium prostratum 'Prostrate Oak.' Low and spreading, excellent trailing from baskets, window boxes, or large tubs. The five-lobed leaf with purple markings is distinctive. Small lavender flowers. Pungent.

P. *quercifolium* 'Skelton's Unique.' A rambling plant
that will completely cover a bare wall in a season's
growth, spreading in all directions for 5 to 6 feet. Small
blooms, orchid colored, in spring and summer. Ruffled,
scalloped leaf, dark-centered, almost purple, with tiny
hairs that give a downy look. Pungent-scented with a
hint of rose.

P. *quercifolium* 'Staghorn Oak.' The finely cut leaf has
distinct purple veining. Choice for window boxes or
trailing from a hanging basket. Blossoms beautifully.

P. *quercifolium* 'Village Hill Hybrid.' Developed by
Dorcas Brigham, it has become one of the most important
of the oakleaf geraniums (P. *quercifolium* and varieties).
Narrow, crenate leaf. New leaves curl and look more
like parsley than geranium. Flowers bright lavender with
purple veining. Upright, not trailing like other oakleafs.
Grows quickly, almost to the point of climbing.

P. 'Rollison's Unique.' A climbing geranium used to
good effect to cover a wall. Grows rapidly, 5 to 6 feet in
one season. Leaves slightly crinkled, mint-scented. Flowers brilliant magenta.

P. *scabrum* 'Apricot.' Handsome with a dark green,
glossy leaf. Pungent odor, with a hint of apricot to some
people. Flowers large, rose-colored with deeper markings.

P. 'Shottesham Pet.' Filbert-scented, one of the most
desirable of pot plants. Beautiful, lacy foliage, a light,
shimmering green. Brilliant reddish pink blooms are
small, but numerous and borne over a long season. Excellent for boxes and pots.

P. 'Shrubland Rose.' Attractive, heavy, glossy foliage
on a vigorous plant that grows tall and spreads. Pungent.
Lovely rose-colored blooms appear freely.

P. 'Snowflake' or 'Roundleaf Rose Variegated.' Attractive with large ruffled leaves of bright, light green
blotched white. Outdoors leaves grow huge and umbrella-
like, quickly covering unsightly places. If potted, brought
inside, and cut back at least once during the winter,
plant stays in bounds. The amount of white on the leaf

is determined by culture: too much nitrogen, water, and not enough sun will decrease variegation. Pungent odor, mintlike and rose all at once.

P. *torento* 'Ginger.' Rounded leaves, fan-shaped with brilliant rose-lavender flowers. Tall plant, rapid-growing, needs to be cut back frequently. Pungent-scented, with a slight aroma of ginger.

SCENTED GERANIUMS IN WINDOW BOXES

I couldn't get along without my window boxes of scented geraniums. The drier the summer, the more I appreciate them. They are on the northwest of the house where there is some shade, with a sphagnum-moss mulch to help hold moisture. Before frost these are brought indoors to my sunniest and coolest window sills. When these are filled, extra plants go to my greenhouse until there is no more space there. Then I trim and cut back, make room for a few more plants, but ultimately some will be left outdoors to freeze after cuttings have been taken.

Scented geraniums grown in containers, indoors or out, need all the sunlight possible each day, evenly moist soil allowed to get dry only occasionally, and coolness in winter (72 degrees maximum). Remove yellowing or drying leaves regularly to keep plants neat and to help prevent the spread of disease.

Boxes or pots for geraniums outdoors need to be at least 5 inches deep, preferably 10 to 12 inches. Good drainage is all-important so that excess water can escape. Use a soil mixture of equal parts sand (or Perlite), garden loam (or well-rotted compost), and peat moss (or leaf mold). Apply liquid fertilizer at watering time every two or three weeks after planting.

Geraniums in box and tub plantings thrive and look best when grouped closely. Here the overall picture is more important than the development of each plant. If you desire specimens, pot plants separately, not in combination.

Italian terra-cotta tub holds large plant of lemon verbena, also scented geraniums. Other herbs shown, from left to right, include *Artemisia absinthium*, perilla, and curly mint.

One of my favorite plantings is made in a box 24 inches long by 6 inches deep and 5 inches wide. A tall broad plant of the rose geranium (*P. graveolens*) is placed at one end. In front of this I plant one 'Apple' and one 'Nutmeg,' this one to trail over the edge. In the center, two or three plants of 'Sunset' ivy geranium cascade over the edge, the pink- and white-marked leaves as pretty as flowers. At the other end, to trail off the side, I plant the velvety peppermint geranium.

'Snowflake' makes a good background in box plantings. I like to combine it with 'Clorinda' in the center, as it blossoms frequently and the dark leaves make a strong center of interest against the lighter green of 'Snowflake.' Toward the back in the same box, I plant 'Ginger' and 'Rober's Lemon Rose.' Favorite trailers such as 'Fair Ellen' and *P. quercifolium pinnatifidum* drape either side, with the taller, more-or-less climbing 'Village Hill' at the back.

My geranium boxes are very full, but I find plants grow well when set close. As I write, one box is particularly attractive. The pale sun of a cold winter morning is shining through the light green leaves of 'Shottesham Pet,' a trailing, lacy-leaved plant also called 'Concolor Lace.' The bright green foliage of the ivy geraniums intertwines with the purple leaves of *Tradescantia fluminensis striata* to give the effect of stained glass against light.

For Hanging Baskets

Many of the scented geraniums do well as basket plants, and I urge you to try them this way. I plant them in sphagnum moss alone. This absorbs water readily and makes a good rooting medium, yet remains light enough for a basket.

Here at Caprilands I use a pair of baskets to break the monotony of a long shed wall that faces the little garden house and the Saints Garden. Tall geraniums—'Rollison's Unique,' 'Skelton's Unique,' and 'Scarlet Unique'—twine up around a statute of St. Francis and trail along the ground to make a distinctive grouping. On either

side there are restful bare spaces. But one year these
were notably lovely planted to 'Beauty,' 'Joy Lucille,' 'Nutmeg,' P. *melissinum* and tradescantia. All grew well in
the dry weather and were attractive until hard frost. Just
before freezing, I transferred them to the greenhouse.

Favorite trailers for baskets or climbers are 'Rollison's
Unique,' 'Skelton's Unique,' 'Nutmeg,' 'Old Spice,' P.
tomentosum, 'Beauty,' and 'Joy Lucille.' I combine these
with English ivy, grape ivy (*Cissus rhombifolia*), the
flowering wandering Jew (*Tradescantia blossfeldiana*),
and variegated periwinkle (*Vinca major variegata*).
Geraniums alone will eventually fill baskets, but the
fast growing tradescantias fill in while the geraniums are
getting started and give baskets a completed look almost
immediately. Also, they contribute color compatible with
the magenta or lavender flowers of the scented geraniums.

Some summers I have found pleasure in creating a
garden of scented geraniums alone. A plan for such a
garden is shown and described in Chapter 1.

Scented Geraniums as Culinary and Medicinal Herbs

We grow the marvelous scented geraniums for fragrance, for interesting foliage and flowers, and find still
other ways to enjoy them. A recipe for rose geranium
tea is given in Chapter 4, and for use in potpourri, see
Chapter 16. Some recipes that call for scented geraniums
and directions for making an alcohol rub are included
here.

Rose geranium jelly is made usually by placing two or
three leaves of P. *graveolens* in the bottom of a jelly glass,
then pouring hot apple jelly over them. They impart a
tantalizing flavor.

Rose geranium sugar is made by layering the leaves
with a pound of sugar in a cannister. Allow eight to
twelve leaves for good, strong flavor. Use the sugar for
cookies, either mixed with other sugar in the recipe or
sprinkled on top.

Sponge cake with geranium flavor makes a simple quick dessert, attractive, unusual, and tasty. Slice a sponge cake into two layers. Spread the layers and the top with rose geranium jelly. Place on a large cake plate, decorate with rose geranium leaves and small blossoms. Top with whipped cream.

Angel cake with rose geranium jelly starts with an angel cake sliced into three layers. Place the first in a 2-quart tube mold, sprinkle with sherry, and spread with rose geranium jelly. Place the next layer in the mold, sprinkle with sherry, and spread with a thick layer of softened vanilla ice cream. Add the top layer, repeat the sherry, spread thinly with the jelly and then with lemon sherbet. Frost with ice cream. Put the completed mold in the freezer until it hardens. Unmold by slipping a knife dipped in hot water around the edges. Turn onto a serving plate previously decorated with geranium leaves. Serve with whipped cream.

Rose geranium pudding cake makes a delicious dessert. Beat together until foamy 3 egg yolks (save the whites), 2 teaspoons dried and grated lemon peel, ¼ teaspoon rose geranium sugar, and ½ teaspoon granulated sugar. Add alternately 1 cup milk and a mixture of 3 tablespoons flour stirred into ¼ cup lemon juice. Fold in the 3 egg whites, stiffly beaten with a pinch of salt. Butter a casserole, arrange 4 rose geranium leaves on the bottom, then pour in the batter. Place in a deep pan of hot water and bake for 1 hour at 350°. The bottom will be a thick lemon-flavored, spongy sauce, the top will be cakelike. Top with whipped cream and decorate with a few geranium leaves.

Rose geranium tea biscuits are delightful for afternoon tea on a winter day, and we have also enjoyed them in fall when appetites are keen and the kitchen is cool for baking. It is then that the geranium plants are most prolific, and I enjoy using them to good purpose. Dissolve 1 cake of dry yeast in ¼ cup lukewarm water to which has been added ½ cup sugar. Add 2 eggs, beaten with 1 teaspoon salt.

In another bowl mix 1 tablespoon shortening, 1 tablespoon of warm water, and 1 cup scalded milk. Let cool,
then pour into the yeast-and-egg mixture. Add 5 to 5½
cups of flour. Mix well.

Put in a pan and let rise until double in bulk. Divide
in half, roll out like jelly roll and spread each piece of
dough with a mixture of 6 large rose geranium leaves
chopped fine, 1 cup sugar, ½ cup melted butter, grated
rind of 1 orange, 1 teaspoon of lemon juice, and 2 tablespoons flour. Roll up and slice into 1-inch pieces.

Arrange on waxed paper in a pan. Again, let rise
until double in bulk and bake in a 400° oven for about
30 minutes. Makes about 48 biscuits.

Rose-scented alcohol rub is made by filling a quart
bottle slightly more than halfway with nearly odorless
ethyl rubbing alcohol, then adding whole rose geranium
leaves to the top. A drop of rose geranium oil may be
added to augment the scent. Set the bottle in a sunny
window where the heat will release the geranium oil and
hasten the diffusion of the scent throughout the alcohol.
Allow about a month. A group of pretty bottles filled with
alcohol and leaves makes an interesting silhouette in a
window.

4. Herb Teas and Tea Parties

The Muse's friend, tea does our fancy aid,
Repress those vapours which the head invade,
And keeps that palace of the soul serene.
                    —Edmund Waller

In midwinter with the garden at rest and spring planting too far away to worry about, I turn my energy to the
greenhouse and writing table, with time left each day
to sip a cup of fragrant tea. Tea-drinking was the favorite
social pastime of the American colonists. We all recall
the story of the Boston Tea Party, and "Liberty Tea."
With the tax on tea representing injustice, patriotic ladies
banished real tea from their tables and turned to other
leaves for a satisfying beverage.

The housewife as well as the lady of fashion tried
mints, sages, balms, rosemary, camomile, and many
others, both for medicinal value and flavor. Many of
these teas proved unpalatable, but some pleasant combinations have remained with us. The name, "Liberty Tea,"
suggests to me a group of women gathered in a drawing
room with thin china cups ready to receive the latest
herbal brew; or two farm wives heating the copper kettle
over the fire on a stormy afternoon while they gossip and
exchange recipes and remedies. For these gatherings,
teas were often sweetened with wild honey and sometimes
made more palatable by the addition of homemade wine
or brandy. As China tea returned to use, most of the
herb teas were relegated to the health department, only
a few were still appreciated for flavor.

43

At Caprilands we sometimes have a tea-tasting party when all the teapots are brought out, each one containing a different herbal brew. Guests are given a small pouring of each kind, with teacakes, breads, and cookies for balance. Years ago at our first sitting of this kind, I served twelve teas, too many for proper tasting, and everyone grew drowsy. Some dropped off completely. The effect was that of an opium party. In those far-off days my guests assisted in the dishwashing, but it was with great difficulty that I got help with my twelve teapots and the cups. I learned that day to use herbs with more caution.

When To Serve Tea

The tea ceremony is a ritual not only for the Oriental and the English, but for herb gardeners and their fortunate friends the world over. The connoisseur of tea finds the garden, the woods and fields filled with leaves and blossoms to lend their essences to fine brews. To the confirmed tea drinker, almost any time is tea time, but for many of us there is a special hour that seems just right for this indulgence. Some have their hour on the terrace in the shadows and coolness of the late afternoon. Others have a cup ready on the kitchen table to sip during a busy day. Many of us remember special times when, in a shadowy old house on a wet spring day, with the garden practically swimming, we have spent a pleasant hour drinking tea from old brown Staffordshire. More often than not this tea was given extra flavor with rum added from a small thick green bottle.

Here at Caprilands, herb tea will always be associated with winter sunsets. This is the time in the short winter day when the pink light of late afternoon colors the snowy fields, and darkness creeping from the shadow of the woods dims the view from my windows. There is a chill on this hour of sunset and a sense of melancholy. This is the hour to bring in firewood for the night, and as I visit the woodshed, passing by the baskets of sweet-smelling herbs, they give off their odors graciously as I brush by them. The windbells are tinkling softly with the rising wind of evening, and the few artemisias left from summer's harvest are swinging from the beams, like ghosts in the gloom.

The wood is piled behind the trappings of the summer garden brought in for safekeeping, and I walk carefully around a collection of weathered wood benches and old wagon seats, past a chest filled with seeds for summer and around a great chestnut table where the figures of our garden saints look as cold as the beadsmen of Saint Agnes' Eve. I choose my armful of wood, retrace my steps to the fragrant warmth of the kitchen and on into the long dark living room. The fire soon rises from the smoldering hickory log that keeps it during the day, and in a few moments the sadness of the sunset hour is dispelled—and it is time for tea.

TEAPOTS HAVE PERSONALITIES

My favorite tea herbs from the garden, harvested in the high noon of summer have been stored in airtight tins and are ready for my many teapots. I am a collector of teapots and find depressing the single cup with teabag string hanging disconsolately over the edge. Teapots seem to me to have personalities molded into their designs that suggest cheer, comfort, or snobbish elegance.

Some days when I am working in the greenhouse, I prepare a mint tea, very leafy, and brewed in my brown clay teapot from Japan. This container is the most practical of all for herb teas as earthenware can stand low but constant heat. It has a deep receptacle, actually a large pottery strainer, that holds eight teaspoons efficiently, keeping the leaves from clogging the spout.

I prefer a more refined pot for rose-geranium tea, and the serenity of pale Lowestoft for my own Caprilands mixture. A celadon pot shows my early predilection for tea. This was purchased with the first money I earned at the age of fourteen, when I played the organ for a wedding in our little Grace Church in Vermont. This pot is reserved for rosemary tea, which, aside from its pleasant odor and good taste, improves the mind and strength-

ens the memory if one may believe the old recommendations.

Two favorite pots have been retired. One is the tall
type of ironstone that held enough for a farm family. It
has developed a crack and now decorates the mantel
along with a lovely old blue hexagonal one. I use teapots
of pewter, antimony, brass, copper, and pottery of various
designs at different seasons and for different types of tea.

How To Brew Tea

When you serve teas made from your own or imported
herbs, be sure to allow ample time for brewing. Otherwise
there will be no taste to it, and all you will have in your
cup will be faintly flavored hot water. I have heard that
herbs get bitter with long brewing, but my experience
has been to the contrary.

Many herbs may be infused more than once as they are
slow in yielding their essence. Often I leave South
American maté and rose hips in the pot for the day,
adding more hot water each time I pour a cup. The old
admonition, "fresh water in the kettle and boiling, the
serving pot warm," also applies to herb teas.

Experimental tea tasting is not always entirely pleasant, either for me or my friends. Many teas are primarily
medicinal, more for health than delight, but some are
truly good even to palates long accustomed to Oriental
tea made from *Thea sinensis,* actually a kind of camellia.

My favorite herb tea is made of rose geranium. The
odor is delightful, the taste delicious. For an ordinary
six-cup pot, warm the pot, add two tea bags or two teaspoons of tea leaves, six cloves, and three rose geranium
leaves. Make certain that you have either *Pelargonium
graveolens* or 'Rober's Lemon Rose' for true rose flavor
and fragrance. Allow the tea to steep for at least ten
minutes for the best taste and let the geranium leaves
remain in the pot during serving. Keep a pot of hot
water at hand to reduce strength as necessary and serve
without cream or sugar. This is a stimulating brew and,
unless your guests know the recipe, you will be suspected

of adding an alcoholic stimulant. Start out with this welcome, but slight change from plain tea in your experimentation, then go on to the more daring innovations.

Mint teas, particularly peppermint, are pleasantly odorous and wonderfully restorative. Use either dried or green herbs, enough to insure real flavor. Be sure to brew for at least ten minutes, preferably fifteen, allowing a heaping teaspoonful to a cup. Old recipes allow a handful to the pot. Mint tea is best brewed in an earthenware teapot, and it is a source of wonder to me that so few people own this kind of pot today. Of course, most herb teas can be made in a cup covered with a saucer while brewing, but this loses heat, and, since half the pleasure is in the pouring which releases the fragrance, it is better to revive the older practice.

There are many other herb teas—as one may read in this little collection of tea tales. But, I hasten to add, I am not trying to give medical advice or to prescribe for illness, except the current ones of tension and boredom. I do advise that you start a tea garden where you can grow some potential Liberty Teas, or make a collection for your kitchen shelf of flowery or herb teas—just so that you can sit down for a little while by the fire or in a sunny window and relax as you sip the hot fragrant liquid. This, yes, I definitely prescribe.

Even in my moments of wildest enthusiasm for the use of herbal mixtures, I am aware that teas made from our gardens are only a supplement to the enjoyment of China tea, and not substitutes for it. Do not believe, however, that in drinking herb teas you are leaving the narcotics behind, as many garden teas contain tannin (maté, for example) and other drugs, in small quantities, but with soporific or stimulating properties. The fact that herbs are green and growing in your garden does not make them completely harmless. Just because a plant comes directly from nature, it is no less narcotic, if it naturally contains such a principle.

One of the pleasantest winter pastimes is making new tea mixtures. For this kind of experimenting, use as a base any good brand of Chinese or Japanese tea. Competition has produced many excellent, if uninspired, types of Oriental tea, and since herbs and spices are to be added, it is well to have a base without too definite a flavor of its own.

SOME HERBAL TEAS

Angelica Tea. Add boiling water to either green or dried leaves and sweeten with honey to make a good tasting tea with stimulating properties.

Anise Tea. Use anise seed which you can grow in your own garden. Brew for 15 to 30 minutes, 1 teaspoonful to 1 cup of boiling water.

Calendula Tea. I use this herb, with mints, in making a mint tea. In the past it was used as an aid to complexion beauty, and it is said to be healing to the heart and good for the spirit. *Calendula officinalis* is a small-flowered, Mediterranean plant from which the large-flowered garden hybrids came. Both make a good tea and add bright color to herbal mixtures. I dry calendula blossoms all through the summer and even into late fall, for they often bloom after frost has killed every other flower. I store the dried petals in airtight jars and have them ready to use in tea mixtures at the rate of ½ teaspoonful per cup.

Camomile Tea. The mature flowers of two plants, *Chrysanthemum parthenium* and *Anthemis nobilis*, are harvested for this. The petals disappear when dry and only the yellow seed heads remain, which yield a slightly bitter brew that is refreshing for headaches and nausea, good for the nerves, and soporific. This is a household medicine and one of the most popular drinks in Europe. Allow a heaping teaspoonful of the seed heads to a cup of water; brew in a teapot.

Caprilands Tea. Remembering the many virtues that herbs have and could contribute to our well being, I have mixed a tea of rich symbolism. If you drink it, theoretically you should enjoy these benefits: wisdom from mint, memory from rosemary, immortality and domestic

happiness from sage, bravery from thyme, happiness
from marjoram, a good complexion and a bright outlook
on life from calendula, and soothed nerves and a good
night's sleep from camomile. Furthermore, this tea tastes
good. To make it, mix equal parts of the dried herbs
and allow 1 heaping teaspoonful to 1 cup of water.

Catnip Tea. This is used in both England and America
for its flavor as well as for its medicinal virtues. Like
sage and rosemary, it is a pleasant as well as beneficial
tea. It should always be infused, never boiled, allowing
a generous teaspoonful of leaves for each cup. Cover to
retain all the goodness. The hot tea is given to relieve
fever and to ward off a cold, for nervous headaches and
restlessness from nightmares.

Costmary Tea. A tea good to the taste; use one teaspoonful of the leaves in a teapot and infuse for 15
minutes, drinking a cupful twice a day. Traditionally
used for catarrh.

Holly Tea. This is the maté from South America and
it is one of the most delightful of teas. It is made from
the dried green leaves of *Ilex paraguariensis,* and the
taste is like that of a good green tea, slightly astringent.
It is very stimulating. South American natives find it
sustaining in place of food. Allow 1 heaping teaspoonful
per cup. Brew 10 minutes.

Lemon Balm Tea. Pour 1 pint of boiling water over
1 ounce of the leaves, dry or preferably green. Let this
steep for 10 minutes. Sweeten with honey. Recommended for feverish colds.

Lemon Verbena Tea. The leaves are used green and
produce a good taste and a wonderful scent in mixtures.
Allow 1 heaping teaspoonful of leaves to 1 cup of water.

Mint Teas. Mint is the herb most associated with teas.
Mentha piperita is the strongest of the flavors and in its
own right without other herbs, makes a good drink for
those who wish to replace China tea or coffee as a beverage. Peppermint was used medicinally for heat prostra-
tion and to avert or cure nausea. I associate my first
real experience with peppermint tea with a visit to a

garden called "Deo Gratias." A lovely, restful place constructed on different levels; it gave the appearance of
great size, although, actually it occupied only the area
of an average backyard. It should have been a place to
enjoy, but my companion was suffering from a severe
headache that spoiled her pleasure in the garden. She
was urged to rest on a comfortable garden seat with the
green "nave" of the church garden stretching before her.
Soon a pot of steaming hot peppermint tea was brought
to her, and never was it more appreciated. The headache
disappeared and the world came into focus again.

Although I had often served herb teas before this
episode, I had not fully believed in them. From that
time on I have felt greater confidence in urging people to
drink them. Apple mint is so prolific I feel it cries to be
used for good purpose. Now we cut it about three times
in the season for a magnificent harvest. We store the
leaves in airtight cans and in the winter use them in a
mixed herb tea with this mint for a base.

Oswego Tea. Known to the Indians and the early settlers this was used by them as a hot beverage. The leaves
come from a plant, commonly called beebalm, botanically
Monarda didyma. It was one of the colonists' substitute
teas. Infuse the leaves in boiling water for 10 to 15 minutes to make a palatable drink.

Rose Hip Tea. Seeds from dried hips of *Rosa rugosa,*
beach roses, and dog roses make this beneficial brew.
Prepare it in an earthenware pot that can stand heat;
allow 1 teaspoonful per cup. Pour hot, but not boiling,
water over it, for you want to preserve its vitamin C.
For this reason, allow it to stand on a warm stove or an
electric plate for 20 minutes. Pour into cups, add honey
as a sweetener, and a little milk or cream, if you must;
then fill your teapot again, this time with hotter water
for the next serving. I leave some in the pot all day
and keep adding water to it. The taste is that of orange
and lemon combined—a real citrus flavor. Bits of dried
and ground orange or lemon peel, with the white membrane cut out, are good to add with the honey. This tea

has a hearty taste for a cold day, a taste quite foreign to the plant that produces it.

Rosemary Tea. The dried leaves of this tender perennial make a special tea. The very steam rising from a cup is a reminder of legends. Rosemary symbolizes the fidelity of lovers and friends. It is said to grow well in gardens of the righteous and where the wife rules the house. Rosemary tea has been recommended since Pliny's time for failing eyesight and loss of memory. To make a large pot of rosemary tea, use a quarter-cup of the dried needles and pour boiling water over them. Allow to steep for 10 minutes. It is then ready to drink, with the addition of honey for those who like a sweet tea. Personally, I like the sage- and ginger-like smell and taste of the plain herb. For nervous headaches and sluggish circulation, try an old remedy, 4 parts dried rosemary leaves, 1 part freshly ground ginger, and 2 parts honey in a 6-cup pot filled with boiling water. Add milk to each cup. This is ginger tea with a difference. Not only a treatment for colds, but for the memory also.

Sage Tea. Put 2 heaping teaspoonfuls of dried leaves from *Salvia officinalis* in an earthen teapot. Pour in boiling water and allow to stand until it obtains a good deep color. Any that is not drunk at once may be left in the pot for use later in the day. According to ancient history, sage tea has a marked effect on the brain and head. The Chinese often preferred it to their own tea. We usually have some brewing on the back of the stove. Pineapple sage leaves, used green for tea, do not yield much flavor but they do produce a fine pineapple odor.

Sassafras Tea. This American drink, beloved by persons in the South and Midwest, is remembered by many as a spring tonic given for a multitude of ills. There are a few sassafras trees in our woods, and we look for the mitten-shaped leaves on walks and pinch them and peel the bark of the tree to get the odor and taste. Rows of these trees grow unappreciated in many new developments, and this is fortunate because to get enough of the root to use, trees may be damaged. We buy our sassafras in large quantities, hoping that in some part of the world where the climate is less rigorous, root and bark can be gathered without damage. Sassafras has a strong flavor and an odor that penetrates the house. As the substance from which the liquid is made is very hard, it takes at least 20 minutes to get the best from it; this, like other seeds and bark, is slow to give off its essence and can be used for several infusions. Allow 1 teaspoonful per cup of water. I confess that I do not like sassafras but it is popular enough to need no recommendation, and you may find it just your "dish of tea."

Speedwell Tea. Both the seeds and plants of speedwell (*Veronica officinalis*) may be used in the brewing of a medicinal tea. This is valued highly for its strengthening properties. At one time it was the universal substitute for tea. Allow 1 heaping teaspoonful to 1 cup of water.

Strawberry Tea. Long before gardeners considered the red berries of this plant for any but medicinal purposes the leaves were dried and employed in the making of tea. It was the woods strawberry or *fraise des bois* that was used. Now I mix strawberry leaves with other herbs in tea mixtures. Try 1 teaspoonful of the dried leaves to 1 cup of water.

Tansy Tea. This makes bitter brew, but it was once used as a spring tonic, and it is reputed to aid digestion, to bring out the measles, dispel rheumatism, and to soothe the nerves. Tansy tea was one of the six remedies for palsy prescribed by the ancient school of medicine at Salerno. It is advised as a tea to produce quiet sleep in cases of insomnia, but it is a mild narcotic and *should not be used to excess.* Allow 1 teaspoonful of leaves per cup of water.

Spring Diary

He who sees things grow from the beginning will have the best view of them.

—Aristotle

There is always one morning in late March or early April when I bundle up and go trudging off in search of spring. There's still a bite in the air and the wind is hardly gentle, but I am tired of fireside planning and ready for the doing.

Here and there I lift the salt hay cover to see how my low-growing herbs have fared. I look under the mulch on the banks of creeping thyme and the hedges of *Thymus vulgaris*. I check the compost around the santolinas. A spring thaw can leave even these fairly hardy herbs bare and vulnerable. As the morning sun warms the air a little, I tamp down a rootlet, firm the slightly heaving soil around the horehound, lift a Christmas tree bough to inspect my germanders, even though I know it is too soon to expect even a greening leaf. I push aside the leaf cover on the lavender bed to find the marker and go off to the shed for a bigger one. Early weeding could easily destroy the seedlings here for it will be mid-June before they show up.

For me, it's spring now; my mind is filled with things to do; I've pots of well-started plants to go out when its warm enough and stacks of notes on what to do and when—and why. Before long daylight hours will be all too short. My hands are aching for the touch of warm soil, and my eyes are ready for the greens and yellows of spring after winter's browns and grays. As I walk back to the house I know that very soon there'll be no time to dream over a cup of tea.

5. Planting the Herb Garden

This rule in gardening never forget,
To sow dry and set wet.
　　　　　　　　　　—Old Proverb

It is fine to have a perfect location for your herb garden, but if this is not possible, don't worry needlessly. Here at Caprilands where I have five acres of lawn and planting, the gardens are not all ideally placed. The Saints Garden, our meditation spot, private and secluded on level but not well-drained land, gets little sun. This is a challenge, but, fortunately, there is an herb for every location and favorites will grow to some extent under trying conditions.

The "perfect" site for an herb garden is well-drained, with a slight slope so that water does not linger around the crowns of plants. A neutral to slightly alkaline or sweet soil is best for most herbs. If your soil is acid and azaleas and rhododendrons thrive, apply generous amounts of limestone to the herb garden each spring. The third requisite is sun. Herbs profit by eight hours of sunshine daily in summer, but if your grounds are shady, you can still grow herbs, although they will grow taller than usual, and those you plant for seasoning will have less flavor.

How To Prepare the Ground

After you select the site, stake out boundaries. Remove any large rocks, other debris, and small underbrush or weeds. Work up the soil to a depth of 12 inches, using a rototiller or spade. As you come upon more stones, sticks,

Photograph by Bamberger

Entrance to Caprilands, the author's fifty-acre herb farm at North Coventry, Connecticut. Plants of note, from left to right, include woodbine (*Clematis virginiana*) at end of greenhouse, dooryard garden of silvery artemisias, sumac against the house, and a tall clump of tansy at right of Caprilands sign.

and bits of wood, collect and remove them, too. If witch-grass is present, as it is here, sift out every last white root you can find.

I recommend three rototillings or diggings: the first to remove the sticks and stones; the second to incorporate well-rotted compost or well-decayed cow manure in soil lacking humus; the third to mix in the garden lime spread on top until the ground is nearly white. Where soil is strongly acid, allow 100 pounds of lime for a garden 12 by 18 feet. Even sweet woodruff, lovage, and angelica will tolerate lime, and thymes, lavenders, and santolinas can't live without it. If mints have enough moisture, they seem to able to grow well in any soil. Therefore, except in areas where the soil is already neutral or on the alkaline side (pH 7.0 or higher), it is wise to apply lime to the herb garden every second or third year in late winter or early spring.

To Put Your Plan into Action

First drive a stake at each corner of the outside boundaries of your herb garden, making the area a few inches larger than you want it to be when completed. Stretch a sturdy cord taut from one stake to the other until the garden is fenced in. Then, with a steel tape measure and more stakes and string, measure off and outline the beds with flour or lime. I sketch in the curving lines with the thin, long blade of a tobacco hoe and true them afterward. Next, lay walks of whatever you prefer—old brick, native fieldstone, woodchips, or even grass. In a contemporary setting, bricks might be used for the walkways with redwood frames rising 2 or 3 inches above the ground to outline each herb bed. This works well if beds have only straight lines, but it is impractical with curves.

Now you are ready to plant. Generally hardy perennial herbs are bought as plants, the biennials and annuals started each year from seeds. If your budget is limited, buy just two each of the perennial herbs you want. As these grow, you can divide or propagate by cuttings. Order your herb plants by mail or visit a nursery as early

Photograph by Bamberger

Author's Dooryard Garden with sundial in the foreground. Plants of interest, from left to right, include *Allium senescens* (slender stems with globe-shaped flowerheads); *Artemisia absinthium* and sumac tree near the house; thymes, artemisia 'Silver King,' *A. frigida* and *A. ludoviciana* in front of the sumac; 'Silver Mound' artemisia and santolinas surround base of sundial; clumps of bedstraw appear at far right.

in the season as possible, so you will be sure to get the kinds you want.

HERBS FROM SEEDS

I find that all herb seeds do better if they are started outdoors where fresh air, full light, and coolness promote vigorous growth. I have tried raising plants in the greenhouse, transferring them later to coldframes for hardening off, but this is hazardous. Often plants started from seeds sown outside are as large as those started earlier in the greenhouse.

The business of planting seeds should be a simple process, as natural as nature. For some reason gardeners like to make a ritual of sterilizing soil, light tests, soil tests, and germination tests with all the protocol of the laboratory. In fact, I know many who get so wound up in all this that they never get around to the actual sowing of the seeds.

When frost danger is past and you have spaded or rototilled the soil until it is in mellow, friable condition, you are ready to sow seeds. Mark out the rows with a hoe, making them wide enough to do a little scattering. Sprinkle the seeds over the prepared area, scatter soil lightly over them, then moisten with a misty spray of water from the hose. The seeds will probably germinate if you do not cover them, but sharp-sighted birds often pick up much of their favorite coriander, caraway, and other seeds if these are left uncovered at planting time. The general rule is to cover seeds to three times the depth of their thickness. If seeds are dust-size, merely press them into the planting medium. I usually sow seeds like this in a protected coldframe outdoors, or in a flat or bulb pan inside, as described later in this chapter.

After sowing your seeds, do not be impatient; some herbs are slow to germinate. Generally, they seem to do better if you don't watch over them too anxiously. But it is important to keep the seeded area reasonably moist until germination is well along. If the weather is cool and wet, no special care is needed, but as the season

Photograph by Bamberger

Entryway Garden at Caprilands, with clump of southernwood to the left side of the chair on the left; potted rosemary and bay between the chairs, and a clump of wormwood at right; foreground plants, from left to right, include camphor-scented artemisia, sage, thymes, rosemary, artemisia 'Silver King,' lavender, and catnip.

advances it helps to stretch burlap, tobacco or cheese cloth across the seed rows to keep the soil evenly moist. If you do this, be sure that this cover is removed by the time seedlings show above the ground.

I learned long ago not to sow all my seeds at one time. First sowings, particularly very early ones, are often washed out in heavy spring rains, or destroyed by unseasonable cold. When this happens, you will want a second sowing.

My own seed-planting methods are not exactly meticulous, but I get good results. For the gardener with a few packets of seeds to sow instead of several pounds, a more cautious method is probably desirable. Prepare the soil carefully, screen out clods and stones, level by raking, then soak with water. When the soil has dried enough to be workable, make drills to the depth of a pencil point and sprinkle the seeds in these, spacing as evenly as possible. Cover lightly, firm the soil, keep moist, and good germination should be the result.

Sometimes in the creation of an herb garden, you can use free-form clumps or groupings of each kind of plant instead of straight rows. You can mark off these spaces inside a bed with the edge of a hoe and redraw them until the effect is pleasing. Then start your planting, broadcasting the seeds of each plant in the area chosen.

Time for sowing varies from one area to another. Your County Agent in the county court house represents the United States Department of Agriculture, and he has up-to-date average dates for the last killing frosts in your locality. It is generally safe to sow all seeds after that date. Here, in New England, I try thyme, rosemary, lavender, hyssop, rue, sweet marjoram, savory, parsley, chervil, chives, calendula, bachelor's-button, caraway, and coriander on the fifteenth of April. I always gamble and plant a few basil seeds then, although I know they are sensitive to cold and will not germinate until the weather is warm. Once in a while April in Connecticut turns out to be warm enough for the first-planted basils to produce an early crop that delights me.

Early planting of herbs is not vital to success. There are many that grow well from seeds sown in summer. I always put in a second planting of basil in late July. I sow burnet seeds as soon as they ripen in order to have small seedlings for potting. Thyme, dill, and parsley are others that may be sown in summer. August-sown seeds provide seedlings for transplanting into winter window boxes, as described in Chapter 2.

Herb Seeds Indoors

If you have to have plants early, start them in February or March in the sunniest and coolest window you have, or under fluorescent lights as suggested in Chapter 2. Annuals to try early inside include basil, summer savory, sweet marjoram, dill, parsley, chervil, and calendula.

For this early planting, use flats or boxes, or bulb pans filled with a mixture of 2 parts sand and 1 part vermiculite. Moisten well, then sow the seeds and barely cover them. Keep in a well-lighted place and water from the bottom as often as necessary to keep the surface soil evenly moist. As soon as germination starts, move containers into the sun. When seedlings are large enough to handle, transplant them to pots filled with a mixture of equal parts vermiculite, garden loam, and compost (or peat moss if you do not have compost). The seedlings need a nighttime temperature of 50 to 60 degrees and plenty of fresh air in the daytime.

As spring approaches and days get warm, harden off the seedlings started indoors by sinking the small pots down in the soil of a coldframe until they take on a healthy outdoor look. Or you can group the seed flats, boxes, or pots on a protected porch for a few days. After this hardening off, the seedlings will be ready for planting directly in the garden.

If you are sowing dust-fine seeds of herbs, such as pennyroyal, ambrosia, or wormwood, half fill a pot with good potting soil and cover with screened sphagnum moss or vermiculite. Moisten, then sow seeds over the

surface, thinly and evenly. Don't press in or cover with
soil, but place the pot inside a polyethylene bag or cover
with a pane of glass. Either will retain moisture so that
the fine seeds will sprout. As soon as they show vigorous
growth, remove plastic or glass, at first just for an hour
or two, gradually increasing the time until the seedlings
are hardened off and no covering is necessary.

Perennial Herbs from Seeds

Perennial herbs that grow easily from seeds include
hyssop, salad burnet, chives, fennel, pennyroyal, rue,
sage, sweet marjoram, *Majorana hortensis*, and thyme
(*Thymus vulgaris*). If you have patience and a place
to start them where they can remain undisturbed, try
the more difficult lemon balm, catnip, horehound, lavender, lovage, mint, rosemary, winter savory, sweet
woodruff, and wormwood. Sweet cicely grows best from
self-sown seeds. Herbs best propagated by division of
roots or from stem cuttings include tarragon, angelica,
most artemisias, santolina, germander, most mints, and
rosemary.

Lavender from Seeds

Lavender seeds are notoriously slow to germinate,
sometimes taking six months. Coolness seems to be an
essential condition for bringing this seed out. For many
years I was determined to grow lavender from seeds. I
bought them from many firms in many parts of the
world. Occasionally I was rewarded with a single weak
plant, but never with any result commensurate with the
time and effort put into the project.

One autumn I dropped a season's accumulation of
lavender seed packets in a row in the garden where, except for cleaning away the leaves, no weeding is done
until the first of June. The next spring I found a small
forest of seedlings, so tiny they did not resemble lavender,
but I had only to touch them to get the wonderful lavender odor. The seedlings grew undisturbed until they were
large enough to be transplanted. Later these plants be-

came the wide lavender border that leads to our side entrance in the dooryard garden.

Now I always grow lavender from seeds sown in November, with sometimes another sowing in March. *Lavandula spica* is the most certain and quickest to germinate, but the plants are generally not very hardy or long lived; they are well worth growing however, for the fragrant white foliage. Blossoms are borne on stems sometimes 2 feet tall, pale in color, and not as sweet as *Lavandula vera* and its varieties.

6. The Versatile Thymes

For he painted the things that matter,
    The tints that we all pass by,
Like the little blue wreaths of incense
    That the wild thyme breathes to the sky;
Or the first white bud of the hawthorne,
    And the light in a blackbird's eye;
                        —Alfred Noyes

Literature is filled with references to thyme—hillsides, banks, and mounds of thyme; old sundials surrounded with thyme in pleasant symbolism; thyme that smells like "dawn in Paradise" and thyme with its clean fragrance in the manger hay at Bethlehem. There are walks and allees of thyme, and old-time gardens with thyme lawns and terraces. There are upright thymes to make little hedges in a culinary garden, and dark green, glossy-leaved kinds cherished for their exquisite lemon odor. There is a thyme as gray as a lichen-covered rock and another that appears to be covered with yellow flowers, but it is the leaves that are touched with gold. There is a silver-variegated thyme, too. Varieties are legion, and many defy classification. Every thyme-filled garden is likely to have at least one that is an unnamed gift of nature.

ABOUT THE NAME

For plants as common as thyme there are usually many common names, but for thyme there are few and *Thymum* has almost sufficed through centuries for these interesting little plants found throughout the temperate

Photograph by Bamberger

Border at Caprilands is fragrant with thymes that carpet the foreground; also artemisia 'Silver Mound,' *Alyssum muralis*, santolina, Roman wormwood (gray border in right foreground); background plants include tansy and tangerine-scented artemisia.

zone, in the Azores, Corsica, England, France, Italy, and
Russia. The greatest number, including commercial
types from which the essential oil thymol is distilled,
grow along mountainous shores of the Mediterranean in
dry rocks under burning sun.

In a treatise on the plants of Shakespeare, Canon Ella-
combe notes that early English vocabularies do not include the word thyme in its present form. A vocabu-
lary of the thirteenth-century lists "Epitime, epithimum,
fordboh," and this may be the wild thyme. In the fifteenth century thyme appears as *Hoc sirpillum*. Gerard
spells thyme "time," and this reminds us that it was once
called "punning thyme" because of its association with
passing hours and the fact that it is difficult not to make
a pun when speaking of thyme.

Several plants not true thymes bear the names "basil
thyme" and "cat thyme." In the time of Theophrastus,
savories and thymes were classed together, and the old
names cling. Perhaps also any small, strong-smelling
plant might once have been given the name of this widely
distributed family. Thus oregano is often called Greek
thyme, though it is *Origanum vulgare*.

In Europe these small fragrant and aromatic thymes
were symbols of energy and activity. To insure his success in battle, the medieval lady embroidered a bee hovering over a sprig of thyme on the scarf she presented
to her knight, and young girls used thyme with mint and
lavender in a nosegay to bring them sweethearts. Little
bushes of thyme were planted on graves, particularly in
Wales, and sprigs of thyme were often carried by secret
orders like the Odd Fellows at funerals to be dropped into
the graves.

According to tradition, thyme was in the hay and straw
bed of Virgin Mary and the Christ Child. It is therefore
one of the "manger herbs" to be included in the na-
tivity scene.

The wild thyme belongs to pastures, rocky promon-
tories, and the valleys of the Alps but it also thrives along
roadsides, in walks, and borders. It is so vigorous that

less bold and invasive herbs must be protected from its encroachment. Breathing in its heady scent, we understand why the ancients believed that where the wild thyme grew, the atmosphere was purified as well as perfumed.

A pleasant summer sound is the hum of bees above a flowering bank of thyme. It is truly the bees' plant, for with the first blooms in May the bee chorale starts, low and controlled. By late June, with the hillside a mass of pink and purple blossoms the hum rises to a fine frenzy. Then the honey gatherers are so thick that I garden in early morning or after sunset to avoid them.

Classic writers tell of the bees and wild plants that covered Mount Hymettus. Then, thyme was a symbol of sweetness, and Virgil, beekeeper as well as poet, wrote, "Thyme, for the time it lasteth, yieldeth most and best honni and therefore in old time was accounted chief. . . . . Hymettus in Greece and Hybla in Sicily were so famous for bees and honni, because there grew such store of thyme."

In parts of England wild thyme is called shepherd's thyme, and it was once thought to bring illness into a house, a contradiction of the belief that thyme cured melancholy.

Virtues of Thyme

Gerard wrote, "It [thyme] helpeth against the bitings of any venomous beast, either taken in drinke, or outwardly applied." And Culpeper reported: "[*Thymus vulgaris*] is a strengthener of the lungs, a good remedy for the chin cough in children. It purges the body of phlegm and is an excellent remedy for the shortness of breath . . . . gives safe and speedy delivery to women in travail. . . . . an ointment made of it takes away hot swellings and warts. . . . . helps sciatica and dullness of sight. . . . . is excellent for those troubled with gout . . . . taken inwardly comforts the stomach much, and expells wind. . . . . And infusion of the leaves of *Thymus serpyllum* removes headaches occasioned by inebriation. It is under

Venus and is excellent for nervous disorders. A strong
infusion tea—a very effectual remedy for headache, gid-
diness, and a certain remedy for that troublesome com-
plaint, the nightmare."

Wild thyme has been used in an infusion as a remedy
for flatulence, also in the treatment of coughs and sore
throat. Culpeper wrote, "If you make a vinegar of the
herb as vinegar of roses is made and anoint the head with
it, it presently stops the pain thereof. It is very good to
be given either in frenzy or lethargy."

To make a tea of wild thyme, mix 3 parts dried thyme
with 1 part each of dried rosemary and spearmint. Store
in a tightly closed teapot; infuse 1 teaspoonful to 1 cup
water. Let brew at least 10 minutes; serve hot, excellent
for headaches and to calm nerves, said to be useful also
in warding off colds and fevers.

To make thyme vinegar, remove a third of the liquid
from a quart bottle of white distilled vinegar, then fill
with the trimmings of thyme, stems and all. Store in a
warm place for a month. The vinegar is then useful as
a sun-tanning lotion in the summer, and, when rubbed
on the skin, it will drive away insects. Useful also in the
treatment of insect bites and bee stings.

Oil of thyme is used as a counter-irritant in rheumatism. Obtained by the distillation of fresh leaves and
flowering tops, this oil, first discovered in Germany in
1725 by an apothecary to the Court of Berlin, was then
given the name, "thymol." It is a powerful antiseptic
mainly for external use as a lotion, also as a salve for
ringworm and burns.

Thymes planted in orchards where blossoms attract
bees assure good pollination of fruit. If the trees are
small and trim so that the thymes beneath them get adequate air and sun, the effect is delightful. The thought
of flowering fruit trees and fragrant mats of thyme puts
me in tune with those ancient scholars who not only were
gardeners and agriculturists, but writers who told of
their discoveries and experiments in verse and prose that
I find inspiring today.

THYME AND ITS VARIETIES—A TO Z

Whether you grow thymes for use in the kitchen, as ground covers or small hedges, or in a selected collection, you will find them a confusing family, with identification sometimes difficult, sometimes impossible. A named collection needs to be planted separated; otherwise species and varieties grow from one bed to another, intermingling and cross-pollinating, with the strong growers ousting the less vigorous.

In two or three years a hillside of the more rampant thymes becomes a rich tapestry of grays and greens, in bloom a rival to heather. Here it does not matter if kinds intermingle somewhat, though the effect is better if they do not mix completely.

There are two well-known species of thyme—*Thymus serpyllum,* the creeping thyme or "mother-of-thyme" and *Thymus vulgaris,* common or culinary thyme.

The *serpyllum* group is further divided into those of flat or creeping growth (not over 3 inches), and those that form mats (to 6 inches while in flower, with well-established plants growing even taller). Some are gold-leaved, some misty blue-green or gray-green, others between dark green and chartreuse. Spring-planted, these thymes will be ready to spread and cover by fall. The next year they will form walks or make lawns to replace grass, and they can be walked upon without harm.

The common thymes (*T. vulgaris*) are used for seasoning, traditionally a part of every culinary garden. However, they are so fragrant and attractive that many gardeners now plant them as shrubby hedges to border paths, outline beds, and assist in the tracing of patterns and designs in formal gardens. These hedges are low, not above 12 inches, and may be trimmed for conformity. Clippings can be dried for seasonings and potpourri, or to make thyme tea.

There are many other species of thyme besides these two common ones. Here are some of my favorites:

T. angustifolius. The narrow, long leaf of this thyme is somewhat hairy, giving the essentially green plant a

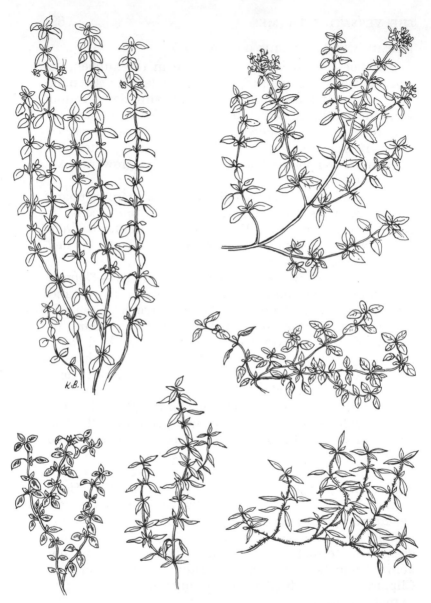

SIX EXCELLENT THYMES. (Left above) Lemon *Thymus
serpyllum vulgaris;* (below) Silver Lemon *T. s. argenteus*
and Narrow-leaf French *T. vulgaris.* (Right above) Mother
of Thyme *T. serpyllum;* (center) Golden Lemon *T. s. aureus*
and (below), Woolly-stemmed *T. lanicaulis.*

70

gray appearance. It is vigorous, spreads rapidly, and flowers in late June.

T. britannicus. A gray-leaved British plant excellent for covering large areas. The leaves, larger than those of *T. serpyllum lanuginosus*, have the same formation and are round, wooly and sweet-scented. They look gray in dry weather, greener in rain, reddish or purple in spring and fall. The pink-lavender flowers appear in late June.

T. cimicinus. A vigorous and hardy import from southern Russia with reddish stems that creep along the ground, never reaching above 3 inches. *Cimicinus* means "smelling of bugs," and when trodden upon, that is just what it does smell like.

T. glaber (syn. *T. chamaedrys*). A delightful plant sometimes called Scandinavian thyme, it makes a low, glossy hedge to 3 inches. The leaves, relatively large for such a small plant, are smooth and shiny, a deep blue-green that is a refreshing sight. The reddish purple blooms appear in July and again in August.

T. herba-barona. A thyme from Corsica with long trailing stems, and leaves that smell of caraway, hence the name "caraway thyme." The specific name is from an early use as a preservative for barons of beef. An exceedingly fine ground cover, and I wish only that it multiplied more rapidly.

T. lanicaulis. Known as the wooly-stemmed thyme, this one develops long trailing arms to grasp whatever gets in the way. It has no respect for boundaries, spreading rapidly with coarse leaves and stems covered with fine hairs. Blossoms are larger than those of most thymes, an attractive pink, and bees delight in them. Good for a difficult spot. I use it, with *T. britannicus* and *T. lanuginosis* 'Hall's Wooly' by my most frequented walk through the dooryard garden to the house entrance.

T. marschallianus. A low mat-forming plant with long, light green leaves and a resinous odor. Flowers are pale lavender.

T. serpyllum. This famous "mother-of-thyme" will grow and perpetuate itself under trying conditions. The dark, shining green leaves vary in size and shape but all give off the true thyme fragrance. Plants grow well among rocks and along the edge of a terrace where they can work their way down a hill.

Mother-of-thyme spreads by root and self-sown seedlings. It thrives almost anywhere except in ground that is constantly wet and shaded. One of my current projects is to transform an extensive area by our roadside into a planting of this thyme. Once established, the place will no longer require mowing, and the mass of shining green leaves all summer and the purple blossoms from August to Thanksgiving will delight all who pass by.

T. s. albus. A tiny white-flowered plant, often overruled by more rampant types. It has the smallest bright green leaves among the thymes and is lemon-scented; in June the lovely white blossoms appear, hovering over the earth as flat as the leaves. Try planting this thyme around a sundial with bushy lemon thyme *(T. s. vulgaris)* growing against the column.

T. s. argenteus or 'Silver Lemon.' Growing to 6 inches in shrublike form this is attractive in a solid bed or used as an accent. The green leaves are variegated with silver. If you have the space, try alternating beds of 'Silver Lemon,' 'Golden Lemon' *(T. s. aureus)* and plain lemon *(T. s. vulgaris).* The color contrast will be delightful and the planting will give off a wonderfully sweet odor. 'Silver Lemon' is not completely hardy if winters are severe. It needs a mild sheltered place where the temperature does not exceed 50 degrees nor go below freezing, with evenly moist soil and ample fresh air on sunny winter days. A cold or pit greenhouse, or well-ventilated coldframe makes a good place for winter storage of tender thymes.

T. s. aureus or 'Golden Lemon.' Green leaves, edged with gold, have a strong lemon odor. Blossoms come late, a light purple, on a shrub about 6 inches high. Needs winter protection as described above.

T. s. 'Caprilands.' Spice-scented plant and one of my best mat-forming thymes, it came to me without indentification. Since I have never been able to discover an official name, I have given it one for convenience. It is the most fragrant thyme in my garden; a leaf picked and rolled in the hand gives off a scent of flowers and spice. The narrow leaves are light green, growing first as mats, later becoming thick cushions. It grows even on the shaded side of my house and has lived for some years in a spot where all other thymes have failed. Blooms appear in late July. As they fade, clip them back. Good to cover arid banks or terraces.

T. s. 'Clear Gold' or 'Gold-leaved.' At certain times of year I must admit that this belies its name and turns a tarnished gold, but seedlings appearing around parent plants in spring have bright clear coloring. An excellent terrace cover, it yields a fine pungent odor when trod upon. It grows well in dry seasons, and in late July and August produces pale lavender blooms that need to be cut back to avoid a ragged appearance. Tops die back in winter and need to be sheared off in spring to allow the new growth to come through.

T. s. coccineus. The popular crimson thyme with small leaves set close, stays dark green until they change to red in autumn. Blossoms are a brilliant magneta-pink with young seedlings late flowering and extending blooming time from June into July. *T. s. c. Splendens* is similar to *coccineus* except that it has larger blooms.

T. s. conglomerata. A green-leaved thyme that grows into a heavy mass. As the roots spread, each group of little branches forms a small circle. It is very hardy in my garden, surviving drought, flood, and cold.

T. s. lanuginosus. The wooly thyme is the lowest growing of the gray ones. It is also one of the most attractive of all the creepers, so gray it is hard to distinguish from the rock it covers. Each spring I fear that winter has destroyed the plants, but usually more have survived than first meet the eye. Soon the gray wisps grow into wooly mats with a few pink flowers in late June.

T. s. lanuginosus 'Hall's Wooly.' Leaves are greener than those of *T. lanuginosus*, yet they are still somewhat

gray and plants are much hardier and better for use as
a ground cover. I grow it along the driveway on the edge
of the dooryard garden. There it spills over the stones,
reaching down into the gravel and sand of the road.

T. s. micans. A low mound-forming type with small
shiny leaves, it makes a compact carpet and bears purple flowers in June.

T. s. 'Misty Green.' An attractive thyme, this has never
had an official name in my garden, yet for many seasons
it has retained characteristics that make it especially
valuable to me. It is almost flat, excellent to trail over
the edge of beds into walks, and transplants easily to
make a thick, misty green carpet with a certain grayness,
as if it were covered by dew. Small pink blooms appear
in August. Similar to *T. s. lanuginosus,* it is not so gray,
and far more vigorous and compact with no problem
of winter-killing.

T. s. nummularius. The marjoram-leaved thyme is a
green plant with a gray cast. It makes a high-cushioned
mat and blooms late in summer with a showy purple
flower.

T. s. 'Nutmeg.' The dark green leaves grow close to
the ground and make a fast cover. When crushed, they
yield a spicy odor. The purple flowers appear in July
and continue through August.

T. s. 'Pine-scented.' A new addition to my garden, and
the name is not official. However, when trodden upon,
leaves give off the unmistakable scent of pine.

T. s. roseus. Leaf and growth habit are similar to
T. s. albus, but the leaf is more rounded and flowers are
rose-colored.

T. s. vulgaris (syn. *T. s. citriodorus*). The much-loved
lemon thyme, a plant of dark green, shiny leaves, beautiful and fragrant. Taller than other varieties of *T. serpyllum,* it has the same trait of rooting at the sides and
once established increases rapidly. It winters well, but
like other hedge-forming thymes, does better if covered
by an airy mulch of salt hay. Lemon thyme makes a good

tea, and provides interesting, fragrant, green material
for flower arrangements.

   T. vulgaris 'Broadleaf English.' The leaf is similar to
that of *T. serpyllum*, dark green and broad. It grows less
shrubby than *T. v.* 'Narrowleaf French,' and is especially
good for cutting as there is an abundance of leaf and
stem. The little bushes thicken quickly so that side roots
can be pulled off for planting, and they in turn are well-
established plants in a few weeks.

   T. v. 'Narrowleaf English.' Similar to 'Narrowleaf
French' but greener. I sow seeds in spring for plants
that will mature the next year and be large enough for
winter window boxes. Seedlings tolerate the change
from garden to house better than older plants.

   T. v. 'Narrowleaf French.' Shrubby with older plants
woody and gnarled like old trees. Young plants are stiff
and straight, the color definitely gray. The odor is sweeter
than that of 'Broadleaf English.' I find it pays to protect
this variety in winter with a salt hay or pine bough covering. It has small, white blooms.

   T. zygis. A visitor from Spain, I find it charming and
it does well for me. It is a tiny shrub, to 4 inches, similar
to *T. vulgaris*, with slender leaves and white flowers. The
variety *gracilis* sends up chartreuse branches from a
creeping stem, to 5 inches, and has lance-shaped leaves
with pale pink flowers in July. These two thymes, along
with *T. vulgaris*, provide much of the thymol of commerce.

How To Plant Thyme

   Thymes need sun and good drainage. Alkaline or
sweet soil, and rocks for plants to clamber over are also
near-requisites. Thymes will exist, though hardly thrive,
on a terrace that receives bright, strong light all day, or
direct sun half the day. My variety 'Caprilands' grows
well on a terrace that faces northwest, a location heavily
shaded until midday but exposed to afternoon sun. In
my small Biblical garden, the paths of thyme that form
a cross have done well although the area is surrounded by

trees and gets only filtered sun all day, with direct sun
for about two hours.

When you plant thyme, be sure roots are well down
in the soil. Otherwise they may work up and be burned
by the sun before they take hold. When planting between
stones in walk or terrace, make a pocket for the roots,
water the soil well, and bury the plant till only one-third
of it is exposed. If you do this in warm weather, cover
the transplant with burlap until it is established, lifting
the cover only for long periods of rain or damp, humid
weather. When you remove the burlap for good, mulch
the soil around the roots with grass clippings or buckwheat hulls.

THYME FROM SEED

Pliny the Elder wrote, "For the sake of honey we have
brought Thyme out of Attica, but there is great difficult
in raising it from seed." This was the experience of the
Roman writer and naturalist who lived in the reigns of
Nero and Vespasian. The *Natural History* was published
in 77 A.D., two years before Pliny's death in the volcanic
eruption that demolished Pompeii. His experience is repeated today by gardeners who try to grow all kinds of
thyme from seed. The seeds of creeping thymes (*T. serpyllum* and varieties) germinate sparsely and the seedlings grow slowly. Because of this, seedsmen seldom collect the seeds. By comparison, the seeds of *T. vulgaris*
germinate freely, though the plants are slow in developing.

If you wish to grow common thyme from seeds, level
a bed of well-prepared, pulverized soil in the place where
you want plants to mature. Make a wide bed, digging out
all grass and weeds and cultivating to a depth of 6 inches
in sandy soil, and to 12 inches in heavy, clayey soil.
Broadcast the fine seeds thickly, cover with sprinkling of
soil, then dampen down with a misty spray. Seeds put
in pockets among rocks will yield fragrant plants that
nestle against the stones in a natural way.

Winter Care of Thymes

Thymes have a genius for survival, although good gardeners do not trade on this fact, but are simply grateful for it. I have found that plants which appear winter-killed often are only damaged back to main roots. For this reason, I do not trim them close in fall, but leave about 3 inches above ground and cover with salt hay for winter protection. If thymes grow near the house where the winter appearance is important, mulch with juniper boughs or pine. (More tips about winter protection are given in Chapter 3). Be watchful of heaving when ground begins to thaw in late winter.

A thick planting of thyme always looks like a weeding problem, but usually mats can be lifted back with care for the main roots, which go down 12 inches or more, and roots of weeds and grass extracted with a dandelion digger. Clover is the worst invader of thyme; it must be dug out vigilantly before it becomes established. But there is no pleasanter gardening chore than removing weeds from a bed of thyme. A cloud of fragrance rises as you lift the heavy mats to extract the offending weeds. And what joy to stand back and view a mound of thyme cleared of every weed.

> He who would know humility
> Must weed a bed of thyme.
> —A. G. S.

7. May Day Party

We've been rambling all the night
And sometime of this day,
And now returning back again
We bring a garland gay.

A garland gay we bring you here,
And at your door we stand.
It is a sprout well budded out,
The work of our Lord's hand.
                    —Old English Song

The May Day party at Caprilands is planned to bring us a little of the charm, wonder, and magic long associated with the advent of spring. We can't ride into the wood on caparisoned steeds or tramp the night through to the lights of Walpurgis Night; we no longer fertilize fields with ashes from fires that burned witches, nor do we drive cattle through flames to keep them safe for another year. Seldom do we go singing with arm-filling garlands or hang May baskets on doors, but at Caprilands we recall these customs as we celebrate the end of winter and salute the new gardening year with a May Day party.

Sweet Woodruff, May Day Symbol

We honor on this happy day a modest plant of the woods, called sweet woodruff, *Asperula odorata*, which carpets the forests in Germany with glossy leaves and tiny white blossoms. Used medicinally in the Middle

SWEET WOODRUFF. *Asperula odorata*

Ages on cuts and wounds, sweet woodruff has long been
loved for its fragrance and valued as an ingredient in

May wine. The green plant has a mossy smell, but let there be one dry leaf and you will sense all the sweetness of May. This is due to the sweet principle of coumarin which has the fragrance of new-mown hay and is a fixative for other odors.

Sweet woodruff makes an excellent ground cover and, as such, is increasingly appreciated by gardeners and landscape architects. A shady site is best where soil is humusy, moist and acid. Gather woodruff for the rose jar and for making sachet; place sprigs in letters to your gardening friends.

From my youth I recall that elusive smell of woods in spring—a sweetness ascending from mold and decay but with the breath of young life rising from it. That is the odor that permeates the house when May wine is poured into the May bowl.

DECORATIONS FOR MAY DAY

My decorations for May Day feature a high-pedestaled, milk-glass bowl with punch cups around it and a deep tray underneath with a little water in it to keep fresh the covering of lilac leaves. I surround the tray with bright herbal flowers from the garden, with basket-of-gold alyssum, myrtle, sweet violets, and Johnny-jump-ups— these interspersed with young camomile plants and crocuses. This garland keeps well and shows off the many cuttings of sweet woodruff which I insert in small containers of moist, mossy soil that are concealed by the other flowers and leaves.

FOOD FOR MAY DAY

To be traditional, food for May Day should come largely from the dairy. Eggs, milk, and oatmeal cakes were the ancient fare, prepared and served around the Beltane fires of Scotland, and similar fires in other parts of Europe. The first day of May was called Beltane or Baltein, and the great event was the *tein-eigen* or "forced fire." This was of Druidic origin and flamed on the highest points of accessible land where dwelt the Druid gods.

Photograph by Bamberger

Kitchen Garden at Caprilands with gravel walkways and old brick edges for the beds. Plants shown toward the back, from left to right, include catnip, dill, mint, chives, small rosemarys, oregano, lovage, sage, tarragon, fennel, Egyptian onion, sweet marjoram, basil and winter savory. Foreground plants include summer savory, Italian parsley, nasturtium, calendula, borage, thyme, and a border of strawberry 'Baron Solemacher.'

Village fires were extinguished so that the hearths might be lighted later in the newness of spring with a faggot from the Beltane fire.

The heat and the flames of this great conflagration streaming up to heaven and exploding in bright showers of rapidly burning birch had properties of magic and healing. In the holocaust old man winter perished; indeed, he was often burned in effigy, a man of straw

81

thrown into the flames after ritual songs and processions. As the straw body, corn husks, and birch boughs were consumed, spectators reached into the fire to retrieve charred bits as good luck charms.

Around the flaming pyre the country people sat at a table made of green sod and large enough to accommodate them all. A cooking fire was kindled, a custard prepared, and a great thin oatmeal cake called a bannock was divided among the company. It was solemnly eaten for it marked an occasion compounded of wild joy and great awe when the evils of death, of which winter was symbolic, were driven out, and the resurrection of life occurred, symbolized by spring.

As you sip May wine, remember that this merry month has been a time of worship as well as feasting since the dawn of history. Truly it is the flower month when Greeks and Romans worshipped Flora, Goddess of Flowers; now May is dedicated to the Virgin Mary. May is a time for rejoicing; the month for Maypole dances, May baskets, and May flowers.

> Upon the first of May,
> With garlands fresh and gay,
> With mirth and music sweet,
> For such a season meet,
> They passe their time away.
> —Old Song

CAPRILANDS MAY WINE

    1 gallon Rhine wine
   12 sprigs or more sweet woodruff
    1 10-ounce package sliced frozen strawberries
    1 cup granulated sugar
    2 cups brandy (optional)
    1 quart fresh strawberries, or 1 twenty-ounce
       bag frozen whole strawberries

Pick the woodruff and heat 3 or 4 leaves in the oven to bring out the coumarin. Let stand in the wine 3 to 7 days to bring out the flavor. Or, follow the suggestion of a German friend and get this woodruff flavor by putting the herb in a bottle of brandy for use at any time through the year.

To prepare the bowl: Put in a block of ice, ladle the wine mixture over it to chill; add the brandy if you wish. Mash sliced strawberries with sugar. Stir into the wine mixture. (Remove the dried woodruff or not, as you wish.) Garnish with fresh woodruff and scatter spring flowers upon the pink surface of the punch, as Johnny-jump-ups and purple and white violets. Put a whole strawberry in each cup and a floating flower as you ladle in the punch. Makes about 50 punch-cup servings.

Hints: Champagne is traditional for May wine punch. Sometimes we use half champagne and half Rhine wine. With champagne, the punch must be served immediately. To avoid diluting the wine too much, especially if you are serving for several hours, pack the bowl in a large vessel of ice. Do not use quick-melting ice cubes, but a large block of ice in the bowl.

For Wine Jelly of fine flavor, use leftover punch, allowing 2 cups of it to 2 cups of granulated sugar with commercial liquid pectin to make it jell. Follow instructions on bottle. To make the jars of jelly pretty—and for a sweet memento of your happy party—place a woodruff leaf in each glass before you pour in the jelly mixture.

PICKLES AND PEANUT CANAPES

Blend well: 1 three-ounce package cream cheese, ¼ cup finely chopped sweet relish, ½ cup chopped salted peanuts, dash powdered garlic, 1 teaspoon Caprilands Mixed Herb Blend. Store in earthenware crock in refrigerator, ready for serving with crackers.

ANCHOVY SPREAD WITH TARRAGON

Mix 1 six-ounce package cream cheese with 1 two-ounce can anchovies and oil, 2 capers, ¼ teaspoon dried tarragon, or 2 top sprigs green tarragon, 1 teaspoon chopped onion or 1 teaspoon chopped chives. Serve on crackers or toast.

SPRING-GREEN SPREAD

This uses that wonderful salad herb, burnet, which often stays green through the winter and is ready for early spring cutting. It has a real cucumber flavor, especially strong if the burnet is left overnight in cream cheese or butter. Blend well: 1 three-ounce package of cream cheese, 4 tablespoons finely chopped burnet leaves, 2 tablespoons chopped chives (garlic chives very good), ¼ cup chopped lettuce and parsley, 2 tablespoons dry white wine, salt and pepper to taste.

DILL STICKS

Prosciutto, the Italian ham, hot as red pepper, thinly sliced. (There is no mild substitute that produces the same effect as this pepper-coated ham.) Sliced Swiss cheese. Kosher dill pickles. Cut all three into bite-sized pieces. Large Spanish stuffed olives. Arrange alternately on cocktail picks, the olive at the top. Or use small, white pickled onions instead of the olives at the top of some picks.

SAFFRON BUNS

An English recipe for yellow buns that look lovely with golden daffodils and forsythia on the table. To get the best results, use the pure Spanish saffron "threads," derived from the dried stigmas of the autumn *Crocus sativus*. This retains its freshness longer than the powdered product and provides much more flavor.

1 cup scalded milk	½ cup boiling water
1 cup shortening	1 whole nutmeg, grated,
½ cup granulated sugar	or 2 teaspoons ground
1 teaspoon salt	nutmeg
2 cakes compressed yeast	2 eggs, beaten
1 teaspoon granulated	8 cups sifted all-purpose
sugar	flour (about)
¼ cup lukewarm (not	1 cup currants
hot) water	½ cup candied fruit peel
1 scant teaspoon saffron	
threads	

SUGAR FROSTING

1 cup confectioners'   ⅛ teaspoon almond
  sugar   extract
2 tablespoons rum or
  sherry

In large bowl, combine milk, shortening, the ½ cup sugar
and salt. Cool to lukewarm. In small bowl, crumble
yeast with the 1 teaspoon sugar into the lukewarm water;
stir until dissolved. Add to milk mixture saffron infusion
(soak saffron threads for 10 minutes in boiling water).
Add nutmeg, eggs, and as much flour as can be stirred
in to make a dough—about 8 cups. Then add the cur-
rants and fruit peel, lightly floured.

Knead dough. Place in greased bowl. Brush top with
butter. Cover with a towel. Let rise in warm place about
2 hours, or until doubled in bulk.

Turn onto lightly floured surface, knead about 1 minute, shape into 4 round loaves or 36 three-inch balls.
Place loaves or balls on greased cooky sheets for good
browning. Cover with towel; let rise in warm place until again doubled in bulk. Bake in a 400° oven for 15
minutes; reduce heat to 350° for about 15 minutes more,
or until done. Cool on wire rack. Frost lightly with the
confectioners' sugar moistened with rum or sherry and
almond extract. Makes 4 loaves or 3 dozen buns.

SORREL SOUP

A variation of the traditional French recipe—easy to
prepare, easy to extend for guests that drop in. Make this
in early spring when sorrel is young and tender, and again
in fall when second-growth leaves have formed. Freeze
some sorrel for use in winter soups. For extra flavor in
spring, use some spears (but not tubers) of Egyptian
onions with the leeks and common onions.

1 cup fresh French sorrel
  leaves
6 leeks or 4 shallots or 1
  medium-sized onion,
  chopped
1 clove garlic, crushed
¼ pound (1 stick) butter
6 chicken bouillon cubes
8 cups water
4 potatoes, boiled, pared,
  and cubed

1 sprig rosemary
1 10½-ounce can cream
  of chicken soup
1 10½-ounce can cream
  of mushroom soup
1 14½-ounce can evapo-
  rated milk undiluted, or
  1½ cups cream
Salt to taste
Chopped parsley or chives
  for garnish

In a saucepan, cook sorrel, leek, shallots or onions, and garlic in the butter until soft but not brown. Add bouillon cubes and water. Cover, cook at medium heat for 30 minutes. Reduce heat to low. Stir in the potatoes, rosemary, soups and the milk or cream. Reheat to simmering but do not boil. Garnish with parsley or chives. Serves 8 to 10.

Hint: For an excellent clear soup, prepare as above but omit canned soups and milk. Serve with garlic-bread croutons.

For sorrel soup in the French manner, use chicken broth instead of bouillon cubes, cream in place of cream soup and egg yolks for thickening. Wonderful, rich, and fine if you take care to keep heat low to prevent curdling.

BROCCOLI CASSEROLE

2 10-ounce packages
  frozen broccoli spears, or
  1 large head fresh broccoli
1 10½-ounce can cream of
  chicken soup
1 10½-ounce can cream of
  mushroom soup

1 cup cubed store cheese
1 onion, chopped
2 tablespoons chopped
  parsley
1 cup sliced cooked mush-
  rooms (optional)
Salt and pepper to taste
Dash garlic powder

Cook broccoli in boiling water until tender, drain. Blend other ingredients together and add to the broccoli. Place in a casserole and cover with Herb and Cheese Topping.

HERB AND CHEESE TOPPING

Brown 2 cups bread crumbs, 1 teaspoon ground sage or 1 teaspoon Caprilands Poultry Seasoning, 1 grated onion, 1 tablespoon chopped parsley in ⅛ pound (½ stick) butter. Spread mixture over casserole. Garnish with grated cheese, parsley, and paprika. Bake in 350° oven until cheese melts and broccoli mixture bubbles, about 20 minutes. Serves 6 to 8.

Hint: For a complete dinner dish, mix 1 cup or so of chopped leftover chicken or turkey with the broccoli mixture, or place slices over the broccoli before the topping is spread.

SAFFRON RICE

An excellent dish for the spring table or indeed for any time of the year. Easy for large parties where food often has to wait before serving.

1 cup rice	½ teaspoon saffron
2 green peppers, seeded and chopped	1 cup boiling water
1 cup chopped celery	1 cup chopped cooked chicken
2 onions, cut fine	Parsley
4 tablespoons (½ stick) butter	Paprika
1 cup cream or 1 10½-ounce can cream of chicken soup	1 teaspoon salt

Cook rice and drain. In a deep skillet, sauté the peppers, celery, and onions in the butter until soft, but not brown. Soak saffron in the hot water for at least 10 minutes. Then add saffron plus water and chicken to vegetable mixture. Pour this over rice and mix in with a fork. Place in 2-quart casserole, cover and heat in 350° oven about 20 minutes. Serves 6 to 8.

Hints: Instead of chicken, use with basic mixture: 1 cup chopped tuna, 2 cups cooked, sliced mushrooms, 1 cup cooked and chopped lobster, or 1 cup cooked flaked crab.

SPICED SQUARES

½ cup butter (1 stick)
2 eggs
2 medium-sized ripe
   bananas
½ cup granulated sugar
2 cups sifted all-purpose
   flour; ½ cup milk
1 teaspoon baking
   powder
1 teaspoon salt
½ teaspoon baking soda
½ teaspoon ground
   cloves
1 tablespoon coriander
   seed
1 teaspoon caraway
   seeds
1 cup chopped walnuts
Confectioners' sugar
with sherry or rum for
topping

Cream butter, eggs, and bananas together. Stir in milk. Combine all other ingredients and blend with creamed mixture until smooth. Spread in a 12"x18" pan. Bake for 25 to 30 minutes in a 350° oven. Cool; cut into about 50 tiny squares or 36 larger ones. Cover each square with confectioners' sugar moistened with sherry or rum to make it smooth and spreadable, but thin enough to run over the sides.

Hints: For a unique and edible decoration cut violets or violas with short stems and press a stem with a flower into the frosting on each square. Or use small unsprayed rosebuds in season. For our cakes we sometimes use the beautiful buds of rambler roses and the opened blossoms of the wild rose. For a Christmas delight, decorate with "holly" leaves of candied angelica and berries made from bits of candied cherry.

SESAME COOKIES

These thin cookies are always a part of our May Day celebration. We make them large to represent the bannocks eaten in the old Scottish rituals of this season.

1 cup sesame seeds
4 eggs, beaten
4 cups light brown
   sugar
1½ cups butter (3 sticks)
1 teaspoon baking
   powder
½ teaspoon salt
1 teaspoon almond
   extract

2 cups sifted all-purpose 1 teaspoon vanilla
   flour   extract

Toast sesame seeds in a large fry pan over low heat until they are browned, being careful not to burn them. Stir frequently with wooden spoon. (Sesame seeds are filled with oil so no extra grease is needed.) Combine eggs, sugar, butter, and hot sesame seeds. Stir in flour sifted with the baking powder and salt, then extracts. Mixture will be thin. Drop from tip of teaspoon onto well-greased cooky sheets, allowing ample room for spreading. Bake in 400° oven until cookies are well browned on the edges, almost to the burning point, about 10 minutes. Cool; remove to serving plate with a spatula. Cookies should be crisp, like a nut brittle. Store in tight container, away from moisture. Do not refrigerate. Makes about 12 dozen cookies.

Summer Diary

Summer in the herb garden is a time of rare delight when days are long but never long enough, when the plans of winter are realized and the labors of spring come to fruition, and harvesting begins in earnest. Come with me in the early hours of day for a walk through the garden.

The folded leaves of Lady's mantle, *Alchemilla*, are then filled with gemlike dew, reminding us that dawn was the hour when dew had magic powers. The plant was thought to impart great virtues to the dew drops that settled on each leaf with its look of a pleated mantle, fresh and lovely enough for the Holy Lady. I have alchemilla planted at the head of a cross of thyme in the Saints Garden where the yellow fragrant flowers rise like a morning offering of pale gold to the Virgin and Child above.

The morning glory opening to the sun has also been named to honor Our Lady. The good Fathers who came to Latin America in Cortez' wake took this plant back to Spain and called the blue flower "Mary's mantle."

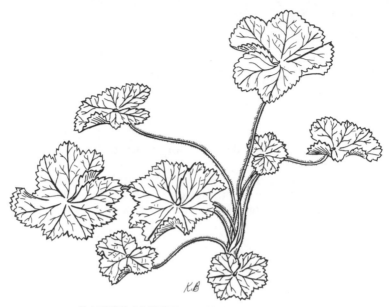

LADY'S MANTLE. *Alchemilla vulgaris*

At one corner of the weathered fence, tall teasels hold-
ing water in the leaf axils tempt me to try an ancient
early-morning beauty treatment—"Who washes her face
in this precious water removes all blemishes." Teasel,
once called "Venus' basin," was later Christianized to "Our
Lady's basin." Hummingbirds drink of this water, and
many insects are tempted by it. Later they will have
eaten out the leaf lining so that the teasel basins no longer
hold water.

At the foot of the statue of St. Fiacre a mass of calendulas, "Mary's gold," reaches toward the sun. "Only to
look on marigold will draw evil humors out of the head
and strengthen the eyesight," so ran the old saying. In
the Middle Ages the flowers were used to decorate the
rich robes of church statues and in the monastery gardens
of southern Europe, calendulas blossomed for every festival of Mary.

Oddly enough, the marigold was not named for the Virgin; this association came later in medieval times. Rather the name was a corruption of the Anglo-Saxon *merso-meargealla*, "the marsh marigold," which is, of course, *Caltha* not *Calendula*. In old English the name was "goldes" or "ruddes," and more recently the marigold. In an herbal dawn we think too, of Shakespeare's Friar Lawrence who collected baskets of potent herbs for Juliet's sleep.

Photograph by Bamberger

The Butterfly Garden at Caprilands, with butternut tree in background, juniper behind statue of St. Fiacre. Plants, from left to right, include *Santolina viridis* (neat clumps in foreground), mints, rue, southernwood, Egyptian onion, rosemary, sage, artemisia 'Silver Mound,' germander, santolina, savory, bergamot, thyme, and lavender.

To look on "goldes" always strengthens me for the day's work as I go up the hill for coffee in the dooryard garden. This is one of summer's special pleasures to be enjoyed from the comfort of a well-cushioned, weather-beaten chair before the day's problems must be confronted.

The dooryard garden at this hour is bursting with sweetness. There are peppermint, apple, and rose geraniums, rosemarys, thymes, lavenders, and a great terra-cotta tub overflowing with a tall lemon geranium. Still other plants beside the door are convenient for picking as we prepare a meal. After coffee, we pause to admire the mints for they belong particularly to summer mornings. The little path leading to the greenhouse spills over with orange mint and frequently is even choked with curly mint. These will soon be harvested, however, for I cut them often, using fresh green leaves for jelly and drying an abundance in onion baskets over the kitchen stove for later enjoyment in teas and potpourri.

8. Herb Gardens in Summer

To have nothing here but Sweet Herbs, and those
only choice ones too, and every kind its
bed by itself.

—Erasmus

The good care you give your herb garden in summer
is the key to its prosperity at other seasons. Now is the
time to rcnew the excitement you felt last winter when
the garden was only a dream sketched on a piece of graph
paper, and to summon up the fine optimism of spring
when it was so wonderful to be outdoors again. Certainly you need enthusiasm now for the many chores of
maintenance. It takes work to keep an herb garden
healthy for a good harvest. The routine is like a three-act
play, with Act I setting the scene (watering, mulching,
and feeding); Act II producing the villains (weeds, insects, and disease); Act III ending happily with the harvest, the sowing of seeds for early fall crops, and surely,
time, too, to gaze upon the garden with pleasure.

WHEN TO WATER HERBS

Established herbs can stand extremely dry weather,
but transplants and young seedlings need plenty of water
until roots are established. In times of drought, herbs
benefit by a slow thorough soaking of roots with the hose,
and a fine brisk spraying of tops to discourage red-spider
mites and also to keep foliage fresh and clean. Rosemary
in particular benefits from this top-washing. But if you

don't have the water or the time to apply it, take hope
because most of the plants will survive.

Early summer is the time for considerable transplanting. To conserve water and insure success, first
moisten the soil well. If there is no rain, soak the area
the night before. When you do transplant, dig a hole
large enough to accommodate the roots of a plant and
pour water into the hole. Then place the plant in position and fill in around the roots with moist soil. Water
again to settle the soil and prevent air pockets; finally
mulch with buckwheat hulls, sphagnum moss, or woodchips. This way you seldom lose a plant, for the moisture lasts for several days.

Wind is probably the worst enemy of transplants, although if this work is done in early spring, chances are
the air will be cool, moist, and fairly still. The problem,
then, is the possibility of late frost. If freezing is pre-
dicted after you have transplanted tender seedlings outdoors, cover them with boxes, newspapers, baskets, or
pieces of blankets. Such protection will save plants unless the temperature drops unusually low.

Later in the season, transplants may be damaged by
hot, dry winds. Cover them then for a few days with
burlap bags propped up with sticks and held in place
with stones. Or use slat frames on legs, and cover with
cheese, or tobacco cloth. Protect individual seedlings by
inserting shingles in the soil on the south and west sides
until the transplant takes hold.

Liquid houseplant fertilizer is beneficial as a transplanting solution when you set seedlings or divide and
replant established herbs. This practice is particularly
helpful as the season advances, and transplanting is done
in the heat of summer.

Mulching the Herb Garden

After your planting is done, weed the garden clean.
Then mulch every bit of bare ground to a depth of
2 inches with buckwheat or cocoa hulls, or other mulch-

ing material available in your area. Mix a little sand or soil with these light mulches or wet them down thoroughly for they have a tendency to blow away. As holes appear in the mulch, replenish it. Some mulches like peat moss and half-decayed leaves work into the soil each winter and need to be renewed in spring. Others like buckwheat and cocoa hulls stay pretty much in place.

A mulch laid in spring after weeding serves several good purposes: it conserves moisture, it helps keep down new weeds, and it gives the garden a neat well-cared-for appearance. Winter mulches are equally vital, and these are discussed in Chapter 13.

FEEDING HERBS

Herbs grown in well-drained soil with plenty of sun and warmth will do reasonably well, but they will really flourish if given fertilizer. Quick-growing annuals like dill and borage benefit from a generous amount of well-rotted manure (or the dried commercial product) worked into the soil before planting.

It is true that over-fertilized herbs are not as good for seasonings; on the other hand, an impoverished soil produces stunted plants and poor leaves for cutting. I find it best to enrich the herb garden scantily with well-rotted manure or compost in spring. Then I water during the season with liquid manure or a commercial mixture with a nitrogen-phosphorus-potassium ratio of 23—21—17.

Potted herbs, such as lemon verbenas in large tubs and window boxes of geraniums, need regular feeding through the growing season with a liquid houseplant fertilizer, applied as a thorough watering once every two or three weeks. Plants in containers have little space in which to send roots out in search of food, and in midsummer the soil dries out rapidly requiring such frequent watering that nutrients leach out quickly. Often a potted herb that looks less healthy than usual will quickly regain good color if given liquid fertilizer with an analysis of approximately 23—21—17.

Photograph by Bamberger
Garden of Esther Larson, Union, Connecticut.
Wide brick paths, formal beds, old roses, thymes,
and heather set the mood for this exciting garden
of many herbs.

As the summer progresses, be vigilant in keeping your
herbs weeded. Every weed takes away moisture, prevents proper circulation of air and mars your own pleasure in the garden. Fortunately, insects and disease are
seldom problems with herbs. Disease almost never oc-
curs if your garden is in a sunny position with well-

drained soil where there is good air. It is also important to keep the dense growers thinned out in spring and fall, as often as necessary to keep them growing vigorously. Transplant the perennials often. Mint sometimes is troubled by rust, a disease encouraged by over-fertilizing and by letting plants go uncared for and unthinned.

If insects attack one of your herbs, do not spray with anything poisonous to humans. Even if the plant you are going to spray is not for cooking, remember that a poisonous spray will drift onto herbs nearby. Methoxychlor and rotenone are two insecticides generally considered safe on foodstuffs. Whatever you do about insect control, follow container directions precisely, keeping in mind that any strong spray or dust will probably leave a residue that, even if not harmful, will dull or ruin the flavor of the herb.

Pause To Appreciate Your Garden

It is in summer that we need time to enjoy our gardens. In the cool of early morning evaluate your plants and appreciate their beauty. Brush fragrant plants, roll a leaf or two in your hand, and breathe in the wonderful aroma. This is a good hour, too, to view your garden objectively; to see if leaf textures, colors, and contrasts are pleasing; whether one clump is too large, another needs moving toward the back of the border, and a third would look better in other company. Make notes of your decisions and pin them to your bulletin board or clip to your desk pad, so that when fall and spring planting times come you can easily make improvements.

In the evening, as the sun goes down, make another tour of your garden. Maybe pull a few weeds always visible at this hour of the day. Then walk in the dusk of evening, forget the weeds, the plans and the problems, and enjoy the tall spires of the artemisias; stay out until the moon touches all with quiet beauty.

Finally, don't be tied down to your own garden all the time. Get away and visit other gardens. You will return

refreshed and inspired. And this we all need. Now the
harvest begins, and the herb gardener's activities build
into a crescendo that concludes only when Jack Frost
brings down his final white curtain.

9. The Mighty Mints

Come buy my mint, my fine green mint!
Let none despise the merry, merry cries
of famous London town.
　　　　　　　　　　—Old London Street Cry

There are few plants in the garden as loved and useful, or as despised for their rankness, as the mints. To know them is to love them—and to be wary also of their bold entrances into every domain of the garden. They are no respecters of the rights of neighboring plants. They run through walks, cover the cowering plants that cannot avoid their advances and often destroy the gardener's dream of order and neatness.

It would be hard to face a springtime garden without the curls of mint pushing through the brown soil. While they are not the first herbs to appear, few plants are as fresh or as perfect upon emerging from the earth. They look like hundreds of small green roses opening to the world of spring, and touching them stirs up rich odors.

SOME WAYS TO ENJOY MINTS

I border grassy paths with various mints, where the lawn mower keeps them cut and they may run at will. As we walk through the garden we can smell the cool odor of mint everywhere. No matter how much you enjoy mint at other times of the year, it is indisputably a plant for tasting and smelling in hot summer weather.

In ancient Greece and Rome, mint was a scent used

101

by rich and poor, and it was the custom to rub tables with it before guests were seated. Today orange mint has many uses in the modern home. To scent a room, hang bunches of mint from open doors or archways where a breeze will release the aroma. This is a practice in India, and I am told that in many hot countries large bunches of mint are tied to screen doors to send cool odors through the house.

On hot summer days when even the coolest garden flowers appear wilted, put bowls of mint on your tables. They will look and smell cool. When you are entertaining, place a sprig of mint on each napkin at the table.

In this day of dining and entertaining out of doors, mints make fine terrace or patio plants. They thrive in redwood tubs, in large clay or pottery containers, or in plant pockets in terrace pavements. In using mints this way, be sure to provide drainage and evenly moist soil. Clip them back occasionally for a neat appearance.

Mints are also excellent house plants. Their culture indoors is discussed in Chapter 2. The many culinary uses of mint are given later in this chapter, and mint will be found as an ingredient in a number of the recipes it this book.

FASCINATING HISTORY OF MINT

Herbals are filled with references to the virtues of mint. After you read the quotations from my notebook I hope you will search out others. Chaucer speaks of, "A little path of mintes full and fenill green," and Gerard tells us: "The smelle rejoiceth the heart of man, for which cause they used to strew it in chambers of places of recreation, pleasure and repose where feasts and banquets are made. . . . It is applied with salt to bitings of mad dogs. They lay it on the stinging of wasps with good success. The smell of minte does stir up the minde and the taste to a greedy desire of meate."

Parkinson wrote, "Mintes are sometimes used in baths with balm and other herbs as a help to comfort and strengthen the nerves and sinews. It is much used either outwardly applied or inwardly drunk to strengthen and comfort weak stomackes."

Culpeper describes cures effected with mint: Rose leaves and mint, heated and applied outwardly, cause rest and sleep. . . . The leaves of wild or horsemint, "such as grows in ditches," are serviceable to dissolve wind in the stomach, to help the colic and those that are short-winded, and they are an especial remedy for those who have veneral dreams in the night. The juice dropped in the ears eases the pains of them and destroys the worms that breed therein . . . [the leaves] are extremely bad for wounded people; and they say a wounded man who eats mint, his wound will never be cured, and that is a long day.

Mint is Biblical and is thought to have originated in Mediterranean lands. Some varieties, slight variations of *Mentha spicata*, came from Egypt and the Holy Land. Mint was brought from the East in commerce and probably was carried by the crusaders into northern and central Europe. In all these places it thrived and, as in our gardens, took over, finding the sites it liked best, usually near water. There it grew luxuriously and was usually considered a native plant.

Mint was once a Biblical tithe. In Matthew 23:23 we read, "Woe unto you, scribes and Pharisees, hypocrites! for ye pay tithe of mint, and anise, and cummin, and have omitted the weightier matters of the law, judgment, mercy, and faith: these ought ye to have done, not to leave the other undone." Peoples of the East and Near East including southern Europeans, Greeks, and Romans used mint as a condiment, in salads, and for flavoring and medicine far more than we do.

Mints have been known as "strewing herbs" since men first thought of such refinements. It was noted that breathing the essence of mint cleared the head and aroused the senses. It also destroyed unpleasant odors when it was scattered over the floors of synagogues, temples, and churches. In medieval Europe, mints with thyme, rosemary, and pennyroyal were scattered among

the rushes that covered the stone floors of castles and
the earthen floors of cottages. Here they purified the air
with fragrance that rose up with every step.

The generic name *Mentha,* was applied first by Theophrastus, a Greek philosopher-scientist and herbalist who
succeeded Aristotle as head of the Lyceum in 322 B.C.
In mythology Mintho was a nymph of great beauty who
was loved by Pluto, god of the underworld. Persephone
became jealous of Pluto's attachment and changed the
nymph into the fragrant but lowly mint. Since that day
mints have been grown in the shady areas of the dark
world of Pluto.

GROWING AND PROPAGATING THE MINTS

Actually mints will grow almost anywhere. They thrive
in moist, humusy soil in shade but also in sun, and few
pests ever bother them. The only problem with mints
is that they spread too rapidly, overrunning other plants
and growing into a mass instead of staying in neat separate clumps. To avoid this, plant each clump of mint in
a metal barrel, with top and bottom removed, and sunk
18 inches into the ground. Or insert metal strips 12 to
18 inches deep around the plantings of mint.

I have never curbed mint this way, but from long experience, I check on the growth of the runners twice a
year, transplanting from the garden any that seem out
of place. I keep them well in bounds in the Butterfly
Garden (see Chapter 1) where they occupy one bed by
themselves. During the growing season I use the plants
lavishly. They are cut in summer to make jellies, vinegars, and an essence for lamb sauce. Leaves are candied
and also dried for teas. They are fashioned generously
in cooling bouquets for hot weather. If you use your
mint beds in this way I am sure they will never be too
large; more likely, they will not be large enough.

MINTS AND NOMENCLATURE

It has been wisely said that the most common plants
were the most difficult to identify because everybody

grew them and gave them names. This is clearly one of the difficulties with the mints. A common belief, and in some instances a fact, is that mints grown near each other cross-pollinate. This does happen, although in the small garden more likely the exploring roots reach into the next bed, resulting in an entangled mixture—hence my suggestion for metal strips. Otherwise it is a matter of eternal vigilance to keep the mints separated.

To classify mints correctly has been the despair of botanists. Dr. Edgar Anderson, long associated with the Missouri Botanical Garden, wrote in a 1938 publication of the Herb Society of America: It is difficult to grow mints without losing faith with botanists. No amateur expects to be able to name all the plants of his garden accurately and well, but he does expect that a professional botanist should be able to do so. Yet if he submits his mint collection for determination, the results are almost inevitably disappointing. If the work is done honestly, some of the mints will be left quite unlabeled, and other names will be followed by a question mark. Our amateur will be even more discouraged if he consults a second botanist and then finds, as he most certainly will, that the two sets of names do not agree. Yet there is no real need for losing faith in botanists and botany. Rather there is needed a better understanding about the whole business of plant naming. Strange as it may seem, the naming of plants is not a finished process, done once and for all time. . . . Had man taken no interest in mints, they would have been less difficult to classify, but his love for them has helped tangle up the snarl. For centuries he has been digging up and carrying them from place to place and letting them run wild again.

I feel sympathy for these learned botanists, when I despair of naming correctly these lovable but errant characters—the mints. Cross-pollination and self-sowing give mint enthusiasts unusual specimens that also present problems of nomenclature and result in the grouping of similar leaves and fragrances under one name with the hope that we are nearly right. But never let nomenclature spoil your enjoyment of the mints. I started my own collection nearly twenty-five years ago and still have many of the original plants.

SOME FAVORITE MINTS

Mentha arvensis. The first mint I grew; it is wild in my area, and was discovered by my mother who loved plants and gardening and associated everything in Connecticut with her Vermont home. This familiar red-stemmed mint has small leaves, comes up late in spring, has a true spearmint flavor, is good for jelly and superlative for summer drinks. It thrives in the moist shade of an ancient ash tree and has been transplanted to other parts of the garden, and to many other gardens as well.

M. citrata. The bergamot or orange mint is a treasure, for it is the most fragrant and manageable of all the species that I grow. The dark green leaves are rounded, broad, and touched with purple. Sometimes the undersides take on a deep shade of red; in early spring the whole plant is distinctly reddish purple. As the season advances, leaves become green and are ripe for cutting. I cut orange mint many times during the summer and use it in the making of a very special punch. Here is the recipe:

1 cup orange mint leaves (green)	12 cups boiling water
½ cup granulated sugar	2 six-ounce cans frozen orange juice
2 cups water	1 cup rum
6 tea bags	

Mix orange mint leaves, sugar, and 2 cups water in large pan; simmer over low flames for 10 minutes. Add to this hot mixture 6 tea bags and 12 cups boiling water; cool. Remove tea bags, then add orange juice and rum, and pour over chunk of ice in punch bowl.

Orange mint appears in many of my summer flower arrangements and frequently surrounds my punch bowl. There, tucked into moist sphagnum moss, it takes root and continues to grow. I harvest the leaves and tender stems two or three times and dry them for winter teas.

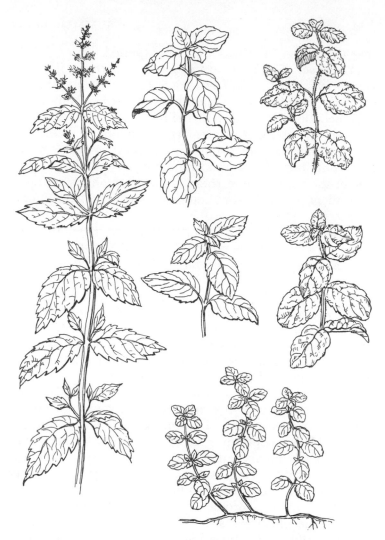

THE MINTS. (Left) Spearmint *Mentha spicata*. (Center above) Orange *M. citrata*; (middle) Peppermint *M. piperita*; (below) English Pennyroyal *M. pulegium*. (Right above) Pineapple *M. rotundifolia variegata*; (below) Apple *M. rotundifolia*.

There is no time when the kitchen smells as good. I tie the stems in small bunches and hang them from the rafters. They are well dried in a day and a night; the leaves remain a dark green and retain their fragrance that is just right for teas and in potpourri.

M. crispa. The curly mint, has a spearmint flavor, a very wavy leaf, and grows to 2 feet, it is a rampant spreader, excellent as a ground cover, but needs to be cut back occasionally. Use it in jellies, for iced-tea garnishing, and in cooling summer arrangements. I would not put this mint in a small garden, unless it could be grown in a container. I use it around the steps on the north side of the house where there is little sun and where it is convenient to pick for bouquets and garnishing cold drinks.

M. gentilis. The gold-flecked leaf has given this the name of golden apple mint. Dark red stems rise from the soil late in spring, similar to those of the wild red-stemmed mint that grows around our farm. It gives a good taste to drinks for it has a fine spearmint flavor.

M. niliaca. This is the Egyptian mint, erroneously called apple. It is a very tall plant with wooly gray, rounded leaves, and may grow to 5 feet, though it seldom goes over 3 feet in the North. I use the leaves for tea, for candying, and in flower arrangements.

M. piperita. Peppermint, sometimes called brandy mint, is most valued in commerce as a source of oil for medicine and seasoning. The finest flavor comes from the English black peppermint, a handsome dark plant with almost black stems and leaves that creep along the ground in early spring and later grow up to 3 or 4 feet with beautiful dark purplish-blue flowers.

Peppermint is vigorous, but tends to die out if grown in the same place for several years. When it is grown commercially, the location is changed every second or third year so the crop will not deteriorate. If you need a quantity of peppermint in your own garden, you may find that it will make its own way and gradually shift to a new location. The state of Michigan in the United States and the township of Mitchum in England have long been known for producing the peppermint of the world, though some is also distilled in Italy, France, and Germany. Today most peppermint oils are produced in Michigan and Indiana in drained swamps and black muckland.

M. pulegium. Pennyroyal, a charming creeper, with a dense aromatic mat of glossy leaves, travels fast and makes an excellent ground cover but unfortunately is not winter-hardy. Sometimes I winter plants close to the greenhouse under cover, but seldom do they live through sub-zero weather. Therefore, to be sure I have some another year, I always take a few plants inside. In a home greenhouse this mint will trail over the edge of a bench and smell sweet as you brush by it. Pennyroyal has long been used for tea, and was a favorite flavoring for puddings in the days when ground meat was termed a "pudding." It is, however, toxic and dangerous to use in any large amount. An infusion of the leaves is used for spasms, cramps, and colds, but it must be taken with the greatest discretion.

Doubtless the best known use of pennyroyal is its effectiveness in warding off insects, particularly fleas. In fact, one of its old names was "flea-away." The oil of pennyroyal was spread in pantries to keep away ants and other pests. The Greeks used pennyroyal as a seasoning for meat and it was called *"blekon"* or *"glekon."* It had many familiar names in England, such as "lurk-in-the-ditch" and "run-by-the-ground." In the days when people wore wreaths to impart virtues to the brain, pennyroyal offered a popular and pleasant way to clear the mental processes.

M. requieni. Corsican mint is so minute and mossy, only 1 inch high, that only by the odor do we identify it as mint. It needs shade, well-drained, moist soil, and a shield from drying winds. Protect it also from rampant thymes or creeping veronicas. Each fall put some sand over the small leaves; this is all the winter protection it needs. Corsican mint grows best for me on the southwest side of the greenhouse where the ground slopes well for drainage, but is still moist from much watering. That this mint will grow in sun was demonstrated when we sank small pots of it in an open field in a moist but light soil.

There it grew so well that it was necessary to pinch it to believe it wasn't the rampant selaginella which it resembles. Corsican mint has the odor of *crème de menthe*, but a far less extravagant essence is used in the manufacture of that liqueur.

M. rotundifolia. The apple mint often starts in the herb garden as a small plant, but it usually ends up growing around the compost pile, in the dump, or perhaps it will jump a fence and grow happily in the pasture or in a neighbor's yard. It was once used in the monasteries of Europe for the treatment of epilepsy. The monks found it valuable in relieving the languor following an attack. Today it still grows around the ruins of ancient buildings, a fragrant reminder of those first centers for the treatment of the sick. I enjoy this mint around an old foundation that needs some cover. It grows either in sun or shade, rich or lean soil, and the soft gray-green, fuzzy leaves and tall growth make it an attractive cover for an unsightly spot. Blossoms are gray-white, shading to pink or pale purple. I make at least three cuttings of it each year and start drying for winter teas in June, continuing the harvest until October. From frequent cutting the leaves are more tender and better for making the candied mint leaves I use to decorate cakes.

M. r. variegata. The pineapple mint is a small form (to 18 inches) of the apple mint with white-splotched leaves that vary with the seasons. I find it needs some winter protection although I wintered it outdoors without trouble for many years. In a cool spot in the house the plant will be attractive from autumn to spring in a hanging basket or trailing from a window box. I use leaves of this and pineapple sage to decorate jellied fruit desserts or fruit cups. While it has little taste, the odor is wonderful.

Pineapple mint makes a fine garden accent. The white-marked leaves somtimes give the effect of flowers. If you have a plant of this variegated mint, do root cuttings to grow in a sheltered spot over winter, or in a window or greenhouse.

M. spicata. The famous spearmint, to 3 feet tall, of easy culture, excellent for iced tea, juleps, candy, salads and as a garnish for green peas, in pea soup, for making sauce and to dry for tea. Keep it cut back so you will always have fresh green leaves for the kitchen.

When the average person asks for mint, he usually means this one. Many think only the one kind of mint exists; some conscious of the existence of other mints, announce they want no "new" ones, just "plain mint." Men usually want a julep mint, women something for iced tea. To describe the many mints that taste like spearmint would be too confusing. Therefore, when I am asked about mints, I lead the way to the plot where we grow what is known as spearmint, and there I have labeled plants of *Mentha spicata.* I make a mental note that this could also be called *M. spicata* var. *longifolia,* *M. sylvestris* (although this name is applied to a distinct species), *M. viridis,* and it could be known by such common names as garden mint, mackerel mint, Our Lady's mint, green mint, spire mint, sage of Bethlehem, fish mint, lamb mint, or Roman mint.

In Mexico and the Southwest, spearmint is *yerbabuena* and it is much used for flavor by the Spanish population. L. M. S. Curtin, in *Healing Herbs of the Upper Rio Grande,* writes:

> The mere mention of yerbabuena will bring a thrill to any Spanish American, he will be enraptured and little murmurs of delight will escape his lips. If he can hold a sprig to his nose he is like a Frenchman in ecstasy over some rare vintage. . . . A tea for indigestion is made of dry or green mint leaves, boiling water, cinnamon, cloves and nutmeg strained and taken hot.

Wounds and sores are washed with the tea and it is a general remedy for diarrhea and neuralgia.

Long ago a decoction of spearmint was gargled to cure the gums and mouth and mend an ill-savored breath—prophetic indeed of our present enjoyment of spearmint chewing gum!

OTHER IMPORTANT MINTS

For years I have grown a plant known only as wooly mint. It resembles spearmint in growth and placement of leaves, but it is almost as gray as an artemisia. It is low-growing, in blossom not over 1 foot tall, although it might grow higher in rich soil. It is decorative and makes a good, not-too-unruly plant for the gray-and-green garden. Its odor, while minty, is resinous and reminiscent of furniture polish.

No discussion of the mints can end with the plants known botanically as *Mentha* species. There are also some important relatives from the labiate family. All are characterized by square stems.

The bergamots (*Monarda* species) can be included but only one is commonly called mint, the delicately colored American horsemint or *M. punctata,* also known as spotted monarda. Historically its use is medicinal—for colic, as a diaphoretic, an emmenagogue, or as a diuretic.

I grow American horsemint for its appearance in the garden. The first spring leaves are green, and as they grow the whitish bracts appear in whorls. The upper lip of the flower is spotted with purple, and bracts that resemble leaves are pink and purple and give the plant the appearance of supporting large blooms. This coloring lasts for weeks in midsummer and causes much admiring comment. Spotted monarda can be grown from seeds; in sections of the South it grows wild. It is hardy in my garden and multiplies, but not rapidly.

I grow an annual member of the mint family which resembles thyme, but smells strongly of mint. It is *Satureja nepeta* (sometimes listed under the generic name *Calamintha*). It grows only 6 inches high and is covered with small, misty blue blossoms that cling to it like drops of blue water. It comes up everywhere in the garden and often has to be transplanted in the interest of order. It contains a volatile stimulating oil in common with other mints; this can be brought out in the brewing of a tea which was once a favorite in English country places.

I grow also the perennial *Satureja calamintha*, a grayish, hairy-leaved plant that forms attractive clumps in the garden. It takes care to keep it in bounds. The bergamot-like blossom appears in shades of purple, paling to white. The leaves were once much used for tea, but they seldom are today, although the taste is pleasant. If it can do all that Gerard claims—"The seed cureth the infirmities of the harte, taketh away sorrowfulnesse which cometh of melancholie and maketh a man merrie and glad"—it would be well worth bringing back into use.

10. Plans for an Herb Show

Herbs too she knew, and well of each could speak
That in her garden sipped the silvery dew;
Where no vain flower disclosed a gawdy streak;
But herbs for use, and physick, not a few,
Of grey renown, within those borders grew:
　　　　　　　　　　　—William Shenstone

A good way to learn about herbs is in an herb study group. This might be limited to herb enthusiasts or it could be a special project for a garden club. If you learn about herbs through organized study, you will want to crown your efforts with an herb show. While it is relatively easy to draw up ideal plans, it takes tremendous work and planning to translate them into actuality.

At the start, make a point of using botanical as well as common names. It is important to be familiar with the correct terminology. Furthermore, make this the horticultural study for the year, and get the most interested members to show their plants from important herb families at your regular meetings.

LEARNING ABOUT HERBS

Here is a six-months' study program. The list of herbs is long yet hardly complete, and well worth a garden club's time. Don't attempt an herb show until at least three members of the club have grown some plants in each classification. If the whole club should attempt the study, suggest that each member keep a notebook of clippings from newspapers and magazines about herbs. The study of herbs is rewarding and leads to a fascinating new aspect of gardening. It will also reveal the modern uses of herbs you grow at home.

This outline is workable, tried and proven in a garden club with 35 members, not one of whom had been deeply interested in herbs at the outset. I presented a twenty-minute talk each month, brought in herbs in dried arrangements, and helped plan for a show composed entirely of dried herb materials. The result was a marvelous display, a delight to all.

Program One. Study the artemisias first. They are so useful in the garden, and there are so many that a show can be planned around them alone. Use Chapter 14 as your study outline.

Program Two. The alliums make a very interesting study as most people are familiar only with onions, chives, and garlic. Study all the species of *Allium* discussed in the Dictionary section of this book: then progress to the ornamental kinds, such as *A. flavum, A. pulchellum, A. giganteum, A. karataviense, A. caeruleum,* and *A. cernuum.*

Program Three. Thymes and other ground-covering herbs are worth considering. Use Chapter 6 as your guide for thymes, or Chapter 7 for sweet woodruff, and the Dictionary entry for ajuga.

Programs Four and Five. Devote two meetings to aromatic and fragrant herbs. Start with mints (Chapter 9), progress to lemon balm, beebalm, the basils, marjoram, oregano, lavender, rosemary, lemon verbena, true myrtle, the laurel tree, and the damask rose. If you have time, talk about the scented geraniums (Chapter 3) and then the preservation of fragrances (Chapter 16).

Program Six. Devote lengthy study to decorative and flowering herbs, some of which will have been discussed in other programs, for example, lavender, bergamot, and artemisia. Point out the usefulness of germander and santolina for low borders, then consider herbal flowers that give color in the garden from late spring until midsummer, such as achillea, angelica, borage, burnet, calendula, dictamnus, dill, galium, hyssop, iris, isatis, lamium, levisticum, marrubium, myrrhis, nepeta, salvia, sorrel, savory, stachys, tansy, valerian, and viola.

ORGANIZING AND JUDGING AN HERB SHOW

The success of your herb show depends largely upon the chairman who carries the responsibility of coordinating the efforts of every committee. "A Guide for the Organization and the Judging of Herb Shows," published by the Herb Society of America, outlines the steps necessary in planning and executing an herb show. This is available at twenty-five cents per copy from the Society at 300 Massachusetts Avenue, Boston 15, Massachusetts.

While the general chairman of your herb show should know a lot about herbs, she must also be a good organizer, able to direct and inspire the other members.

You will need committees for planning, to draw up and have a schedule printed, to direct staging, to handle entries, to pass on arrangements brought to the show; also committees on conservation, publicity, housekeeping, hospitality, and information. Hostesses, judges, and clerks to aid the judges are most important.

If you are going to have an herb show, do follow the suggestions of the Herb Society of America. This procedure will give your show the authenticity and direction necessary to make it a satisfying venture for all concerned.

SUGGESTED THEMES FOR HERB SHOWS

Horticulture needs to be dramatized when it is taken to the exhibition hall. Pieces of herbs stuck in milk or Coke bottles will not inspire anyone, but displays of full-size, growing plants will delight as well as instruct. Arrangements with historical background and a theme that unifies the whole will help you create a show that is a credit to your club and the community.

"Herbs Are Kitchen Magic" would be a good theme for a show with recipes on large placards displayed throughout the hall. Instead of individual horticultural displays, do a series of four small kitchen gardens which could include household herbs. Have one exhibit on drying herbs, with a chart to tell when and how. Arrangement classes should be largely compositions, as many herbs are not dramatic in themselves but are charming in combinations.

"Shakespeare Sets the Stage with Herbs" could be an exciting theme. Give this exhibit a theatrical touch with handbills displaying the cast of characters with quotations from Shakespeare on herbs. Naturally, a knot garden would be featured in this show.

For a fall show of dried materials, plant an autumn garden in front of a drying shed filled with hanging herbs being dried for winter use. Emphasize dried materials in each arrangement class. The horticulture for this theme could be a garden showing green herbs ready to cut. Include decorative and practical plants with instructions for their drying and use.

"Herbs and Flowers Mark the Hours" is another possibility with the insigne a sundial with four or more small plantings around favorite sundials. These could be early American wooden ones, the armillary type, a dial on a stone with a flat planting around it and perhaps one modern sundial. Arrangement classes for this show could be inspired by the hours of the day: "Dawn in the Herb Garden," gray plants, pink flowers, and crystal; "High Noon," an arrangement of fully open flowers suggesting the sun, or of flowers dedicated to the sun; "Dusk," purple and darker tones from a summer garden, tea herbs, and ornamental basils; and "Moonlight," sweet-scented leaves and flowers, ghostly artemisias, white roses, white candytuft, alyssum, bedstraws, and sweet cicely.

For the kitchen herbs in this show have arrangements portraying "Just Gathered" in baskets, "Fine Herbs for the Omelette," "Salad Savories" and "The Herbs That Came To Dinner." To enhance this class, show recipes from favorite cookbooks and interesting containers and accessories, all of interest to cooks.

SUCCESSFUL HERB SHOWS

When you are exhibiting herbs, conditioning is all-important. Long-stemmed mints, particularly apple mint, much used in arrangements, must be hardened in deep water for several hours. Early in the season, artemisias will often wilt and need to be *immersed* in water over-night. Basil leaves usually go into vases without wilting if they are picked before the sun is out. All rose-scented geraniums, if cut with any length of stem, will need soak-ing. The purple leaves of perilla, so beautiful and crisp in the garden, will go limp the moment you bring them in, but if they are left in a deep pail of water overnight, they will crisp up again and last for days. Pick or cut early in the morning or at dusk if arrangements are made at night.

In selecting materials for arrangements in an herb show, check varieties used to make sure they have herbal backgrounds. If "marigold" is mentioned, for instance, this does not allow the use of the hybrid *Tagetes,* na-tive of Mexico, but calls for the herbalists' marigold, the calendula, or pot-marigold. Some judges allow the use of larger hybrid calendulas, but if you can get the origi-nal Mediterranean native, use it.

How can you be sure a plant is an herb? Many answers have been given to this question, but I advance this one: Plants of use to man—for flavor, for fragance, or for medicine—are probably herbs. Many beautiful flowers come on medicinal herbs and can be safely used in your arrangements. These include foxglove, rose, peony, lily (particularly the Madonna) and iris (especially dwarf types, *Iris pumila,* also *I. florentina, I. germanica,* and the old pale yellow and swamp types).

Many trees can be included in an herb show, as wil-low, birch, wild cherry, common ash, apple, almond, olive, fig, sassafras, senna, pine, larch, common oak, cedar, lime, linden and juniper. Trees usually enter the herb world on a medicinal passport, although some have culin-ary or fragrant values.

Shrubs for an herb show include witch hazel, broom

(*Cytisus*), holly, mistletoe, viburnum, and February daphne. And you can certainly use English ivy because of its ancient association with music, legend, and medicine.

To give your herb show a fresh look, have members grow a number of herbs in pots or tubs. These can be moved to the show without disturbance, and there they will last as well as if they were still in garden. In choosing containers for plants to be taken to a show, keep in mind that small pots dry out quickly and that larger ones have stability and give herbs sufficient root space to develop good growth. Members are likely to want to experiment with potted herbs, since container-gardening is very popular today.

11. Harvesting and Drying Herbs

And on his left he held a basketfull
Of all sweet herbs that searching eye could cull:
Wild Thyme, and valley-lilies whiter still
Than Leda's love, and cresses from the rill.
—John Keats

Drying home-grown herbs is one of the great pleasures of herb gardening. It is rewarding to use your own fresh seasonings, and if you dry them, you will doubly appreciate each savory leaf. Drying processes are simple, and the work need not be done all at once for plants mature at different times. Almost all herbs produce two, sometimes three, crops if they are harvested frequently.

The best time to cut plants for seasoning is before noon after the dew has dried but before the sun has leached the essential oils that keep herbs fresh and flavorsome. Of course, herbs should be dried out of the sun.

When you look at your garden in midsummer consider that herbs are grown to be harvested. Their function is to be of use to man in seasoning, in medicine, and for fragrance. If they are left uncut, yellow-ripe or dying leaves will result. Cut plants back and you will be rewarded with new growth far into fall. No garden is perfect all the time. If gardening does nothing else, it teaches patience.

Cut the leafy herbs, basil, savory, chervil, and marjoram, just before blossoms form. After blooming, leaves change color in some varieties; savory becomes very dark and the already-small leaves look black and shriveled when dried. This doesn't mean that leaves cannot be cut *after* blooming. If you do forget them, don't despair. They will still be full of flavor, though color and texture will not be perfect.

WHERE TO DRY THE HERB HARVEST

Dry herbs in the shade, but not in a damp place. Sometimes in very dry weather an outdoor shed can be used, but moisture seeps in at night and drying is slowed. For best color, quick drying is advisable, but heat should not exceed 150 degrees. One method is to spread leaves thinly on a tray of fine wire mesh. This is placed in a slow oven with the door left open. Watch carefully as drying should be completed within a matter of minutes, the time dependent on the thickness of the leaves.

Herbs are decorative hung from a ceiling to dry, or strung on a pole across the front of a fireplace, the original way of curing them. If they are not allowed to hang so long they pick up dust, these methods may still be used. Brown paper bags may be used for drying but many holes will have to be punched in them to let air in and moisture out. Brown wrapping paper spread on boards in an attic or an unused room works well. Of course the attic, or what used to be known as the "woodshed chambers" in Vermont where my grandmother's sage for sausage was always drying, is ideal. Few modern houses have attics or a space to be used for long-time drying, however, so the quick method is usually best.

A few herbs need no washing before drying, especially if the rows where they grow are mulched thickly with salt hay. However, I wash all leaves excepting herbs gathered for seeds, and an occasional tall mint. Small herbs that grow close to the ground, such as marjoram, parsley, and thyme and those with thick, wrinkled leaves like horehound and sage need special treatment and go through three waters before they are ready for drying. The warm water bath is first, then a cool water rinse and draining on a screen in the sink before leaves are put into the dry-

Drying shed at Caprilands filled with harvest of herbs for seasoning, the making of fragrant potpourri and all kinds of dried floral decorations.

Basket in left foreground holds rose hips; table at center has herb grinder and material for potpourri; bunches of apple mint hang from the ceiling beams; comfrey hangs in corner at right; teasels and artemisia dry in other containers; finished arrangements of dried materials can be seen at center in the background.

ing rack. Washing needs to be done quickly, as warm water releases oils and flavor may be lost if leaves are wet very long.

Herbs to dry in trays include chervil, lovage, myrrh, lemon verbena, parsley, thyme, and rosemary. Leaves of parsley and lovage are so thick that they can be spread only one layer deep. Thyme holds so little moisture that a basket may be piled full and it will dry well in any place that is not damp. Lemon verbena leaves are usually removed separately when plants are brought in for the winter. It is wise to take leaves from plants at this time, as they will drop as soon as they are brought inside, and they may be lost or soiled if they fall of their own accord. Dried rosemary needles are sharp if left whole; I run these through a coffee grinder and they emerge at just about the right length for coating a chicken, seasoning a gravy, or spooning out for tea.

Herbs that dry well hanging in bunches include sage, savory, mint, oregano, marjoram, basil, lemon balm, and horehound. If the bunches of basil are too large, leaves blacken quickly; the flavor will be there if they do not mold, but the color will be unattractive. Dill may be dried in this fashion if the green leaves are desired. In a warm room all these plants dry in two days, sometimes overnight in my kitchen, but our stove burns constantly, and the kitchen is dry even in humid weather.

Chives needs to be cut or shredded for drying. If you have plenty, perhaps a border in your kitchen garden, you will cut it back as the season advances but be sure to let a border of it blossom. Cut and dry some for winter bouquets. When blooms left on plants begin to fade, pull out the flowering stalks and cut the whole plant back to the ground. There is much sorting in chives as some leaves yellow quickly and only the tender green ones are of value. These are cut into pieces about half an inch long or finer. I put these into baskets hung over my stove and they are ready to package in about two days. I dry dill in much the same way, cutting it into bits while it is green. This is one of winter's most useful seasonings.

Herb seeds to dry include those of coriander, cumin, caraway, dill, and fennel. Watch these carefully or seeds will fall and be lost. Cut the whole plant, and place it, seed head down, in a paper bag so as to catch all the seeds. Hang up until dry and the seeds will drop out readily. As these seed herbs mature at different times,

caraway not until the second year, you will have to be
vigilant to save your harvest.

Some herb gardeners find pleasure in pressing leaves
and flowers between folds of parchment or old Bibles just
like the ancient specimens in herbariums. These old dried
pieces often retain characteristic shapes and odors, reminding us as we open the books in winter of bright summer days in the garden. Some of my friends make their
own designs for notepaper with pressed pieces of herbs,
and it is pleasant to open a letter with leaves and flowers
placed in interesting designs. There is something magical about a little grouping of herbs, no matter how humble or how dry they may be. Each year I press dozens of
costmary leaves in our heaviest books, and use them in
collections of Biblical herbs at Christmas. Pick costmary
all summer in order to get leaves in good condition. They
need no special drying; just choose perfect leaves and
press them in a heavy book or between pieces of newspaper weighted down by a brick.

Sweet geranium leaves also make good bookmarks and
retain fragrance better than other plants. For bookmarks,
I like the cutleaf forms of 'Dr. Livingston,' the fernleaf,
old-fashioned rose, and many of the variations. The
leaves of lamb's-ears are also easily pressed. Mullein
leaves and rosettes cut through the summer and put under heavy pressure are useful in winter arrangements.

I also press thyme, bedstraw, rosemary, and pennyroyal, which with costmary leaves, are used in Christmas
crêche decorations or sent in little cellophane packages
to friends during the holidays. These are all picked in
summer, pressed, and put away for future use. Cards
with the story and symbols of each herb make distinctive Christmas remembrances.

Many herbs can be dried for winter arrangements. I
try anything from my garden or the roadside that looks
interesting. Plants I recommend highly include amaranth, ambrosia, artemisia, bachelor's-button, broom,
delphinium, globe amaranth, helichrysum, lamb's-ears,
lanceleaf goldenrod, lavender, mullein, oregano, pepper-

mint, perilla, red orach, statice, St. John's-wort, sorrel seed heads, tansy, teasel, woad, and yarrow.

When I gather foliage and flowers for drying, I often find dried seed pods that are interesting for arrangements. Some of these I wait to gather after frost, others I pick at various times from midsummer on. Searching for interesting herb seed pods for arrangements is a fascinating business. I look for agrimony, baptisia, broom, flax, horehound, Japanese iris, lily, okra, peppergrass, rose hips, rue, shepherd's-purse, thermopsis, and veronica.

How To Store Dried Herbs

The faster herbs are processed, the better. If they hang too long they will lose flavor. Have clean glass screw-top jars all ready or, if you cannot process immediately, leave stems on and store in a large, airtight metal container. Herbs keep better on stems. If leaves are pulled off and shredded, they must be bottled at once to preserve the essential oil that determines flavor.

Herbs need to be "chip dry" when they are processed. Strip the leaves of thyme and savory, crumble those of basil. I do not powder herbs, as the oils in whole leaves or parts of large leaves keep better. I use an old-fashioned corn grinder, just right to break up a leaf without powdering it. Parsley may be prepared this way, or put through a coarse sieve, as for basils. Most leaves I leave whole, but I grind some for special uses. Handling tends to destroy flavor, so put the finished product in jars at once and screw on the tops. Work in a dry place and check jars for moisture. If any shows on the glass, remove the herbs at once and dry them again or all your efforts will be lost. Green herbs must be kept out of strong light or sun, for the color fades quickly. Store in a closed cupboard.

Keep seed herbs in their original form until they are to be used. Ground coriander and cardamom deteriorate rapidly, but if the seeds are stored whole they keep indefinitely. If you wish, powder or crush these just before using with a rolling pin or use time-proven mortar and pestle. Almost all left-over herb seeds will germinate if planted out the next year. Excess seed also makes good winter bird food.

Leafy herbs need to be renewed after one year, but seed herbs are good for several years if containers are tightly closed.

Storing herbs for flower arrangements is less complicated than for kitchen herbs. It is important after they are dried to keep them in a dry, airy, dustfree place. As the branches cure, they get brittle, and require careful handling. They can be left in bunches hanging from a ceiling if covered with polyethylene plastic to protect them from dust. Or stand bunches in boxes and baskets, and cover with a large sheet of thin plastic.

SOME SPECIFIC HARVEST NOTES

Amaranthus. A popular medicinal herb in seventeenth- and eighteenth-century gardens. I first grew it in a small garden devoted to dye plants. The progeny of those first plants still come up annually and self-sow for the next year. *Amaranthus caudatus* has a dark red stem or trunk and purplish leaves. Blossoms are tasseled and should be cut before they start to lose color. Dry upside down in a dark place as the color fades quickly if exposed to sun, and stems bend under the weight of the heavy tassels if they are set upright before drying.

Ambrosia. Watch the green plumes and when each segment of the blossom has developed, pull up the whole plant. To dry, place in a container that will hold it or at least half of a large clump. In the house away from the sun, it will stay almost the same green as outdoors. Dried ambrosia is used in many of my late summer and early fall arrangements. When these are replaced by holiday decorations, I store the harvested plumes in a protected place outside where they absorb enough moisture to make them easy to rework into backgrounds for dried wreaths or winter arrangements. Ambrosia is occasionally made into little trees for the model landscapes used by architects. For this purpose, they are sprayed with a plastic emulsion so that the fragile material becomes lasting and workable.

Angelica. When this blooms (in its third year), there will be more seeds than you care to plant. Store these in tight containers until ready to use for seasoning. If seeds are to be planted, do so within a month after harvesting or germination will be poor. If they are held until spring, they will not grow at all. Stems of angelica are candied at this time for use later with pastries, cakes, and Christmas cookies. You will like the small stems, finely cut and made into jam. Angelica tastes like gin and juniper.

Artemisia. Time to pick varies even among varieties grouped under *A. ludoviciana albula.* For pure whiteness that lasts indefinitely I cut 'Silver King' when each blossom segment is well formed and the branch ends are completely developed. Here the time to start cutting is in September, but I go on gathering into October. The largest amount is cut for its laciness and whiteness. The second early cutting, at the end of September or early October, has well-formed brown seeds, and the plant looks like felt and feels wooly. These later branches turn dark and lose their whiteness, but they yield variety in tone. Some straggling groups of this prolific plant are usually left until late fall to be cut even in snow. Wind shapes the woeful wisps into basic lines for arrangements. I save some of the windswept pieces, strip off the leaves, and use them as finials in line studies of pale branches that suggest a winter landscape.

Artemisias transplanted in spring produce the most fully formed heads for drying. They dry easily in a barn loft, a shed, or a corner of the kitchen. If you plan to make artemisia Christmas trees, one tree will require all the plants of an average garden. For this purpose, hang clumps upside down, remembering that they will dry stiff and straight—fine for the trees and some arrangements, but too unyielding to use in a design that needs curves. For these, put part of your harvest in jars or vases to dry in curves as they will.

Large seed heads of artemisia are too thick for arrangements and must be torn apart carefully. Save every little curl to make attractive nosegays for favors, or to decorate packages. Artemisias are refined enough for exquisite containers and so pliable in the green stage that they may be shaped at will.

Cut plenty of the true wormwood (*Artemisia absinthium*) when blossoms are fully formed and seeds are evident. For very large bouquets I find this bitter plant invaluable. The odor, however, is strangely half-sweet as it rises from even the oldest and driest branch. The taste will cling to your hands for hours after you have worked with it.

A. abrotanum camphorata is a variety of southernwood that I save for blossoms. Since it is usually planted as a low hedge and maintained in some order, trimming is a common practice. I cut it as green as possible after seeds have formed and dry it quickly out of the light. It makes nice spiky backgrounds to use with other brown or gray plants.

Bachelor's-button. I grow this *Centaurea cyanus* in abundance, and pick buds each day but not the full-blown flowers. Using florist wire, I bunch about six together and hang heads down in a dry place. Overnight they are dry enough for storage.

Baptisia. The black seed pods are stunning for modern arrangements. This is a dye plant, often called false indigo, and it spreads rapidly to make a handsome summer hedge. The blue, pealike blossoms resemble lupine and are good to cut though you can't cut blossoms and have seed pods, too.

Basil. A problem herb to dry because leaves darken easily. I remove leaves from stalks of the lettuceleaf variety as they are very large and contain more water than the smaller ones of bush and common basil. Pull off each leaf of the lettuce variety and place in a single layer in the drying basket or tray. Bush and common basil, which grow on longer stalks, can usually be tied three to a bunch and suspended tops-down where air circulation is good.

Broom. Great sweeping branches of broom *(Cytisus scoparius)* as green as summer rise against my weathered gray fence in winter. There are always a few long pieces to cut for dried arrangements, but not too many as I remember I am losing some of the golden blossoms that will come out in spring. Broom is a foliage most suitable for line arrangements. In using it, few recall its herbal past—for chronic dropsy, with dandelion roots as a purgative and for kidney disorders.

Broomcorn. This sorghum is the broom of commerce from which brooms are made. It has also been used in the treatment of kidney disorders, but is reported to be poisonous to cattle if they eat the green tops of the second growth. Seed heads are used but stems are too stiff to be of value for most arrangements.

Camomile. Both *Chrysanthemum parthenium* and *Anthemis nobilis* are grown for their daisy-flowers which are dried for tea. Cut the flowers when the outside ring of white petals turns back and the yellow center rises up in a cone. Snip the heads into a shallow basket and dry over heat. Sometimes I hang whole plants from the beams in my kitchen. There they dry quickly and sometimes drop. It is a temptation to hang them to dry for they are decorative and the apple-like odor is delightful. However, cutting seed heads is more practical. When the flowers are dry, put them in an airtight container. To use, measure out a generous spoonful to a cup, infuse in a teapot, serve, and infuse again.

Catnip. I allow catnip to blossom and then cut off most of the plant, leaving only enough to grow for a second harvest of leaves. If it is only for cats, the plant is hung up to dry in an open shed, barn, or attic. If it is for tea, it should be dried inside away from dust. Keep out of the sun so that it will stay green and attractive in leaf. Blossoms will dry gray. For tea, leaves are only partly crushed, because they keep better this way.

Delphinium. The spires bring welcome blue to arrangements. They can be dried by cutting before the blooms have matured and hanging head-down in a warm, dry, dark place. Or they may be dried in a covering of sand, borax, or silica gel.

Dock. The seed heads are indispensable for emphasis in arrangements, and also for line, but they have been so overused that some arrangers now ignore them. I start cutting blossoms early in summer when they are green. Sometimes I find a stalk that is reddish pink and most effective for arranging. Docks dry well standing in a basket or a metal container with sand in the bottom and where the air circulation is good. While we do not generally grow dock in our herb gardens, it is classified as a medicinal herb and so is suitable for herbal arrangements.

Globe Amaranth. Gomphrena globosa is a charming, dainty old-fashioned annual that yields purple, pink, and white everlasting flowers to add color to Advent wreaths. It is lovely all summer in the border, too, especially the dwarf kinds.

Japanese Iris. In winter I walk nearly every day, around the garden, and while my main purpose is the adjustment of snow covers or salt hay over plants that tend to be tender in winter, I always bring home some forgotten treasure from the rows or hedges. Sometimes it is green and growing like the creeping thymes that spread out from under the snow and project the fragrance of summer into a winter arrangement. More often rather than disturb these winter-happy plants I pick the seed pods of Japanese iris, stiff and sculptured and turned slightly silvery by cold. These combine with many of the gray plants for line and emphasis in arrangments.

Lamb's-ears. Stachys olympica is frequently used as a border and then must be kept from blossoming for good effect. I try to grow some plants also for drying. These are rounded and rise in spikes from a cluster of low leaves. In bloom, spikes are covered by purplish petals, but these dry out and disappear when the stalk is cut. Stalks are hung upside-down in a warm place to stiffen, otherwise tips are limp unless wired. Leaves of lamb's-ear resemble mullein but are softer and less like felt. They may also be pressed.

Lavender. For good color and scent this favorite herb must be cut early, as soon as the blue blossoms are at their best, and arranged at once, allowing it to lose moisture naturally.

Lovage. The leaves are particularly good in soup and potato salads and dry with much of their flavor intact. In gardens where roots can be spared, these may be dug in the autumn of the second year. Wash carefully, slice crosswise, and dry artificially at 100 to 125 degrees. Lovage seeds are tasty but you usually need to plant all of them.

Mullein. The common mullein rosettes of the field can be pressed easily, or dried in their natural shape to create wonderful accents for arrangements. Mullein is a medicinal herb, used in the past by homeopaths and those who practiced country medicine. I have found, in making arrangements, that one of the great lacks is large leaves of a quality useful in composition. Mullein is just right, and available almost everywhere.

Oregano. The most fragrant of dried herbs, this is spreading in growth and can be cut freely for it grows again quickly. Cut early, so blossoms will retain color; dry quickly by hanging bunches in a shadowy barn or kitchen corner. Oregano keeps from year to year, and never, no matter how old, does it lose that wonderful fragrance.

Perilla. This native of the Orient has attractive foliage for the border and thrives along our driveway where it produces a luxuriant effect in mid- and late summer. After the purplish blossoms go to seed, seed stalks appear and turn brown. I cut these before they shatter and use them for secondary backgrounds in arrangements.

Red Orach. This was once a pot herb, used like spinach, but now it is grown mainly for its decorative red, yellow, and brown seeds which bleach out quickly in the sun. It is an annual, usually self-sowing, that will grow high in rich soils, but seldom to more than 3 feet in my garden.

Rue. Interesting seed pods come after the flat yellow flowers. The tiny pods are like hand-carved Chinese wood, and, if picked early enough, do not break. They may be used in wreaths like pins to hold easily shaken materials in place. They are good, though small, accents in a design and lend interest to herbal compositions.

St. John's-wort. Both the wild and cultivated types of hypericum are attractive for winter bouquets. The dried tops are a rich red-brown and add warmth to bouquets and wreaths. Pick to dry when blossoms turn brown.

Shallots. Harvest when they rise in clumps bulging out of the ground, usually in late August and early September. Remove excess soil and hang in an open, airy place, for example, a garage with the door open. If clumps are large they will need some breaking apart to allow the air to circulate around them and prevent mold. Keep at least two out of every clump to plant the following year.

Sorrel. Both the French and broadleaf garden sorrels have blossoms worth drying when they go to seed. These are related to the docks and resemble them at the seeding stage. They are of more delicate texture, however, and the color is a light red-brown. Sorrel leaves for winter soup may be harvested when they are fresh and perfect in the spring, or the second growth of late fall may be frozen. Sorrel bouillon is a favorite here in fall.

Statice. *Limonium* provides delicate wisps that last forever in dried bouquets. *L. vulgare* is called sea lavender and fills salt marshes along the shore. *L. sinuatum* is the papery flower sold on street corners in late summer in colors almost too brilliant to bear. In the garden it is planted early in May to give a long growing season.

Strawflower. You can grow these at home and pick early for lovely everlastings of a color and size in keeping with other herbs and preferable to the big artificial-looking ones of commerce. Listed in some catalogs under helichrysum.

Sweet Woodruff. After the days of May wine (Chapter 7), the woodruff ground cover will spread rapidly once it is established. In shady moist spots, it needs sharp cutting back to let air into the thick plants, particularly in humid weather. When trimming plants, always leave the foliage closest to the ground. Dry cuttings for pot-pourri or for a winter woodruff bowl. Or you can pre-serve this plant in Rhine wine, keeping the leaves in the wine for a strong essence, reducing it with more wine or fortifying it with brandy as you use it.

Tansy. In the autumn I cut a huge bouquet of tansy flowers for the old copper bucket on the hearth. We keep water in it for a few days, then allow the flowers to dry for later use. To have the very best tansy flowers of clear yellow, watch carefully until they are fully opened and developed. Cut these on dry days when the sun is high and the dew has dried, with 18-inch stems. Strip the leaves away, and tie the blossoms in bunches of a dozen. Store where there is no dampness. Tansy flowers work nicely into tiny nosegays. They are made miniature by pulling the flowers apart to the desired size. For large ef-fects, put several full blossoms together to form one. I use tansy in wreaths and swags, sometimes combining it with a variety of pine cones. I find the rusty gold-browns of the last harvested blooms (almost in the seed-ing stage) excellent in a brown-and-gray wreath. In this wreath, artemisia is the background, but scarcely shows through the decoration. A circle of dark tansy follows the outline of the wreath; in the center there is a fringe of oregano blooms; and the outside circle is made of a fluffy everlasting. Decorate with tiny brown spruce cones and add a bow of brown-and-beige velvet ribbon for a finish.

Tarragon. When I first grew herbs, it was thought that tarragon did not dry well and could be used only green or "put down" in vinegar. In my early days of gar-dening I cut everything that could be cut with shears for bouquets—and I still do. Tarragon was rich and green with its delicate pointed leaf and went into many flower arrangements. These were long-lasting, and I noticed that a fragrance came from arrangements when tarragon was used. It was sweeter than new-mown hay, but just

as pervasive an odor. Soon these dried bits found their
way into potpourri for they added a lasting sweetness.
Cut tarragon early for drying, then use the second cutting
for vinegars.

Teasel. This tall plant is striking in the garden. A
biennial, it needs two years to develop the impressive
spikes which we depend upon for dramatic effects in
dried arrangements. This thistle needs no drying, just let
plants go uncut until seeds fall to insure a stand for the
coming year. Then cut and place the stalks upright wher-
ever they will be effective. I do not dye these interesting
spiny heads, but sometimes gild them for Christmas
wreaths and swags. Teasel heads are almost indestruc-
tible and can be used for outside decorations.

Thermopsis. The seedcases of this herb are an interesting oddity, following the impressive yellow pillars of
pealike blooms. Silhouetted against the deep green of
a shady area of ferns and arching trees, thermopsis is
a garden sensation in summer. The dried seed pods are
long and gray-brown, stiff and hard to use effectively,
but they can be worked into designs if the challenge is
accepted.

Woad. This dye plant, *Isatis tinctoria,* has large umbels of yellow blossoms in spring. It is biennial, so let
some seeds fall each year to insure blooms the next. The
lime-green seed pods if gathered promptly, retain color
for a long time. They need careful handling, but are
worth the effort because of the effects they make possible in dried arrangements.

Yarrow. No matter how many of these I grow (*Achillea filipendulina* and its varieties), I never have enough
for all the ways I would like to use them. They dry into
solid plates of color valuable for colorful designs. Depending on variety, yarrow dries into muted tones of
pink, gold, or grayish white that combine beautifully
with the browns, grays, and golds of other herbs. Blossoms may be cut at height of beauty, grouped in bunches
of six to a dozen, and hung top-down in a dry, airy place.

12. Midsummer Party

Then doth the joyful feast of John
The Baptist take his turne,
When bonfires great, with lofty flame,
In everie towne doth burne;
And young men round about with maides
Do dance in everie street
With garlands wrought of Motherwort
Or else with Vervaine sweet.
                                —Anonymous

The folklore of herbs takes us down many delightful paths. Here at the farm we hold pleasant little celebrations on days that in the past were of significance to gardening and farming people. We meet in the garden to discuss the legends, the plants, and the personages of the day or the season. We eat the foods that once had special meaning (though often in a modern form) and drink the beverages—or their equivalents. These celebrations are usually on the saints' days since whatever their origin, a saint's name has been given them with the passing years. Many of the foods and customs go back before recorded history, where truth, legend, and magic merge.

We have a celebration for midsummer, usually the twenty-second and twenty-third days of June, the time of the summer solstice, the longest days of the year. After this, days are shorter as the sun retraces its steps and drops toward the harvest season.

135

In the past, as long days gave way to earlier darkness, fear attacked ancient people, fear that the light would go forever, so fires were built on midsummer's eve throughout Western Europe. These fires were to hold warmth in the heavens, to keep the sun from losing its heat, to insure good growth of grain and flax, and health for cattle. Like the fires preceding May Day, they were kindled to burn witches and other dispensers of evil.

As Europe was Christianized, the summer solstice and St. John the Baptist's day sometimes coincided with the twenty-third and became the Eve of St. John, and the fires became St. John's Fires. In sixteenth-century Germany, almost every village had its bonfire on the Eve of St. John. Men, women, and children gathered round to dance and sing, pray, and repeat charms. The herbs, mugwort or St. John's herb and vervain, were made into chaplets to wear for the ceremonies.

Bunches of larkspur were held up to the flames. If the fire was gazed upon through the larkspur, eyesight would be keen for the rest of the year. As fires died down, herbs were thrown on the embers with the wish, "May ill luck depart, burnt up with these."

Wheels to represent the sun were wrapped with straw and smeared with pitch, lighted and rolled down hill toward water, this to insure good crops for the year. Cattle were driven through the fire to protect them from sickness and bewitching. Young couples jumped over the flames, the higher they leaped, the taller their crops would grow. Charred bits from the fires were preserved in the fields: a burned broom upright in the field insured the flax, fire-blackened sticks were crossed at the entrance to a grain field, a charred wreath was treasured above a peasant girl's couch.

A piece of this wreath might serve to propitiate the thunder, or cure sick cattle, or cleanse the house from pestilence. Great were the blessings of the midsummer fires. In Sweden, Balder's Balefires are still a joyous occasion. Then the air is filled with witches flying to the Great Witch who dwells in the mountains; caves open, rocks split apart, and spirits come forth to dance until the rising flames drive them back into hiding.

As we make our herb chaplets of mugwort and vervain and give them their fiery baptism, we too wish for the old magic, "May ill luck depart, burnt up with these."

JUNE WINE—THE CLARET BOWL

Here the chief flavor derives from borage, an herb that makes you happy. It grows quickly and prolifically from seed, and self-sows early for summer use. The large coarse leaves, stems, and lovely delicate, bright blue blossoms make a pretty punch with a cool cucumber flavor. Some of the floating blossoms turn pink in wine, so you have a claret cup with pink and blue flowers in red wine.

    1   stalk borage—stem, leaves and blossoms, or 12 large
        leaves and blossoms—for garnish
    1   gallon claret or dry red table wine
    Juice of 3 limes
    1   cup granulated sugar (about)
    1   sliced lime for garnish

Steep borage in wine, lime juice, and sugar at room temperature in large open-mouth jug for at least 3 hours before serving; if possible, in a refrigerator for 24 hours —the longer the time the better the flavor. At serving time, pour wine mixture over a block of ice in the punch bowl. Decorate with lime slices, fresh blossoms, and leaves. Makes 36 punch-cup servings.

Hints: Sweetened lemon juice and a sliced lemon may be substituted for the limes. For a stronger punch add a fifth of gin to each gallon of wine just before serving. In late summer we heap the cake of ice with sugared peach slices and ladle a slice into each cup.

MELISSA PUNCH BOWL

Lemon balm, with its fragrant wrinkled leaves so strong of lemon that in France it is called *citronelle,* is the herb for this cool summer punch.

>   6 tea bags or 6 teaspoons of tea leaves
>   2 quarts boiling water
>   1 cup crushed lemon balm leaves
>   1 cup granulated sugar or honey
>   1 cup lemon juice
>   1 12-ounce can frozen lemonade (undiluted)
>   2 quarts dry white wine
>   6 sprigs lemon balm for garnish

Prepare tea with boiling water. Cool. Add remaining
ingredients. Pour over cake of ice. Garnish with sprigs
of lemon balm or, as I sometimes do, with tiny blossoms
of the lemon-scented marigold (*Tagetes pumila*), or the
Scotch marigold. Makes 40 punch-cup servings.

Hint: For a more delicate flavor, omit lemon juice and
rely on the lemon balm alone.

ORANGE MINT COOLER

This is a different kind of mint drink, very popular
here at Caprilands when the heat hangs heavy over the
fields and thirst-quenchers are most appreciated.

>   2 cups crushed orange mint leaves
>   1 cup granulated sugar
>   6 cups water
>   6 tea bags
>   1 12-ounce can concentrated orange juice
>   ¼ cup mint or basil vinegar, or 1 bottle white rum
>   Sugar to taste
>   Mint sprigs for garnish

Bring to boiling, orange mint leaves, sugar, and the
water. Simmer for about 30 minutes. Add tea bags.
Steep for 5 minutes; remove tea bags. Stir in orange
juice diluted according to the directions on can, and the
vinegar. If flavor is too sharp, add more sugar. Cool
and pour over cake of ice. Decorate with sprigs of mint.
Makes 18 punch-cup servings.

Hints: For Pineapple-Mint Cooler, use the herb pine-apple mint, substituting pineapple juice for orange juice, and 2 cups white rum for vinegar. Float slices of whole fresh pineapple in punch bowl.

ANISE BREAD

A quick bread is always welcomed by the cook and her guests on a hot summer's day. This is one of our favorites.

    3 cups sifted all-purpose flour
4¼ teaspoons baking powder
    ½ teaspoon salt
    ½ cup granulated sugar
    2 eggs, beaten foamy
    2 cups milk
    2 tablespoons melted butter
    5 teaspoons anise seed

Sift together the dry ingredients. Stir in the eggs and milk, and add the butter and anise seed. Beat well and spoon into two regular greased tea-sized loaf pans. Bake about 30 minutes in a 350° oven.

SUMMER SQUASH SOUP

Here is a delicious way to make use of an abundant squash crop.

    3 medium-sized summer squash
    3 cups water
    4 chicken bouillon cubes
    4 cups water
    1 cup chopped celery
    3 onions, sliced
    ½ cup chopped parsely
    1 clove garlic, crushed
    1 sprig rosemary
    1 sprig thyme
    Salt to taste

Scrub, cut up, and cook squash in the 3 cups of water

until soft. Run through a sieve or food mill. In 3-quart kettle, put other ingredients and stir in the puréed squash. Simmer all together until celery and onions are soft. Serves 6 to 8.

Hint: For cream of squash soup, run the cooked mix through sieve or blender. Then stir in about 2 cups of cream or milk, enough for the consistency desired; or instead of cream or milk, stir in 1 ten-and-one-half-ounce can cream of celery soup, undiluted. Garnish with parsley and chopped chives.

GREEN BEAN CASSEROLE

Cook until just tender 1 quart of green beans with ¼ teaspoon savory in salted water to cover. Drain and add freshly grated pepper and more salt if required. Hard-cook 12 eggs. Shell and cut in half lengthwise. Remove yolks. Mix these with 1 teaspoon Caprilands Poultry Seasoning, 1 tablespoon grated onion, a pinch of cayenne pepper, and salt and pepper to taste. Moisten with mayonnaise. Stuff eggs with this mixture. Spread the egg halves over the bottom of a 2-quart casserole. Sauté 1 pound of fresh mushrooms in ¼ pound (1 stick) of butter. Cool a little and then spread mushrooms over the eggs. Cover with the green beans and spoon the Cheese Sauce over all. Top with fine bread crumbs, dot with butter, and sprinkle with finely chopped parsley and paprika.

CHEESE SAUCE

Cream ¼ cup (½ stick) of butter with 4 tablespoons of flour. Add 1 cup evaporated milk and 1 pound of mild cheddar cheese, cut up in small pieces. Stir over low heat until smooth. Add an ounce of sherry and salt and pepper to taste.

Hint: Pulverize ½ teaspoon marjoram, ½ teaspoon rosemary, and a pinch of sage and mix with ¼ cup of chopped parsley. Substitute this for the poultry seasoning in the egg-yolk mixture.

SALMON PUFF WITH DILL BUTTER SAUCE

Fourth of July calls for traditional salmon. Our recipe is adapted from Mother's old Vermont one.

4 eggs
2 cups of milk
1 cup finely ground sal-
   tine or soda-cracker
   crumbs

1 16-ounce can red
   salmon
¼ cup parsley
Pinch tarragon
Pinch thyme

Beat eggs until light and mix with milk and cracker crumbs. Remove dark skin and bones from salmon and drain. Stir salmon into egg mixture. Stir in parsley, tarragon, and thyme, and turn into a buttered 3-pint casserole or a long shallow fish dish. Bake in 350° oven about 25 minutes, or until mixture puffs up and browns. Remove from heat, spread with butter, and return to heat for 5 more minutes. Makes 8 to 10 servings. Serve with Dill Butter Sauce.

DILL BUTTER SAUCE: Melt ¼ pound butter with 2 tablespoons chopped dill leaves (no seeds) in ¼ cup hot water. Serve hot. (Dried dill weed may be used.)

GREEN SAUCE FOR MEAT

Good with potatoes, too, barbecued dishes and cold meats. To ½ cup olive oil and ¼ cup lemon juice, well blended, add: ½ cup finely chopped parsley, ¼ cup chopped chives, 1 chopped shallot, ½ cup chopped sorrel leaves, 6 chopped borage leaves, 1 teaspoon minced capers, 2 stalks chopped celery and leaves, 2 minced hard-cooked eggs. Blend and season with salt and freshly-ground black pepper to taste.

CAPRILANDS FAVORITE GREEN SALAD

Summertime is salad time when the herb garden yields exciting tastes and new flavor combinations. Gather at least three kinds of salad greens for the basic mixture. Red lettuce and oakleaf lettuce, both green and bronze, survive the heat of summer. You can cut red lettuce every week and always have new tops within seven days. Small amount of kale and spinach leaves, Chinese cabbage, and Italian parsley are also good in the mixture. But with all these fine fresh greens, you still need 'Iceberg' lettuce for crispness. Gather, wash and thoroughly dry greens in early morning. Unless leaves are tiny, cut and tear them into bite-sized pieces. Store in a large plastic bag in the refrigerator until you are ready to use them. For this salad, also store, but in three separate bags, 6 finely grated carrots, ½ bunch cut-up celery, and 2 green peppers seeded and sliced.

1 cut clove garlic	½ cup finely chopped salad burnet
2 quarts mixed salad greens	½ cup finely chopped curly parsley
2 large leaves lovage, chopped	4 calendula blossoms pulled apart
1 tablespoon chopped tarragon	1 cup finely cut Mozzarella cheese
½ cup chopped chives	
4 leeks	

Rub salad bowl with the cut garlic. Combine other ingredients (except the cheese) and toss with just enough Caprilands Herb Dressing (below) to coat every leaf but avoid a dripping mixture. Spread over the greens colorful, alternating rings of the chopped carrots, green peppers, and celery. Mound the cheese in the center. Serves about 25.

Hint: When they are in season, I also garnish the bowl with a ring of chilled and sliced tomatoes or tomato wedges sprinkled with minced basil leaves.

CAPRILANDS HERB DRESSING

Whip together in a blender or beat with a wire whisk until smooth: 2 cups olive oil, 1 two-ounce can anchovies with oil, 1 three-ounce wedge blue cheese, 1 crushed garlic clove, I teaspoon paprika, ½ teaspoon freshly ground black pepper, ¼ cup tarragon vinegar, 1 teaspoon Caprilands Mixed Herb Blend. Salt to taste. Store in refrigerator for use as needed.

HERB AND HONEY SALAD DRESSING

Blend well: 1 cup honey, ¼ cup basil vinegar, ¼ cup each of chopped chives, salad burnet, basil, and parsley, 1 tablespoon chopped tarragon leaves, 2 crushed garlic cloves, 1 teaspoon chopped savory. This makes a thick, green dressing. Spoon it over a salad of slices of tomatoes and Italian onions arranged on a bed of lettuce and curled parsley. Makes about 2 cups.

JELLY-FILLED ROSE COOKIES

1 egg	3 teaspoons baking
1 cup granulated sugar	powder
½ cup shortening	1 teaspoon rose water
½ cup milk	or vanilla
2½ cups sifted all-purpose	Rose geranium jelly
flour	

Cream together the egg, sugar, and shortening. Add the milk and the flour sifted with the baking powder. Add the rose water or vanilla. Blend well. Divide dough in half. Roll out one piece thin. Cut with a 2½-inch cooky cutter. Spread with rose geranium jelly. Roll out the other piece of dough thin and cut out the rest of the cookies. Slit the tops of these and place one on each of the jelly-spread cookies. Pinch edges firmly together. Sprinkle with Rose Geranium Sugar (below). Arrange on greased cooky sheets and bake at 400° for 20 to 25 minutes. Makes two dozen cookies.

ROSE GERANIUM SUGAR

Crush leaves of rose geranium to get the old-fashioned sweet rose flavor in a garnish or a jelly. It takes 6 or 7 leaves for 1 pound of sugar. Or use either a drop of rose syrup or essential oil of roses to 2 pounds of sugar. This essence is powerful, so take care not to use too much or sugar will taste very strong.

SUGARED ROSE COOKIES

1 cup butter or margarine	½ teaspoon cream of
1 cup sugar	tartar
2 eggs, beaten light	2 tablespoons rose water,
2¾ cups sifted all-pur-	or 1 teaspoon rose syrup
pose flour	2 tablespoons caraway
1 teaspoon soda	seed
	Raisins for garnish

Cream together butter or margarine and sugar, and add eggs. Sift in the flour mixed with the soda and the cream of tartar. Stir in the rose water or rose syrup and the caraway seeds. Drop mixture from a spoon onto greased cooky sheets. Press down a little and put a raisin in the center of each cooky. Sprinkle with rose geranium sugar. Bake in a 375° oven until lightly browned, about 25 minutes. Makes 3 dozen cookies.

Autumn Diary

For there is hope of a tree, if it be cut down, that it will sprout again, and that the tender branch thereof will not cease.
—Job 14:7

The herb garden in autumn has a special charm. Now that the competition of surrounding flower gardens is banished by frost, the calm beauty of massed plantings of greens and grays is seen at its best. Now is the time to appreciate leaf formation, texture, and the distinctive growth that marks a green garden for contemplation, a place where delightful odors, pungent, sweet, and heady, carry us back the remarkable way that only odors can do.

The gray border garden at Caprilands is planted in a semicircle around a weathered shrine. Here a medieval figure of Virgin and Child smile on herbs arranged in formal half-moon beds. These look fresh until late December. The back border of *Artemisia albula* is stark white against the blue fall sky, or a ghostly shadow in the light of the hunters' moon.

Close to the shrine a variety of santolina makes miniature round trees with leaves like silver filigree. Tall branches of southernwood (tangerine-scented) wave gracefully about the shrine. Mats of gray thyme interspersed with golden thyme emphasize the year-round color of this garden—gray, green, gold, and white. Two semicircular beds in the center are separated by walks of old brick bounded with soft masses of easy-growing lamb's-ears *(Stachys olympica)*. The whole border is edged with lacy Roman wormwood *(Artemisia pontica)*,

145

kept reasonably trim by cutting back twice a year, and by pulling roots to keep lines even. Santolina, also called lavender-cotton, forms a chain of white coral growth the whole length of the garden.

Some beds are bordered with sage, two with camphor-scented southernwood, others with hyssop and rue. Snow-on-the-mountain *(Euphorbia marginata)* falls in gray cascades over the walls and draws attention to a small rock garden below, where rows of artemisia 'Silver Mound' make silk cushions. Bushes of hyssop are still in bloom, and pot-marigolds *(Calendula officinalis)* are tossing heads of yellow and deep orange, untouched by frost, against the cloud of artemisia 'Silver King.' Other marigolds *(Tagetes* hybrids) have succumbed to frost.

In the thyme terrace below the border garden, armies of Johnny-jump-ups are awake after a summer sleep, ready for winter blooming. Sweet alyssum is foaming in fragrant waves all through the garden. Costmary or Bible leaf *(Chrysanthemum balsamita)* has a fine second blooming and looks up over the bank toward the tawny plumes of its more glamorous relatives, the chrysanthemums. Thymes are at their greenest and grayest now, reaching out exploring arms to anchor safely under protecting rocks for the winter. Many have late blooms. Mother-of-thyme often blooms for Thanksgiving.

To walk among these herbs on a late November day is an adventure. The day should be sunny with the frosty mist of autumn hanging over the hills, shutting you and the garden into gratifying solitude. The smell of the damp earth, the mingled fragrance of thymes, mints and lavenders rises with every step, and your eye is held by garden beauty in somber key.

13. Winter Protection for Herbs

The gilliflower also, the skilfull do know,
doth look to be covered in frost and in snow:
The knot and the border, and rosemary gay,
do crave the like succour, for dying away.
　　　　　　　　　　　　—Thomas Tusser

One of the problems in the first years of herb gardening comes at the approach of fall. What to cut back, what to leave; what to mulch and what not to mulch; and what to bring into the house and what not—these decisions have to be made every autumn. Fortunately, most herbs are hardy perennials that need no winter coddling. If you familiarize yourself with the plants you grow, determining whether each is annual, biennial, perennial, or shrub, putting the herb garden to bed for the winter will be less puzzling and more an excuse to get outdoors and enjoy the brisk invigorating weather of the season.

To Cut or Not To Cut

Basically, plants in the garden are cut back after frost to make the garden neat. Certain perennials, and most shrubs and trees are exceptions, because they will sprout again when the sap flows again in spring. After an herb gardener harvests all summer and fall for winter arrangements and seasonings, there will be somewhat less material left in the garden for winter to paint with a frosty brush. However, no matter how diligently you gather

147

herbs, there will always be some left standing in the garden. Your choice, then, is to cut these back in autumn,
or wait until spring. If neatness is all-important, you will
trim them back evenly to within an inch or two of the
ground, gather up clippings, and add them to the compost pile.

Having the herb garden come through winter in good
condition is my primary concern, so I usually let the
frosted tops stand in the garden. There they catch the
snow and hold it as security against blustery winds. I
do my cutting back on those first days of spring when it
is too early to remove mulches, or to dig and plant. I
am glad then that tops were not taken off in fall, for as
I cut in spring, I press them loosely over clipped-off stems.
This way, they act as a mulch that prevents spring sun
from thawing soil by day when it is sure to be frozen at
night. If this happens, roots are torn apart and often
heaved out of the ground. When spring comes to stay,
I go over the garden, gathering up all the clippings, bringing neatness out of the jumble, and adding what I collect to the compost pile.

To Mulch or Not To Mulch

My whole garden is mulched in autumn, some plants
more heavily than others. Salt hay covers tops of santolinas, and many of the low growers. Thymes winter well
under this light protection. My New England upbringing
and French heritage promote a frugality that makes me
roll up this salt hay in spring and store it for next year.
Evergreen boughs are often used as winter cover, a fitting
use for Christmas tree and greens which have had their
great moment, and now return to the earth to begin their
journey again. In nature all things are planned to be
useful, and it is good to have a part in this continuity.

Santolinas, both green and gray, and germanders need
a heavy covering of salt hay, and also evergreen branches
over the top growth. I cut favorites back in spring when I
put the garden into shape, trimming only to make cuttings and to keep bushes neat. In autumn my method is

to push back tops enough to let me swirl hay around the roots for winter protection. Then I place pine, juniper, or spruce boughs over the tops. The results are certainly worth my time and trouble.

At first, I was led to believe that lavender was not hardy here, but I have found it one of the most satisfactory perennials if grown with perfect drainage—never any water standing over it—and with lime and more lime, lots of sun, and "a rock to lean on." This is an easy form of protection in Connecticut, but perhaps not so easy in other regions, or in a long decorative border. Unquestionably lavender grows best in the shelter of a wall, and protection for a few plants can be provided by rolling some sizable stones to their windward side. These help to stabilize the temperature of the ground and insure against root damage caused by alternate freezing and thawing, but a good mulch of salt hay will also accomplish this.

I do not mulch until the top inch or two of soil has frozen. If a deep mulch is placed before top soil freezes, field mice and other rodents may find a warm refuge and cause damage. However, if you wait to mulch until after some sharp freezes, soil will have frozen, and plants will have been put to sleep by the anesthetic of autumn's decreasingly warm days and increasingly cold nights.

From January to April, I walk the hillside garden, whenever there is no complete snow cover, checking plants for trouble. The banks of creeping thyme and hedges of common thyme often get bare and cruelly exposed when the first spring thaws come. I tamp down rootlets and fork compost over them to cover the heaving ground around the base of the plants. Without this care, roots would be exposed causing tops to brown, and encouraging a rush of growth doomed to suffer the bite of frost.

When spring finally comes—insofar as I can determine after years of trying to outguess New England weather— I begin the annual cleaning up and cutting back. Large herb branches and leaves that would not decompose readily if left on the ground are raked up and added to the compost pile. Twigs and leaves that quickly change to humus are scattered out as a mulch, and this practice over the years has improved my soil.

Herbaceous perennials like the mints, most of the artemisias, lemon balm, rue, and tansy are cut back to the ground. Woody perennials, such as lavender, santolina, and germander are not cut back at all, except to remove damaged growth. My lavender bushes are never pruned except to remove blossoms, to make cuttings for propagation, or to clip for seasonings and wreaths. It is late May when the old wood shows green and I can ascertain which parts are dead and need trimming off. This can be a touch-and-go time, as some plants are slow in starting up again and often appear dead when they are not. Cutting to the ground frequently kills lavenders; and, if not fatal, this practice will prevent your having large bushes the same year. These take three years to develop, so it is important to preserve the wood from season to season.

HERBS TO TAKE INDOORS

If your garden lies in an area where winters are severe, then your tender perennial herbs should be carried over in a sunny, cool window, in a greenhouse, or in a frost-free coldframe. Here are the herbs I bring indoors in winter; your experiences may indicate others.

African baby's-breath—*Chaenostoma fastigiatum*
Camphor tree—*Cinnamomum camphora*
Cardamom—*Amomum cardamon*
Dittany of Crete—*Origanum dictamnus*
Heliotrope, fragrant—*Heliotropium arborescens*
Lavender, fernleaf—*Lavandula multifida*
Lavender, French—*Lavandula stoechas*
Lavender, fringed—*Lavandula dentata*
Lemon Verbena—*Lippia citriodora*
Pennyroyal, English—*Mentha pulegium*
Rosemary—*Rosmarinus officinalis*

Sage, pineapple—*Salvia rutilans*
Sage, tricolor—*S. officinalis 'Tricolor'*
Scented Geraniums—*Pelargonium species*
Sweet Bay—*Laurus nobilis*
Sweet Marjoram—*Majorana hortensis*

The culture of herbs brought inside for the winter is outlined in chapter 2. Chapter 3 includes suggestions for the care of scented geraniums as house plants.

14. The Artemisias

> What savour is best, if physic be true,
> for places infacted than wormwood and rue?
> It is as a comfort, for heart and the brain,
> and therefore to have it, it is not in vain.
> —Thomas Tusser

To the herb gardener, the words artemisia and autumn are synonymous. I could add another alliterative *A*, for art goes along with them, too, because of their many uses in landscapes and arrangements. Properly managed, artemisias can be the backbone of a well-planned herb garden; however, they cannot be counted on for early spring, as many do not develop fully until August. Then they become the glory of autumn, providing accents and graceful patterns both day and night.

Belonging to the composite family, artemisias are generally divided into four groups: mugworts, wormwoods, southernwoods, and decorative types. Tarragon *(Artemisia dracunculus sativus)* stands alone as it is primarily a seasoning herb. The confusing nomenclature of artemisias is sufficient to drive one to madness, but the poet Andrew Fletcher wrote,

> These for frenzy be
> A speedy and a sovereign remedy,
> The bitter wormwood, sage and marigold.

Authorities differ on the origin of the name "artemisia." I have always accepted the explanation that, since the artemisias, particularly the mugwort or *A. vulgaris* type, and the wormwoods were used for women and their many

152

ailments, these plants took the name from Artemis or Diana, goddess of the hunt, of the moon, and of virginity. There is also the story of Queen Artemisia of Halicarnassus, wife of Mausolus, King of Caria, who gave us the word "mausoleum" from the tomb she erected for her husband at his death. In any case, the moon is a fitting patroness for artemisias as they are at their best in the light of a harvest moon, or in the cold white nights of November when the last wispy stalks wave their goodby to the old year.

The Mugworts

Three artemisia species are placed in this class. *A. annua*, the sweet mugwort, grows in one season to the height of a small tree, is green, very fragrant, and excellent for dried arrangements. *A. lactiflora*, also called sweet mugwort, has fragrant white blossoms with leaves greener than they are gray on a plant 5 feet tall. *A. vulgaris*, the common mugwort or German *beifuss*, grows to 4 or 5 feet, has silver-backed cut leaves, and is decorative if controlled.

A. vulgaris is the magical herb in this group, venerated in many lands and used as a charm by both Eastern and Western people. Few persons dare to plant it in the garden for it is reputed to be a weed; but if the space is large enough, it can be used effectively like any large shrub. Common mugwort is one of the most spectacular herbs in the garden at the old Captain Paul House, now the home of Esther Larson, fashion artist by profession and herb gardener by avocation. There they stand on either side of a planting of other artemisias that leads into a brick terrace surrounded by beds of old roses. These mugworts grow to 6 feet, and they are the wonder of many visitors who know herbs but do not recognize this most common member of an aristocratic family. Each year the circle of roots increases and it is necessary to cut away many roots every year to keep plants under control. Seedlings also must be removed to prevent new clumps starting and getting ahead of us.

Mugwort is at its best in midsummer and that is when I cut it lavishly to make crowns for all our guests at the Midsummer Festival. There is an old belief that these worn on a midsummer day and singed with fire will drive away last year's evil and bring good luck through the coming year. Mugwort is also known as St. John's plant and is dedicated to St. John the Baptist. It was worn by the young saint in the wilderness and was reputed to have protected him. Mugwort gained an early reputation for allaying fatigue because of Pliny's recommendations, and in the Middle Ages it was known as the plant of the weary traveler, helpful if worn in the shoes.

Mugwort is used as a charm in China at the time of the Dragon Festival when it is hung up in the principal room of the house. It is said that Chinese lives were spared if this herb was found in their houses during rebellions.

The name "mugwort" for *Artemisia vulgaris* came from England where it was used to flavor ale, and today it is added to stuffing for the Christmas goose in Germany. A tea made from the leaves was once recommended as a brain tonic for hysteria in epileptics, as a stimulant, a tonic, and an emmenagogue.

I dry mugwort for arrangements, use it in the Christmas goose, and revive an old custom by using the dried leaves gathered on St. John's Eve in a wreath to prevent our being overcome by "evil powers." It is said that, "Made into a cross and put on the roof, mugwort will be blessed by Christ himself, hence it must not be taken down for a year." Also, if some mugwort, or *muggins* in Scottish, is eaten in May, "It will protect the eater from consumption, poisoning, physical exhaustion, wild beasts and the necessity of paying too many bills."

THE WORMWOODS

The plants in this classification are the most familiar of the artemisias, and they have a great history. *A. absinthium* is the true wormwood, a large gray shrublike herb that grows 2 to 4 feet tall. It needs sun, but will

VARIED ARTEMISIAS. (Left above) Tarragon *Artemisia dracunculus;* (below) Silver King *A. albula.* (Center) Mugwort *A. vulgaris.* (Left above) Southernwood *A. abrotanum;* (below) Wormwood *A. absinthium.*

155

grow in partial shade. *A. frigida,* the fringed wormwood, grows to 18 inches and makes a good gray accent. *A. pontica,* the Roman wormwood, grows 1 to 2 feet tall, depending on soil, has fine lacy foliage but does not bloom in my garden. It is gray and decorative in borders. *A. stelleriana,* the beach wormwood, grows to 1 foot by flowering time, and because of its white leaves is called "old woman," or dusty miller.

True wormwood (*A. absinthium*) is a native of Europe and one of the great plants of the past because of its medicinal value. In fact, it is used today in the well-known product, "Absorbine Jr." My Wood and Bache handbook, the United States Dispensatory, published in Philadelphia in 1847, a mine of information of that day, states that, "Wormwood known to the ancients was highly tonic and probably enters the circulation as it is said to render the flesh and milk of animals fed with it bitter. Before the introduction of Peruvian bark it was much used in the treatment of intermittants [fevers]." A narcotic property has been ascribed to it by some writers in consequence of its tendency to occasion headaches and when long continued to cause a disruption of the nervous system. In large doses wormwood irritates the stomach and stimulates circulation.

An elderly man who came to talk to me about wormwood said that he drank three wineglasses of it a day, and to this he attributed his incredible age and good health. I, being young at the time and ignorant in the use of herbs, decided to try his dose and persisted in drinking this in a weak solution for three days. At the end of that time I was unable to enjoy food or drink. I decided that the penalty paid to live to a ripe age was too great and that I would rather relish the joys of the table and die young. (At this point, dying young is an impossibility for me.) Later I learned that wormwood in very small doses is reputed to revive appetite, but that, taken persistently it will have the same effect that absinthe has on the addict, stimulating the appetite at the same time it produces inability to eat food or a distaste for it.

In an old herbal we read: Wormwood is of benefit for strengthless flatulent indigestion. An infusion may be made of an ounce of the dried plant to a pint of boiling water and given in doses of from one to two tablespoonfuls three times during the day. This infusion with a few drops of the essential oil will prevent the hair from falling off.

In Dioscorides' day wormwood was declared to be a preventive for intoxication, and that I can believe. In fact, it was a remedy for the ill effects of any such excess. Dr. Fernie wrote, "It keepeth clothes from moths and wormes," and Gerard, "Taken in wine it is good against the biting of the shrew mouse and of the sea dragon." The latter seems a safe recommendation, but another writer, a Dr. Maignan, concluded after experimenting on animals that, "Absinth [wormwood] determines tremblings, dullness of thought and epileptiform convulsions. Hence it may be inferred that absinth contains a narcotic poison which should prevent its being employed as a liqueur or as a homely medicament to any excess."

It would be easy to take any one of the virtues of wormwood out of literature and use it in home treatment with disastrous results. Let us resolve to leave green medicines alone unless like John Dryden, we can say with truth,

> Medicine is mine;
> What herbs and simples grow
> In fields and forests,
> All their powers I know.

Old records tend to attribute the same virtues to both mugwort (*A. vulgaris*) and *A. absinthium*. Both are often called wormwoods, along with many others, and this adds to the difficulty of determining their uses. I have always believed that the Bible referred to the true wormwood, but Harold N. Moldenke in *Plants of the Bible* points out that *A. absinthium* is not native to the Holy Land. The word "wormwood" was a synonym for bitterness and in some

passages simply means "a bitter thing." It is thought now
that *A. judaica* and *A. herba alba,* also aromatic, bitter,
and camphorous, are the true wormwoods of Palestine.

Moldenke says, All the [Bible] translators continue to
use [the word] wormwood in the Revelations reference
[8:10-11], but Goodspeed renders the passage far more
lucid: "Then the third angel blew his trumpet, and there
fell from the sky a great star blazing like a torch, and it
fell upon one third of the streams of waters. The star
is called Absinthus, that is, wormwood. Then one third
of the waters turned to wormwood and numbers of people died of the waters for they had turned bitter."

But what of wormwood in the garden? It grows large
in the third or fourth years, the crown spreads, and the
stems may go to 4 feet. Foliage is an interesting blue-
gray color, and leaf shape is so like that of chrysanthemum that visitors often mistake it for that. Wormwood
is a good accent where grayish, bold leaves and late, tall
flowerheads, brown with yellow seeds, are welcome. It
grows in sun or shade. Seeds are slow to germinate, but
those self-sown usually furnish some sturdy plants in
spring. Old clumps gradually die out and it is well to
have some new seedlings to fill in as the older woody
specimens disappear.

I grow wormwood freely in my Saints Garden for it is
known not only for Biblical references, but as a plant
used in the medicines of monasteries.

The fringed wormwood *(A. frigida)* is from the western plains and mountains and is a native from Texas
north to Alaska. It is a fine addition to the garden. Early
in the season, it resembles 'Silver Mound' *(A. schmidtiana
nana),* but at maturity spikes grow to 2 feet and are hung
with yellow blossoms. I sometimes pick these for drying
although generally neither of these artemisias dries well.

In the Southwest, according to L. M. S. Curtin, there
are many other artemisias unknown in the East. One
called *A. filifolia* 'Romerillo' resembles southernwood. It
grows in the mountains and is revered by the Indians.
Like other artemisias grown in the West, this one is called

sage or silver sage. Curtin writes, "Silver sage is a favorite remedy with the New Mexican Tewa Indians and those at Hano, Arizona. They chew and swallow it with water or drink it in a hot decoction for indigestion, flatulency and biliousness. In addition they compress on the stomach a bundle of the plant that has been steeped in boiling water and wrapped in a cloth to drive away pains. It is used also for rheumatism, the entire bush being boiled and a bath taken in the water. The penitents, after receiving their lacerations, wash them with the astringent tea."

Roman wormwood (A. pontica) is a delicate, attractive gray herb with a lacy look that makes it effective in the garden and in flower arrangements. Each year in autumn I cut this artemisia to the ground once and it grows back again to make a low border by frost. This gray hedging remains attractive through the winter, and serves to catch its quota of snow. I have grown A. pontica for twenty years and never in all the spots where I have planted have I seen it in bloom. The roots spread mightily and need to be curbed sharply twice during the year. Early writers give this species medicinal values that I have never detected. In The Modern Herbal, Maude Grieve states that the "aromatic flavor with which its bitterness is mixed causes it to be used in making Vermouth." Culpeper considered the plant to be excellent to strengthen the stomach and "the juice of the fresh tops is good against obstructions of the liver and the spleen, a tincture is good against gravel and gives great relief in gout." Dr. John Hill speaks of a wine famous with the Germans, made with the Roman wormwood, "of such an efficacy to give an appetite that the Germans drink a glass with every other mouthful and that way eat for hours together without sickness or indigestion."

Beach wormwood (A. stelleriana) has a thick white leaf and grows in great white patches along our Connecticut shore. Descriptions indicate that this is the same as A. maritima, found wild in England, in northeast Ireland, and the Channel Islands, but the species are separate

according to L. H. Bailey. This is the plant frequently
called "old woman" and planted beside doorways, with *A.
abrotanum* to represent the old man of the house. It was
named for Georg Steller, a German plant collector of
the eighteenth century. To grow this wormwood properly, very sharp drainage and sandy soil are required.
I cut the plant back once a year and root new cuttings
in wet sand and vermiculite. Grow this artemisia in large
patches and keep the flowering tops cut back flat. Its
uses today are purely decorative, though no doubt it does
have some of the same medicinal properties as other
wormwoods.

THE SOUTHERNWOODS

All plants in this classification come under the name
Artemisia abrotanum, and they are known by scents of
lemon, camphor, and tangerine. Two other species, *A.
borealis* and *A. glacialis* (or *A. laxa*) are sometimes
grouped with the southernwoods. *A. borealis* is lower
growing than the others and makes a compact small
shrubby perennial with very gray foliage. *A. glacialis* is
from the Alps and makes a delightful mound of fine,
gray leaves not above 4 inches.

All southernwoods are propagated by cuttings taken in
spring or summer, or by removal of side roots in spring.
English writers note that southernwoods never, or seldom bloom, but my lemon and camphor varieties put
forth blossoming heads in late August and September.
These are cut back to keep the hedges trim and even,
but are left where I want accent spires.

Southernwoods are among the most attractive plants
for the herb garden. The odor is pleasing and household uses are many. They are natives of the south of
Europe, indigenous to Spain and Italy. The finely divided
leaves, reduced to ashes, were once used to make an
ointment to promote the growth of a beard. Thus it came
to be called "young lad's love," only one of many quaint
names. Sprays of the plant were put into country bouquets presented by young lads to their lasses. The scent

Photograph by Herman F. Marshall

Magnificent clump of southernwood at entryway to Caprilands.

of southernwood is said to be disliked by moths, hence branches of it are used in chests and closets.

Historically bunches of southernwood and rue were used together to protect judges and prisoners from jail fever, and it was also reputed to ward off drowsiness. In days when church services and sermons were long, bunches of southernwood and balm were taken to church to stimulate the listener and prevent his falling asleep.

Culpeper wrote, "The seed as well as the dried herb is often given to kill worms in children. The herb bruised helpeth to draw forth splinters and thorns out of the flesh; the ashes mingled with old salad oil helps those that have their hair fallen and are bald, causing the hair to grow again either on the head or as a beard."

I had grown southernwood in my garden for years just because it was decorative, when I received a letter from a nun who was trying to find a plant used in Alsace, her home, to keep moths away. Her name for it was "armoise and garde robe." We sent plants of our southernwood to her convent where the sisters grew it in an herb garden. They used the branches to pack away their black wool habits and I was assured that it was an efficient protection. A long correspondence began with this letter and covered the whole country, as she wrote to other herb gardeners, both ecclesiastical and secular. In turn they wrote to me. Though we never met, the nun's letters were an inspiration. She is gone now, but my southernwood hedge remains a lovely memorial to her.

It is a wonder to me that only one southernwood is generally known, for the camphor variety is a most obliging plant. Officially it is *A. abrotanum camphorata* and resembles the lemon-scented type to the extent that it is hard to tell them apart in certain seasons. "Old man" or *A. a. limoneum* (lemon-scented) is grayer than the camphor type. It is also harder to propagate by root divisions and more upright in growth. It flowers less often, usually when a bush is quite along in years, grows slowly, and is later to show green in spring. In fact, each year I find myself breaking twigs of it to be sure that the little nodes along the branches are still living. The camphor artemisia is likely to sprawl along the ground if not frequently transplanted. When properly cared for it makes an attractive hedge, 2 to 3 feet high. It is winter-hardy and emits an odor like camphor which should be the death of a moth.

Tangerine-scented southernwood is a tall, willowy herb, to 7 or 8 feet, that combines well with the lower-growing artemisias. It is notably late to leaf out in spring and presents long, naked branches well into June. Cutting it back reduces its height, though sometimes in desperation I do this and then have to wait for it to grow again. At its best this artemisia is like a great plume, Oriental in effect.

THE DECORATIVE ARTEMISIAS

Of the countless artemisias, there are some species I cultivate for their landscape value and to dry for winter bouquets. These include *A. ludoviciana* and its variety *albula* or 'Silver King,' *A. purshiana*, *A. schmidtiana nana* or 'Silver Mound' and *A. tridentata*.

A. ludoviciana, native from Utah to Texas and Arizona, grows to 6 feet and makes a stunning accent along a fence. The foliage is nearly white. Propagate it by root division in spring or fall. *A. ludoviciana albula*, the popular 'Silver King,' is valued for its cloud effect in the garden and dried for winter bouquets, wreaths, swags, and tree-like effects. During late summer and early fall, this makes a row of silver, and I have to summon my willpower to cut it down. I know that if it stands too long the almost pure white seed panicles will turn brown or black, but if I cut it, the garden will be bare of this gray beauty. So, I compromise and grow two rows of *albula;* the back one I cut completely, the front I leave until the seed heads have ripened.

After *albula* is cut in early autumn, it is bunched and hung from rafters in an open shed. There it sways in the breeze and dries into decorative material, to be used in fall while it it still pliable. Instructions for making some

of my favorite decorations are given at the end of this
chapter, and an artemisia wreath is described in Chapter 18.

A. *purshiana*, sometimes known as cudweed wormwood, has a broader leaf than 'Silver King.' It grows to 2
feet and makes an excellent gray note in the border.
Early writers sometimes speak of this as a "fattener of
cattle."

'Silver Mound' artemisia, A. *schmidtiana nana*, is the
chinchilla of the herb world—so elegant and extravagant
looking that it seems too much to expect the plant to be
hardy, easily divided, and generally well behaved. In the
autumn my rows of young plants are at their best. The
older plants, that were cut back in spring to produce the
young ones, have been cut again to the ground and are
beginning to show a beautiful gray color. I plant long borders of 'Silver Mound' in front of chrysanthemums, and
these come through winter without cover. I divide two-
year-old clumps between September 1 and October 1,
giving them as much time as possible to get set before
cold weather. They thrive in dry, sunny places and once
established, succumb to winter only in heavy, rich soil
that holds so much moisture that the crowns rot.

The sagebrush of the western plains (*A. tridentata*)
grows ever onward and upward, sometimes to 12 feet,
and for this reason it is difficult to have in the garden. It
is native from British Columbia to California and Ne-
braska. The leaves are highly scented, and if you have a
sunny, arid location where a 12-foot shrub is needed, this
artemisia might be a good choice.

TARRAGON IS AN ARTEMISIA

The French tarragon used for seasoning, in the making
of vinegars, and for various other flavoring purposes, is
A. *dracunculus sativus*. It is a hardy perennial that grows
to 2 feet. It is propagated only by root division, spring or
fall, of established clumps, and it needs sun, good drainage, and some fertilizer each year.

DECORATING WITH ARTEMISIAS

To make an artemisia tree, cut 'Silver King' when it is completely headed, probably in the middle of September. Try to cut just before the brownish seed heads have formed so that the plants will dry white and not be wooly. Dry only overnight or not at all, as it is stiff and will be more workable if not dried. Make a half or full circle of chicken wire 6 inches across. Half trees made on a semi-circular, cone-shaped frame are more practical than full-circle ones, as they do not require as much material or space.

Start the tree with the best, most perfectly formed and upright bush of artemisia. Fix this in the wire for the main trunk. Place two lesser stalks in opposite directions and at right angles to the trunk. Let these rest on the table to give stability, and place so that the ends curl. Then proceed up the sides of the tree. Put the branches into the wire or into other interlaced branches, as they will soon hold each other. Always turn the curls up and break off any branches that you will not be using so that a thick, unmanageable mass does not build up.

The finished tree can be 18 to 36 inches high, made on the same frame. Larger artemisia trees take an enormous amount of material—cuttings from about six large plants —while small trees can be made from one well-grown plant.

Each year I add to my stored trees, keeping the basic materials which I wash under the kitchen faucet to remove dust, dry slightly, and to which I add fresh artemisia. This saves the long first process. Some mantel trees are made with scraps or the lovely tops of silver that are already miniature trees without effort on my part.

To decorate an artemisia tree for autumn, I use the full-blown chartreuse ambrosia. If the tree is made in early fall, the ambrosia will be easy to work with, somewhat sticky, pliable and very fragrant. Fresh tansy heads picked when they are bright yellow and fully formed add more color to the trim. Oregano blossoms yield a rich brown, green, or purple, depending on when they are

picked and how they are dried. Roadside everlastings
(*Gnaphalium obtusifolium*) impart a soft flowery texture
to the decoration, and tiny spruce cones may be wired into
the branches. Bright yellow blossoms of yarrow lift up
the deeper tones of the tansy. White yarrow and bits of
baby's-breath may also be added. The trees are best if
kept to autumn tones—greens, browns, and yellows—or
made white and gold with the addition of gilded leaves
and cones for Christmas. I sometimes gild the small rose
hips from *Rosa chinensis* (hedge rose) as they are in pro-
portion to the rest of the decoration. The trees look best
if left quite natural; artificial decorations are to be
avoided. This should be an herbal tree, made from the
harvest of your garden.

Swags of artemisia are fixed to our worn red doors on
the first of October. They include harvest corn, a sign of
hospitality, and branches of rue to "ward off evil and the
attacks of witches." Fresh-cut branches of rue dry to
brilliant green. A branch of elder and large umbels of
dill also "hinder witches of their will," and rosettes of pine
cones tightly wired make a firm center motif.

To make a swag, place large well-headed sprays of 'Silver King,' with tops going in opposite directions, and bend
the tops to a semicircle. Bind stems together in the center
Then wire in other sprays of artemisia down the sides.
Long sprays of mugwort and wormwood blossoms are
decorative when placed to follow the lines of the basic
'Silver King' and contribute their own symbolic protection
and good fortune. A large rosette of cones wired firmly
together can be used with the Indian corn hanging as a
pendant below, or teasels may be inserted at the top and
bottom of the design with rose hips in the center.

Christmas swags are made for inside decoration much
the same way as the autumn ones, but then they are often
background for a string of bells. I add dull green, brown,
or gold velvet ribbon. These swags stand like gray lace
against the deep reds of the walls or the black panels of
the old doors. They are truly elegant and can be used to
good effect in most settings.

I once decorated the Georgian panels of the Captain Paul House with these swags. The dull green fireplace walls with a fine old portrait and priceless shining brasses were just right for artemisia. The two semicircular swags faced the portrait; their colors, silver-gray and dull gold with creamy white flowers as central motifs and dull green and gold, faded velvety bows, repeated the rich tones of the brass sconces, the gold damask cornice draperies, and the fine bindings of the books. They were at home with the polished mahogany, oriental rugs, and the textures of the upholstery. Once placed they did not drop leaves or branches into the immaculate room and they remained crisp and fresh from early December through the long holidays.

15. Harvest Party

"The spirits of the air live on the smells
of fruit; and Joy, with pinions light, roves round
The gardens, or sits singing in the trees,"
Thus sang the jolly Autumn as he sat;
Then rose, girded himself, and o'er the bleak
Hills fled from our sight: but left his golden load.
—William Blake

St. Michael's Day, September 29, is a delightful time for a party. There is a hint of autumn in the air though days are still warm and sunny. Basil rows are full and fragrant in the sun, green and purple against the long background of gray artemisias. Unharvested savory is in blossom, reddish now in leaves and stems, and covered with minute white blooms. Mints sprawl along the paths, and thymes have burst all bounds, spilling onto driveways and over the lawn where the mower cuts a fragrant path.

Everywhere the harvest is ready. The kitchen rafters are hung with drying mint for winter tea, with bunches of sage for holiday seasonings, and flowers to add color to winter arrangements. The air is filled with good harvest smells and with the opening of the kitchen door the heady incense of heated spice and baking bread is wafted through the house.

This is the incense burned for St. Michael, patron of soldiers, coopers, hatmakers, haberdashers, and grocers, the saint of the great soldier-lords of the manors, of the middle-class merchants and purveyors of food. St. Michael is one of the three archangels mentioned in the

168

Scriptures who appears with a flaming sword to protect Christians from the snares of the devil and to lead them to light eternal. The pagan gods Mercury and Wotan were ousted from their high places by the Christian Michael. His most famous deed was the raising of his flaming sword against the plague in Rome. One of the most beautiful of all churches, Mont St. Michel in Normandy, was built in his honor and has survived countless wars and changes, remaining a shrine for Christians everywhere.

St. Michael's Day was celebrated throughout Europe. This was the end of the harvest time in medieval Europe, when herds were driven home from mountain pastures, when laborers hired on St. George's Day (April 23) were given wages and discharged after much feasting and gaiety. Many left with a gift of a live squealing pig under their arms or a roast of pork, a fresh ham, or a goose. Pork and goose were the foods used for the feasting and the outdoor spits turned all day in their preparation.

In French cities the pancake-maker was busy on St. Michael's Day at his place in the shadow of the great cathedrals, for it was his business to make a sweet, crisp cake, much like a waffle, called *"gaufre."* The long-handled iron pan in which he baked the cake over charcoal fire had beautiful religious designs embossed in it and these left their imprint on the waffle. The iron pans are collectors' items today.

In Scotland St. Michael's Day was remembered with a rich fruit cake called St. Michael's Bannock. This was made with wild and cultivated fruits and a mixture of all the harvest grains, oats, rye, and barley, a multitude of eggs and much butter and cream, with honey for sweetening. All represented the bounty of nature and the richness of the harvest.

RECIPES FOR AUTUMN

Thus our theme is set by the harvest festivals of the past for a Michaelmas Festival. The recipes for this harvest party are my adaptation of the traditional meats and sweets served as the bounty of St. Michael.

170

THE PUNCH BOWL

The punch bowl stands in the center of an old barrel head in which ivies grow happily through the year in sphagnum moss; for special days we insert other plants in this green circle. Woodruff grows around the May bowl, thymes and mints decorate midsummer parties, and in the fall mints are supplemented with Michaelmas daisies, cut and inserted in the moist moss. The punch bowl rises like a white flower out of this mass of fragrant green.

Traditionally this harvest festival was celebrated with libations of foaming ale and various types of home-brew, but our guests prefer a more delicate refreshment like this dry punch which stimulates the appetite for a harvest feast.

1 quart dry vermouth (which contains many herbs)

2 quarts dry white wine
Juice of 2 limes
1 lime, sliced

Combine all and pour over solid cake of ice in a punch bowl. Garnish with leaves of lemon balm. Makes 25 punch-cup servings.

AUTUMN RED WINE PUNCH

24 sprigs burnet, bruised

2 quarts claret

2 cups orange juice

1 cup granulated sugar

6 ripe peaches, peeled and quartered
2 bunches green grapes, separated
1 bunch purple grapes, separated

Marinate the burnet, which has a cucumber flavor, in the wine and orange juice for about 4 hours, allowing the mixture to stand at room temperature. Sugar the peaches. Arrange the peaches and the grapes over a flat cake of ice. Pour the wine mixture over the fruit. Have extra quartered peaches and grapes ready for second servings. Makes 20 punch-cup servings.

Hint: For a non-alcoholic drink substitute grape juice for the claret and add a sprig or more of thyme to cut the sweetness.

GINGER SPREAD FOR CANAPES

Whip to a smooth bright yellow paste: 1 six-ounce package cream cheese, 2 teaspoons ground ginger root, 1 teaspoon chopped candied ginger, 2 teaspoons curry powder, ½ cup crushed pineapple, ¼ cup granulated sugar. Serve on crackers or on fingers of homebaked bread, white or dark.

BEER AND CARAWAY SPREAD

Heat in a saucepan 1 pound cut up cheddar cheese with ½ cup beer or ale and 2 tablespoons of butter. Add 2 crushed cloves of garlic. Stir in 1 tablespoon caraway seeds and ½ teaspoon salt. Cook until beer and cheese blend. Remove from heat and beat with a wire whisk until smooth. Store in the refrigerator in crocks. Serve on rye crackers or whole-wheat crackers, or rounds of rye bread.

CAPRILANDS CHEESE ROLLS

2 cups sifted all-purpose flour	¼ teaspoon margarine
4 teaspoons baking powder	¼ teaspoon oregano
½ teaspoon salt	Pinch of rosemary
¼ pound butter, softened	Powdered garlic
¾ cup milk	Dried parsley
⅛ pound butter, softened	Paprika
	1 pound sharp "coon" or store cheese

Blend flour, salt, and baking powder, which have been sifted together, with the ¼ pound of butter. Add milk to make a dough that can be rolled into a piece about 6 by 12 inches. Spread with more butter. Mix sage, margarine, oregano, and rosemary and sprinkle very lightly over the buttered dough. Then powder lightly with garlic. Grate the cheese over all and roll like jelly roll. Slice into sections about 1 inch thick. Arrange in a 12"x18" pan. Dot with remaining butter and sprinkle with the parsley and paprika. Bake in a 450° oven until center rolls in pan are done. Makes about 2 dozen rolls. Serve hot or cold or reheat in foil. Excellent all ways.

Hints: Chop some green sage leaves into the herb mixture; sage is very good with this cheese or add about ½ teaspoon chopped rosemary to the biscuit dough and then add no other herb except finely chopped parsley. Or replace all herbs with Caprilands Poultry Seasoning.

FRUIT GINGERBREAD WITH CORIANDER

A rich and wonderful gingerbread which is a great favorite here. This is superior to quick mixtures in taste and keeping quality because of the filling. In New England we make this for the Michaelmas Festival to represent the Scottish fruit-filled bannocks, appropriate to this day.

2½ cups sifted all-purpose flour
2 teaspoons soda
1 teaspoon salt
1 cup boiling water
2 eggs, beaten light
1 cup molasses
½ cup granulated sugar
½ cup (1 stick) of butter
2 teaspoons ground ginger root

1 teaspoon powdered cinnamon
1 teaspoon ground cloves
1 tablespoon coriander seed, crushed
½ cup raisins
½ cup chopped nuts
¼ chopped candied fruit
Confectioners' sugar or whipped cream for topping

Sift flour three times with the soda and salt. Beat in the boiling water and then mix with the other ingredients. This makes a thin batter. Pour into a 12"x18" well-greased pan. Bake in a 350° oven for about 40 minutes or until cake tester inserted in center comes out clean. Sprinkle with confectioners' sugar or, at serving time, top with whipped cream.

Hint: This is also good made without fruit and served with a topping of applesauce flavored with caraway or coriander seed.

CAPRILANDS CHILE BEAN POT

2 28-ounce cans red kidney beans
¼ cup basil or garlic vinegar
¾ cup brown sugar
½ cup chutney or tomato preserve
1 large clove garlic, crushed
3 green rosemary tips, or ¼ teaspoon dried rosemary

2 teaspoons Caprilands chili powder
6 whole cloves
1 teaspoon dry mustard, or 2 tablespoons Caprilands Herb Mustard
2 bay leaves
½ teaspoon dried thyme
½ teaspoon basil
Salt to taste

Combine all ingredients in a 3-quart bean-pot. On top of bean mixture, spread:

2 large onions, sliced   4 slices bacon

Cook in a very slow oven overnight, or at 350° until liquid is thickened; 3 or 4 hours. Half an hour before serving, remove bean pot from oven and pour in ½ cup of strong black coffee. At serving time add 2 ounces of brandy, rum, or sherry to the hot beans. Serves 8 to 10.

ROAST PORK WITH ANISE

1 five-pound pork loin with pocket
2 tablespoons anise
1 cup white wine
¼ cup (½ stick) butter
1 onion grated

1 teaspoon Caprilands Poultry Seasoning
1 teaspoon sweet marjoram
1 teaspoon salt
2 cups fine bread crumbs

Place pork in open roasting pan. Simmer anise and wine for a few minutes. Melt butter in large sauce pan with seasonings. Add crumbs and cook until mixture browns a little. Then force crumb mixture into the hollow of the pork. Spoon some of the anise and wine over the meat. Wrap in foil and roast at 250° to 350° for 4 hours. More of wine mixture may be spooned over the meat during the roasting by opening the foil and letting the liquid seep down. Serves 6 to 8.

Hint: For an excellent pork salad, combine red apples, cored and sliced but not peeled, bite-sized pieces of cold pork, chopped shallots or onions, and cut-up celery. Bind with mayonnaise.

CAPRILANDS SWEET POTATO CASSEROLE

This rich golden mixture is particularly attractive and delicious for a harvest meal. First make a sauce of 6 red apples, cored and sliced, but not peeled, 1 cup granulated sugar, 1 cup of water, and 1 teaspoon caraway seed.

Let the apples cook until they are soft but not mushy; avoid a runny sauce. In a long, narrow 2-quart casserole, arrange sweet potatoes from an 18-ounce can. Sprinkle with ½ teaspoon oregano. Cover with ¾ cup of brown sugar and ½ cup raisins, preferably a Muscat type. Spread with the applesauce and pour in ¼ cup of sherry. Top with bread crumbs mixed with cinnamon or with just a sprinkling of grated nutmeg. Bake in a 350° oven about 30 minutes, or until ingredients are well blended. Serves 6 to 8.

PEARS IN PORT WINE

6 firm fresh or canned pears
1 cup port wine
1 3-ounce package cream cheese, or ½ cup cottage cheese
½ cup pear or orange juice

Mint leaves—orange, curly, or spearmint
Ginger root and nutmeg, grated
½ cup chopped candied ginger
Mint jelly

Drain pears, if canned, and reserve juice. Place pears in a deep bowl. Pour wine over them and refrigerate for 4 hours or overnight. Mix cheese with the pear or orange juice. At serving time drain pears and arrange on a bed of mint leaves. Fill hollows with the cheese mixture. Sprinkle generously with the grated ginger and nutmeg. Dot with the candied ginger and top with a dollop of mint jelly. Serves 6.

Hints: Use green minted pears and red maraschino cherries, instead of mint jelly, for a holiday green and red salad. If you like, alternate pears with slices of pineapple; decorate the cheese with candied mint leaves, but be sure to serve these at once.

BROWN AUTUMN COOKIES

2 cups sifted all-purpose flour	2 tablespoons sesame seed
½ cup (1 stick) butter	1 tablespoon caraway seed
¼ cup brown sugar	2 cardamom seeds, shelled and crushed
3 eggs	
2 cups brown sugar	2 tablespoons lemon juice
1 cup shredded coconut	
½ teaspoon salt	1 teaspoon grated lemon rind
1 cup raisins	
½ cup chopped walnuts	

First combine the flour, butter, and the ¼ cup brown sugar. Pack into a well-greased pan, approximately 9″ x 12″. Bake in a 350° oven for 10 minutes. Next beat eggs to a froth and mix with the two cups brown sugar, coconut, salt, raisins, walnuts, and herb seeds. Stir in lemon juice and rind. Spread this egg mixture over the slightly cooled baked mixture in the pan. Bake 25 minutes. When cool, cut into about 2 dozen squares.

Herbal Hints for Autumn

At this season most of us are eager to use herbs in cooking. Here are some of my "secrets" which I hope you will try. Add a little cardamom to mincemeat. Try coriander in ginger mixes. Spread sliced apples thinly with mayonnaise, sprinkle with caraway seeds, and serve on mint leaves. Garnish fruit salads with pineapple sage leaves. Add chopped, fresh marjoram to 8 cups of soup, made with caraway seeds. Season a casserole of zucchini squash, with basil. Add a pinch of marjoram to boiled onions or an onion pie.

Christmas Diary

I saw a stranger yestere'en;
I put food in the eating place;
Drink in the drinking place;
And in the sacred
Name of the Triune,
He blessed myself
And all my house,
My cattle and all my
Dear Ones.

And the lark said in her song
Often, Often, Often
Goes the Christ in the stranger's guise.
—Old Gaelic Rune

Christmas is the peak of the herb gardener's year, a time of long preparation, great anticipation, and much excitement. The dark days of Advent overflow with Christmas plans, and the best celebrations follow the true meaning of the season. They emphasize family traditions, but also borrow colorful customs from many lands and eras to weave a rich tapestry of prayers, parties, giving and receiving, dining and decorating.

The herb gardener has a wealth of materials—decorative aids from the garden and dried seasonings for cooking. This is the time to use your herb garden; to make the personal gifts that money cannot buy; to serve the foods of many lands made exceptional by herbs; a time to use the spices symbolic of the Wise Men; to serve the wassails of Merrie England and the lands of the far North.

The Christmas season ushers in the happiest and busiest time of my year. The house is filled with the color and sweet odor of evergreens that adorn every corner and frame the long living room where our activities take place. Greens are of many varieties, and all have herbal histories and uses, from the tall pyramidal junipers in the four corners of the room, to the bits of pennyroyal in the manger bed of the Christ Child.

In a large window that looks across the fields, great rosemary shrubs with shining needle leaves make a fragrant silhouette against a snowy or bleak brown world. Theirs is the true scent of Christmas, spicy with a hint of ginger, that permeates the room as the sun strikes the leaves or we brush them in passing.

Juniper, from nearby pastures and overgrown farmlands, with its frosty resinous berries and silver-backed branches, cedars, thick-branched and yellow-green, long-needled pine, and the satiny luxuriant yew, elegant, dark, and mysterious—all these evergreens make the frame on which our Christmas decorations are built, and provide the background for a joyous season.

16. Capturing the World of Fragrance

Not all the ointments brought from Delos Ile,
Nor that of quinces, nor of marjoram,
That ever from the Ile of Coös came,
Nor these, nor any else, though ne'er so rare,
Could with this place for sweetest smells compare.
                                        —William Browne

The fragrant things of the world have romantic appeal
—flowers, spices, aromatic gums, the resinous tree barks,
even wet or burning leaves, the acrid odor of wood smoke,
the earthy smell of new-turned soil—all touch the imagination. Spice may recall apple pie fresh from the oven or
the different experience of incense in the gloom of a
Gothic cathedral. The sweet breath of island paradises
is caught in the scent of the fabulous clove. Fragrances
have also proved to be the pot of gold at the foot of the
rainbow. Continents have been discovered, islands colo-
nized, industries developed, and fortunes made to insure
the sources of some valued scent. The imagination of the
churchman, of the lady of the manor, and the humble
housewife have been stirred by the smell of incense, of
strewing herbs, of medicinal plants. The merchant has
found these a rich source of income; apothecaries have
won fame by compounding them into love filters and
charms for eternal youth; the priest has used them rever-
ently in the rituals of worship.

179

In stillrooms and apothecary shops, it was discovered that certain garden plants had odors similar to those of valuable spices. There were roses that smelled like cinnamon, and carnations, like cloves. Since spices were costly, it was desirable to extend these with herbal elements.

Ships brought strange gums, barks, beans, seed pods, even animal products to the apothecary. These provided fixatives for plant materials. The spice ball, the pomander, potpourris, and sweet bags with their combinations of spice and fruit scents were developed and preserved by the fixatives.

Ambergris, civet, and musk are three evil-smelling animal secretions that, with age, proper application, and blending give to perfumes a quality both rich and haunting. These were difficult ingredients to procure, so floral fixatives were sought and found in the root of the Florentine iris, patchouli leaves from Malay, tonka beans from South America and Africa, and vetiver roots from many places. These added a musky quality to mixtures. The lemon verbena plant from the Southwest, the new world of Spanish conquest, was brought to England in 1784 and added its fresh, cool lemon odor to many fragrant preparations.

Potpourri was originally not a luxury but a necessary nicety. In the days before good sanitation when fresh air was considered dangerous, castles and cottages alike needed the clean smell of flowers and the masking odor of spices. It was the duty of a proper housewife to make potpourri, sweet bags, and pomanders.

The rose jar was kept on the table in the best room, and, after the cleaning was done, it was opened and stirred to scent the room and freshen the air. Sweet bags, filled with lavender, lemon verbena, with herbs and spice mixtures, were fitted to the backs of chairs and placed in closets and linen presses. Sweet herbs were strewn on the floors of church and home to modify the accumulated odors of the rushes that covered the stone or earthen floors.

Many recipes for fragrances were concocted. The lady

of the manor, proud of her stillroom skill, spent hours compounding mixtures worthy of her efforts. Some of these recipes found their way into stillroom books and were treasured as family heirlooms. Others were included in popular herbals and are our common inheritance.

To walk in a garden of fragrant herbs is rewarding at any time of day, but to plant and tend such a garden is a rare pleasure indeed. Choosing plants that have sweet-smelling leaves and flowers that retain their ordors is an interesting avocation, placing them in proper patterns, a fascinating occupation. To the herb gardener, there is also the reward of drying fragrant materials that will bring the garden inside for winter enjoyment.

The fragrant plants listed here can be grown in any garden that has some sun and a well-drained soil.

FRAGRANT LEAVES

Bay
Lavender
Lemon balm
Lemon geraniums
Lemon thyme
Lemon verbena
Narrowlcaf French thyme
Orange mint
Oregano
Peppermint
Peppermint geraniums
Rose geraniums
Rosemary
Strawberry
Sweet basil
Sweet marjoram
Sweet woodruff
Tarragon

FRAGRANT SEEDS

Anise
Coriander

FRAGRANT PETALS

Lavender
Pinks
Roses

COLORFUL PETALS

Bachelor's-buttons
Blue salvia
Calendula
Daffodil
Delphinium
Forsythia
Lavender
Pansy
Pinks
Viola
Violet
Zonal geraniums

Spices for Potpourri

Allspice (*Pimenta officinalis*) of the myrtle family grows naturally in the West Indies, especially Jamaica, and some trees are found in Mexico. The spice docks of Kingston are fragrant with this highly scented berry. Great casks of them fill the air with wonderful odor not unlike bayrum.

Calamus root, and the oil derived from it, adds a mellow and somewhat spicy odor to potpourri. This product of *Acorus calamus* comes from France and Belgium.

Cinnamon bark or sticks (from *Cinnamomum zeylanicum*) of the laurel family yield a spicy element which was once the chief ingredient in the manufacture of the holy oils of the Bible. These were used for anointing priests and favored persons and the cleansing of the holy vessels. The cinnamon tree grows to 60 feet in nature; in cultivation it is a bush to be propagated from seeds. The young shoots are brilliant red, the bark speckled green and orange. Cinnamon is made from the inner bark which is cut in cylinders or quills from the time the trees are three or four years old; the best grade comes from young branches. India, Ceylon, Malaya, China, and the East Indies have groves of this beautiful tree.

I grind the stick cinnamon with whole cloves and add this coarse mixture to orris root. Sometimes I grind a handful of tonka beans and mix this with the powdered frankincense and myrrh, to make an excellent fixative. The mixture is stored in jars and sprinkled through the potpourri.

My recipe calls for ½ pound of stick cinnamon, 1 ounce tonka beans, 1 cup of orris root with 10 drops rose oil, ½ cup of frankincense, and 1 tablespoon of myrrh.

Cloves (*Eugenia caryophyllata*, of the myrtle family) come from trees 25 to 30 feet high that grow in Zanzibar, British Malaya, Ceylon, India, Madagascar, and Penang. Two annual harvests are made by the native villagers who pick the unexpanded flower buds by hand. The bunches are dried on mats, and the green buds removed from the stems. In about a week they were brown, ready to be sorted and graded for the market.

Frankincense (*Boswellia carteri*) gives us the most used and treasured of all the sweet odors from the East. Incense was a vital part of Herbrew worship, and several written versions of the temple mixtures are extant. The compounding of these was something of a secret and proportions were carefully weighed. One used four ingredients: stacte, onycha, galbanum, and frankincense. Another was comprised of thirteen elements, including myrrh, cassia, spikenard, saffron, costus, cinnamon, sweet bark, and an herb known as a "smoke raiser." The compounding was also a secret handed down through generations of incense makers. It is recorded that two pounds of incense were used every day in the temple.

Frankincense in our time comes not only from Arabia, but from India, Ethiopia, and Somaliland. To procure the gum from which the essence of frankincense is obtained, incisions are made in the bark of the tree and the gum oozes out in large drops.

The odor of frankincense is not discernible in potpourri unless the mixture is warm or moist. However, it is a fixative and adds stability to a mixture. If you wish to burn something very fragrant sprinkle a little rose and spice potpourri with frankincense over hot coals from the fireplace. If you wish to burn frankincense and myrrh together, follow the old Hebrew rule of six parts of frankincense to one of myrrh.

Myrrh comes from a tree, *Commiphora myrrha*, that grows in Arabia, Ethiopia, and along the Somaliland Coast. Wood and bark are fragrant, and the gum flows slightly without cutting; it is dark brown and bitter tasting. In the past it was used to soothe a sore throat, for dentifrices, and as a purifying agent. The dead were embalmed with myrrh in Egypt and Palestine, and it was valued by Hebrews as a perfume. Kings, gods, and temples were censed with this distinctive gum from the time of the sun worshippers at Heliopolis, where it was burned daily at noon, until the reign of George III in England.

Sometimes it was burned alone, sometimes in combination with other spices. Today myrrh is used as a fixative in potpourri, either as powder or oil.

Patchouli (*Pogostemon cablin*) from Singapore, Sumatra, and British Malaya cannot be classified as a "spice," yet it is a fragrance that we import for potpourri. This is a tropical shrublike plant of the mint family with large musk-smelling dark leaves from which an essential oil was distilled in the 1850's, when it was a popular scent in Paris. The odor has been described as fruity, earthy, and of very warm character. I find that patchouli gives depth to potpourri, and has certain fixative powers as well.

When the bales of big patchouli leaves are first opened at Caprilands the odor is overpowering. A few leaves will scent a room and in my experience they never lose their odor. Patchouli and rose buds with orris root and a few drops of rose oil make a good mixture for a rose bowl to be left open. I add a large crushed leaf of patchouli to every rose jar as well as to each bag of potpourri.

Sandalwood (*Santalum album*) grows 30 to 40 feet high, is native to the Malabar Coast, and found also in New Caledonia. From early time the wood was valued for its sweet odor and employed in the making of musical instruments, particularly those used in sacred ceremonies. It was also burned at sacrifices to idols and was later incorporated in incense for synagogues. There were domestic uses, too; fans were made of it and boxes lined as protection against moths.

Sandalwood chips are best for potpourri; they add that indefinable something that those who remember the old rose jars search for—sometimes in vain. For burning, both chips and larger pieces are effective. The chips mix well with other ingredients, such as frankincense, myrrh, vetiver, spices, and lavender flowers.

Vetiver root (*Vetiveria zizanioides*) comes mainly from Java and the Reunion Islands, small amounts from Louisiana and the West Indies. Vetiver is an 8-foot grass in its native climate. It has a fragrant root with the odor of violets or sandalwood. As a fixative in potpourri, it never seems to lose its fragrance, although this is more noticeable in a warm, moist atmosphere. In the South, Vetiver root is put in bureau drawers and closets to keep away moths and ants and to scent clothing. It is effective as incense and at its best in oriental mixtures.

FIXATIVES TO HOLD FLOWER FRAGRANCES

Fixatives from the animal or plant world are used to hold the fragrance of potpourri ingredients. Animal fixatives include ambergris, civet, and musk. Ambergris is a substance from the intestines of the sperm whale, and it is found on beaches or floating on waters of the South Seas. The odor is disagreeable, but like many fixatives, when combined with fragrant things, it absorbs and enhances the essences.

Civet is extracted from the scent glands of the African civet cat. The animal is confined so that the secretion may be collected at regular intervals. The odor is repulsive while fresh, but it adds alluring tonalities to oriental perfumes. Musk comes from a sac in the male musk deer, a small, hornless, rapidly disappearing species from the mountains of Central Asia. Today most of the musk is synthetic.

The plant fixatives I use most are orris root, benzoin, and tonka bean. Orris root comes from *Iris florentina*, a variety of *I. germanica*. The fresh root is dug, peeled and sun-dried, then stored for two years to develop the scent. It is then ground and emits the violet odor for which it is known. Orris root is the most common fixative for potpourri as it is easily obtainable. I use it generously, at least 1 cup to 1 pound of rose petals, along with spices and other essences.

Benzoin, once called "Benjamin," is often found under this name in old books that give the early recipes for sweet bags, jars, and astringent lotions. In the fourteenth century gum benzoin was called "Java frankincense." In 1461 benzoin was sent as a present by the Sultan of Egypt to the Doge of Venice with gifts of sugar, candy, carpets, and china. Apparently the benzoin was pleasing to the Doge and the Venetians developed a fondness for the aromatic scent. Records show that the beginning of the sixteenth century a good trade in this gum was established with Venice. By the seventeenth century, England received supplies of benzoin regularly from Sumatra and Siam.

Benzoin is a gum that oozes from cuts made in the tree known as *Styrax benzoin*, native to Java, Sumatra, and Siam. Plants are grown from seed and when they are about seven years old, the first harvest is made. Trees produce for about twelve years and are then cut down. Benzoin is used in church incense, and is also valuable for cosmetics because of its astringent and preservative powers.

The tonka bean *(Dipterix odorata)*, sometimes called tonquin bean, provides one of the most concentrated of floral odors. It is overpowering in its sweetness, heavy with the smell of coumarin. The ground beans are important for good potpourri, since they act as fixative and an intensifier, sharpening other odors while losing their own identity. Beans are imported from Brazil, Ceylon, Venezuela, British Guiana, and Africa.

Oils Essential for Potpourri

When essences or essential oils are included in recipes, the distilled plant oil is indicated. These are generally volatile oils that evaporate at room temperatures. They occur in secretory cells, reservoirs, glands of flowers, barks, fruits, and leaves. Most oils are obtained by steam distillation.

Attar of roses, of all oils, is the most fabulous and desirable. There is a charming story of the origin of attar in the year 1562 the time of the Grand Moguls. For the wedding of Princess Nour-Djihan to the Emperor Djihan-gugr all pathways the royal pair would use were strewn with the sweet roses of the East. The canals surrounding the palaces were so filled with roses that the royal barges could scarcely be propelled through the floating petals.

In the heat of the day, bride and groom sought refuge in the royal barge. As they drifted along, the princess noticed a thin film upon the water. She trailed her hand in it and found it slick with an oil sweet beyond belief. This was indeed the very essence of the rose. Her discovery, carried to the royal apothecary, resulted in the valuable oil of roses.

The first rose oils came from the East. At one time rose perfume was the only one known. Rose water was first made and recorded in the eleventh century by Avicenna, a Persian Moslem of unusual intellect and learning. Rose oil was first made by steeping roses in oil, not by distillation. Much of the attar of roses produced later came from Bulgaria, out of the famous Valley of the Roses where the *Rosa damascena,* a native of the Orient introduced into Europe during the Crusades, was cultivated by hundreds of rose farmers. Many of them distilled their own essences in old-fashioned stills. It is said that it takes ten thousand pounds of rose petals to make one pound of oil. Hence the high cost of attar of roses, or "rose otto" as it is sometimes called.

Other oils used in the making of potpourri include oil of violet, carnation, jasmine, lemon verbena, and orange blossom.

WHEN TO MAKE POTPOURRI

Through the summer and far into autumn, the good herb gardener is busy harvesting. Airtight tin containers hold chip-dry rose petals, aromatic lavender, lemon verbena, orange mint, and others of the mint family. Large boxes or drawers in an old dresser hold a colorful selection of dried flowers, not necessarily fragrant, for decoration within the glass jars of potpourri. When gardening demands are less strenuous, there is no task quite so pleasant as the making of potpourri.

It is always a matter of surprise and perhaps disap-

pointment, to the novice to discover that while the chief
ingredient of potpourri is the rose, much of its lasting
fragrance comes from exotic materials that bring out,
preserve, and add to the basic scent. A bushel of carefully dried petals, tinned and stored in a dry, cool place,
will emit an odor like tea with very little sweetness. This
is partly due to the difficulty of getting the old fragrant
damask roses, partly because few remember what went
into Grandmother's rose jar.

Plan to add many ingredients to your potpourri. Get
them well in advance and make your mixture by late
November so that it can ripen for one month before
being transferred to jars or bags for gifts.

CAPRILANDS POTPOURRI

 1 pound of dried petals
 2 ounces dried rose buds (those from the south of
    France or northern Africa have the best color and
    shape)
30 grams each of frankincense and myrrh (gum);
    lavender, lemon verbena, and patchouli (leaves);
    sandalwood chips and vetiver root
¼   cup gum benzoin
 4 to 6 tonka beans
½   vanilla bean
 6 cinnamon sticks
¼   cup each ground cinnamon, ground cloves, cori-
    ander, and dried tarragon
¼   pound orris root
¼   to ½ ounce oil of rose essence (only 1 drop if attar
    of roses is used)
 4 drops oil of violet
 2 drops oil of jasmine

In a 20-inch wooden salad bowl put dried rose petals, rose
buds and the grains of frankincense, lavender, lemon
verbena, myrrh, patchouli, sandalwood, and vetiver.
Crush or grind to powder the gum benzoin, tonka beans,

vanilla bean, cinnamon, cloves, coriander, tarragon. In a separate container mix the orris root with the powdered spices, then add the essences. Add all to the roses and dried leaves, turning over carefully many times. Store in airtight tins for one month.

Package in glass apothecary jars, placing rose buds on the top so that it will be pleasant to look at. Use pressed pansies, delphinium florets, violets or violas against the glass for decoration. Tie the jar with ribbon, with perhaps, a dried flower in the bow. Place in a clear plastic bag and store until the holidays.

LAVENDER POTPOURRI

½ pound lavender flowers
1 ounce orris root with 6 drops oil of lavender
2 cups dried red geranium blossoms stripped from stems
1 cup each dried larkspur blossoms and white rose petals

Mix together thoroughly, then enjoy in an open pewter bowl or in a glass jar.

LEMON VERBENA JAR

1 cup dried lemon verbena leaves
1 cup dried lemon balm leaves
Peel of 1 lemon, dried and grated
½ cup dried petals from forsythia, calendula, lemon-scented dwarf marigold
1 ounce orris root with 6 drops of lemon verbena oil
Few leaves of lemon-scented thyme if you wish

Combine all ingredients, then turn into small apothecary jars. Press some of the yellow flowers against the sides of the jar for color. Tie the top with yellow and green velvet ribbon.

POTPOURRI OF HERBS AND FLOWERS

    1 cup each of dried thyme, orange mint, and
       bergamot leaves
    1 cup of mixed blossoms
    ¼ cup each of dried tarragon and rosemary
    1 ounce orris root with 6 drops of oil of bergamot

Prepare as for lemon verbena jar; tie with a ribbon of
appropriate color.

MINT POTPOURRI

    2 cups dried lavender
    1 cup dried mint leaves (peppermint, spearmint, and
       orange mint)
    ½ cup dried culinary thyme
    ¼ cup rosemary
    Few drops of essential oils of lavender, thyme, and
       bergamot
    Dried red geranium petals, blue bachelor's-button, and
       delphinium

Combine ingredients and store in apothecary jars. When
you are entertaining turn some of this mixture out into
a pewter or silver bowl. Stir it slightly and the smell of
a fresh clean breeze will permeate the room. An excellent potpourri for a desk or worktable, perhaps in a wide-
mouth, antique sugarbowl of stoneware or old blue Staffordshire.

ROSE GERANIUM JAR

    1 cup each of the dried leaves of *Pelargonium graveo-
       lems* (old-fashioned rose geranium), 'Dr. Livingston'
       geranium, and any other rose-scented geraniums
       available
    ¼ cup orris root with 2 drops geranium oil
    Rose petals for color

POTPOURRI OF HERBS, FLOWERS, AND CITRUS

6 cups rose petals
1 cup each of culinary thyme (preferably narrowleaf
   French), rosemary, sweet marjoram, lavender, and
   sweet basil (narrowleaf bush)
6 crushed bay leaves
1 tablespoon allspice, crushed
Rind of 1 orange and 1 lemon, dried and crushed
1 teaspoon anise seed

MOIST POTPOURRI

3 cups dry rose petals
1 cup bay salt
1 teaspoon each of allspice, cinnamon and, coriander
1 tablespoon each of cloves, grated nutmeg, and anise
1 cup lavender
½ cup each of patchouli and powdered orris root
¼ ounce each of oil of rose and oil of rose geranium
3 cups of a mixture made of dried rosemary, lemon
   balm, and lemon verbena leaves

In a covered crock mix rose petals with the bay salt and
leave for one week. Turn once each day. Add spices and
let stand for another week, turning daily. At the end of
the two weeks add the lavender, patchouli, orris root, and
oils. Let stand for a few weeks, then mix in leaves of
dried rosemary, lemon balm, and lemon verbena. Stir
frequently with a wooden spoon or cinnamon stick.

ROSE JAR

1 quart dried rose petals
1 cup each of lavender flowers and rose geranium
   leaves
½ cup patchouli
¼ cup of sandalwood chips and vetiver, mixed
2 teaspoons of frankincense and myrrh, mixed

1 teaspoon each of powdered benzoin, cinnamon, and
   cloves
2 tonka beans, ground
¼ cup allspice
10 drops rose oil
1 cup orris root

Mix first eight ingredients thoroughly; then add the rose
oil and orris root. Mix again and stir well. If this amount
of orris seems excessive, remember that this is a basic
mixture to which you can add flowers of the season right
up to fall. After it is finished, close the jar for at least
two weeks (a month is better), then it will be ready to
enjoy.

Ingredients and recipes for potpourri are legion. Other
fragrant leaves, roots, or blossoms you may wish to add
to mixtures include sweet woodruff, myrtle (*Myrtus communis*),
sliced angelica root, and eglantine leaves.

How To Make Sachets and Scented Pillows

Sachets are made simply by tying up a fragrant dried
mixture of potpourri in a square of organdy or fine net.
Decorate with little dried roses or everlastings and a bow.
Antique glass containers with a sachet in them make
delightful gifts.

Covers for scented pillows are made of organdy, fine
net, or silk; but put the more sturdy fragrances of pine
and patchouli into soft felt or homespun. Pieces of brocade,
velvet, and chintz also make useful covers. For
these small pillows, make an attractive case of one of
these materials and a slightly smaller lining of muslin
to hold the fragrant mixture.

Use prolific plants from the herb garden for the bulk
of fragrant material for pillows. Lemon balm is one of
the most leafy herbs; lemon and camphor southernwoods
also produce an abundance of foliage with a clean, penetrating,
and lasting scent. Combine any of these with
cuttings of rosemary, bergamot, thyme, and bay leaves,
and a generous amount of dried orange and lemon peel.

17. Wreaths from the Herb Garden

Joan can call by name her cows,
And deck her windows with green boughs;
She can wreathes and tutties* make,
And trim with plums a bridal cake.
                              —Thomas Campion

In the last days of November, when it would be pleasanter perhaps to stay by the fire, I start down the hillside with a basket to fill with herbs for making wreaths—part of the garden's contribution to Christmas decoration. Any garden that has santolina, germander, horehound, rue, lamb's-ear, lavender, sage, winter savory, and thyme provides a wealth of material for holiday cutting. I take rosemary from the greenhouse where it winters in large terra-cotta tubs and bushelbaskets. All this fragrant material stands in water, in a larger copper bowl, until I can use it.

The History of Wreath Making

The making of wreaths is an ancient and honored art that began about a thousand years before Christ. A crown of oak leaves adorned the warrior, ivy rewarded the poet, and statesmen were dignified under their laurels. Laymen did not wear these crowns, only men of distinction. Roman generals were crowned as they returned from war with wreaths made of grass and wild flowers from the battlefields.

*Tutties are tussie-mussies.

At Christmas the wreath is symbolic of Christian immortality. The circle and the sphere are symbols of
immortality. Traditionally, the wreath has been worn
at festivals, at sacrifices, at weddings, and banquets. The
priests wore henbane, vervain, and rue, plants long associated with the other world and religious rites. Crowns
for victors were made of laurel *(Laurus nobilis)*, oak, olive,
parsley, palm, and poplar. Brides wore coronets of orange
blossoms, myrtle, or rosemary. Funeral wreaths were
made of daffodils, poppies, and other plants that meant
remembrance or everlasting life, as amaranth, statice,
tansy and yarrow.

How To Make a Living Wreath

Start with a hollow circle planting-form about 12 inches
across and fill it with moist, unmilled sphagnum moss.
Place this on a black or dark green metal tray, or on an
old pewter plate. Insert cuttings of green santolina thickly
all the way around the circle so as to cover the brown
moss. All this forms the base of the wreath and stays
fresh and green indefinitely. Next make an inside edge
of gray *Santolina chamaecyparissus*, and repeat on the
outer edge. Then group lavender and a rosette of lamb's-
ears on one side, spreading out the leaves to make a
flower-like shape. On the opposite side, insert a rosette of
young horehound plants.

The tops of clary sage and seasoning sage make decorative accents when used at intervals around a wreath.
The deep purple-gray of *Salvia purpurascens* and the
variegated foliage of 'Tricolor' sage are also interesting
additions. Insert sprigs of silver and gold thyme for a
different leaf form and the lemon aroma. Continue the
wreath by inserting stiff silvery cuttings of the gray, narrowleaf French thyme. The blue-green tops of rue make
fine accents around the wreath. At this point, I often put
a design of rosemary at the base of the wreath; if it is a
perfect circle I make two designs, one for the top and one
for the bottom.

Photograph by Herman F. Marshall

Caprilands herb and spice wreath has an artemisia base, with bay leaves, rosemary, cardamom, nutmegs, cinnamon sticks and packages of herb seeds for seasoning.

195

The secret of success with this wreath design is to keep the outer edge a solid line of gray or green with one kind of plant for this basic line. Hold contrasting material generally to the center, and do not place large leaves so that they break the neat outline of the circle. If you do not have enough green santolina, use substitutes, as *Myrtus communis*, small-leaved English ivy, periwinkle or myrtle (*Vinca minor*), sweet woodruff, and *Euonymus japonicus microphyllus*.

To keep the wreath fresh, provide plenty of moisture and light, but no hot sun. My wreaths stay healthy and even form roots in a west window where there is good light all day but no sun. The living wreath will fare better if it is in a cool place at night. If, despite all precautions, some materials dry, the wreath can still be made attractive by adding other dried herbs.

You can make this wreath into a hanging door decoration by lacing the frame lightly with florists wire. Carefully cover the back of the wreath with heavy aluminum foil so that moisture will not mar your door. Tie on a moss-green and white bow, add bayberries, and attach the wreath, firmly, top and bottom, to the door.

The Advent Wreath

Thanksgiving week is the time to gather materials for the Advent wreath made of herbs associated with the Holy Family. (Illustration 13) I use Savin juniper, rosemary, Our Lady's bedstraw, thyme, pennyroyal, rue, lavender, horehound, sage, true myrtle (*Myrtle communis*) and the purple, white, and pink flowers of dried globe amaranth (*Gomphrena globosa*). Mechanics are the same as for the living wreath.

Cover the moist sphagnum moss with clippings of Savin juniper inserted thickly and deeply right into the wire frame. Press four pieces of floral clay, each of a size to hold the base of a 12-inch candle, and place these clay holders equidistant around the wreath. Complete the wreath with other herbal materials and small bows of

Photograph by Herman F. Marshall

Holiday preparations at Caprilands. Copper pan at left includes pomanders curing in spice bath; Advent wreath in foreground is described in Chapter 17; pomanders in the making are shown at right.

purple velvet, changing these to pink for the third Sunday.

Traditionally, the Advent wreath was hung, but today the table wreath is usually preferred because it serves as centerpiece for the dinner table, and the candles may be watched during the meals. The German custom was to light a candle each Sunday of Advent, and for the family to read and memorize scriptures from the Old and New Testaments. At the end of Advent all candles were lighted, the final verses read and the celebration of Christmas begun.

An Everlasting Wreath of Artemisia

The form for this wreath is a circle to represent eternity and the projection of this world into the next. The herbal flowers symbolize immortality, with golden blossoms signifying the gifts of the Magi and also representing the light of the world. This artemisia wreath is made to last, not just for one year but for several.

Basic materials include an abundance of artemisia stalks (preferably those fresh from the garden), two dozen or more dried or freshly cut tansy blossoms, dried yarrow flowers, oregano blossoms (dried for deep browns, and fresh flowers which will dry first to purple or green), everlastings (preferably the roadside gnaphalium, dried, then shaken outdoors to remove the fluff), seed pods of rue, ambrosia, and the dried brown tips of St. John's-wort. You may experiment with other materials such as sumac berries and various pine cones. Before starting to make the wreath, have at hand a roll of florists wire, sharp clippers to cut it, and a circle of heavy wire from 8 to 12 inches in diameter.

Arrange the artemisia stalks thickly and evenly around the circle of wire. Let stems overlap and press them down then bind them lightly into place with florist wire, leaving 1 to 2 inches between the strands as you wrap it around the wreath. Flatten the artemisia with both hands, adding more wire if necessary. This forms the base on which to place your best cuttings.

Take your whitest artemisia (if you want a brown effect, use plants harvested later), remove the curls or stems from the treelike blossoms, or cut the tops from the wispy ones that have not properly developed, and cut with stems long enough to insert in the base. Turn the curls toward the center, working clockwise until the circle is filled. Shape the outside line carefully as you work to keep a good circle. If the material is unruly, run a wire lightly around the whole wreath, lacing in the errant pieces, then cover the wire with more artemisia sprays. Save some of the laciest pieces for the center. Push these firmly into the framework, being careful to maintain a circle.

The wreath is now ready for floral decoration. Add a circle of tansy, then use yarrow toward the bottom. Make a circle of the everlastings, pressing their soft stems among the sturdier ones already in the wreath. Follow these with a ring of oregano, then ambrosia on the inside of the circle or pushed into the design for a green, mossy effect. Use the St. John's-wort and rue pods as pins and add small sprigs of dried lanceleaf goldenrod to give the design liveliness.

When the flowers are all placed, reshape the artemisia and add small curving pieces. Bows of yellow and brown velvet with a group of small cones or a rosette of tiny brass bells complete the festive appearance of this everlasting wreath. It may be used inside or in a sheltered doorway where wind and rain will not harm it. When not in use, wrap carefully in polyethylene film and store in a safe place. Restoration the second and following seasons is a simple matter of showering briefly under a spray faucet, hanging to dry in a warm place, and then adding some of the current season's artemisia and herbal flowers.

AN HERB AND SPICE WREATH

This fragrant and decorative circle makes a perfect decoration for the kitchen. Use the artemisia base, adding a circle of bay leaves with the lower edge left open. Point the bay leaves toward the center of the circle. In the lower edge arrange one of two nutmegs. Group three cinnamon sticks and wire them into the nutmeg, then add cardamom in the same cluster. The finishing touch consists of sprigs of rosemary inserted all around the outside of the wreath for a green frame. If you make this wreath as a gift, add two or three clear cellophane bags of seed herbs, such as coriander, caraway and anise. Make a bow of brown or moss-green velvet ribbon and with it secure the seed packets to the wreath.

In making an herb and spice wreath, you may wish to add whole, dried ginger root, whole mace, groups of sage leaves, sprigs of thyme and savory, both winter and summer types.

18. How To Make Pomander Balls

Here is a pomander rare
  A ball of spice to scent the air.
Before its fragrance moths do flee
  Hang it high, then, fortune come to thee.
                                    —A. G. S.

Two of the most wonderful odors in the world come from baked bread just out of the oven, and a bowl of pomander balls, curing in a brown sea of spices. In November and December my house is filled with these enchanting smells which, with the wood smoke puffing out of a corner of the fireplace, seem like seasonal incenses.

From the first frosts until the last hurried days before Christmas, I am likely to be found with a wooden bowl of cloves and an orange started on its way to becoming a pomander ball. Trips to the grocers have preceded this holiday exercise. Carefully I select perfect oranges, not too thickly skinned, not too large—though it is diffcult to find the right size, and I often end by being extravagant with the cloves and using whatever oranges are available even if they are large. A juicy orange certainly has a headier bouquet, but will exude so much liquid in the making that you will find yourself quite sticky, brown with spice, and smelling like a cross between an apple pie and a wassail bowl.

I ruined many cloves in my first pomander days by putting the unfinished juicy orange in the same bowl with

201

the cloves. I learned to use a separate small wooden bowl for the orange, or a round metal mold. The liquid, if not contained, will make the cloves too soft to insert in the fruit.

HISTORY OF POMANDERS

Originally pomanders were not made of oranges or apples but were small balls of various materials that would hold perfumes, herbal odors, and spices. Sometimes beeswax was used for the medium. Other bases included garden earth, mold, or apple pulp with the juice drained out. Balls made only of gums and spices were costly and not available to the average household.

There were many types of pomanders, for through the years, spices, essential oils, and green herbs, including rue, sweet bay, lavender, and rosemary, were used not only for their sweet smells but also for protection against contagion. Medicinal pomanders, some for the curing of fevers, some for insomnia, many for the medieval counterpart of our "nerves," were a part of stillroom activities and a source of revenue for the professional apothecary. Silversmiths and jewelers made exquisite cases for balls containing expensive perfumes, and these were worn as ornaments about the waist, while tiny ones were fashionably worn as lockets. They were one of the most appreciated gifts for "fayre ladyes" at Christmas, even for the great Queen Elizabeth who received a "gyrdle of pomanders" as a gift from an unnamed courtier.

The early word for these spice balls came from the French, *pomme d'ambre,* but the word *"pomme"* did not mean then (as it does now) that the balls were apples, but rather that they resembled apples. The name was applied originally to the small ball itself and later came to the container as well. The word "amber" was derived from ambergris, the whale sperm that was the chief fixative, so "pomme" and "amber" became "pomander."

Pomanders were also carried by men in many professions. Doctors, while visiting the sick, carried them against contagion. Lawmakers and judges who argued and heard cases in close courtrooms with prisoners infected with jail fever considered them invaluable. The dandy on the battlefield drew long breaths from a scented box to mitigate the stench of battle, and the traveler who walked along the streets lined with open sewers often carried his herbs and spices in the head of a cane which opened at will.

Courtiers traveling luxuriously in sedan chairs lifted languid hands to hold a pomander against the odorous crowd. It was natural that the cottager as well as the master of the castle should wish to have the fashionable and useful spice balls. The ingredients used in the aristocratic product were beyond the purse of the housewife. It was a strain to obtain the oranges which were eventually substituted for the first rich bases. It was discovered when oranges were unavailable, that apples could be used, and these became the receptacles for the treasured cloves and spices. Until the last fifty years, in America, oranges have been scarce and expensive. Therefore, many of the Colonial and Victorian pomanders were made of the fruit that was native and common, the apple.

Today the pomander is devoted to household use rather than to personal adornment. Our lives are lived under more sanitary conditions, and the doctor and the druggist provide necessary disinfectants. I am glad, however, that there are still many uses for these sweet-smelling balls. The clothes closet is one place where they may be hung— smelling more fragrant than mothballs. Blanket chests, bureau drawers, storage places for furs, and rooms that get a musty odor on damp days benefit from the presence of pomanders.

In pioneer New England the spice balls, clove apples, or clove oranges were placed in the homemade coffins that were kept in many attics ready to receive the bodies of those who did not survive the long winters. Often the graves could not be dug until spring, and farms were too isolated to call on the services of professional embalmers. Pomander balls were then put to their ancient use of preservation and fumigation, and known as "coffin balls."

To turn to a happier use of clove apples and clove oranges, it was an English custom recorded in the time of Henry VIII to give one to each guest at New Year's tied with a sprig of rosemary for remembrance. This was not only a sign of esteem but of good luck, a charming custom worthy of revival. I make a pomander spice tree from which on New Year's Eve or Twelfth-night each guest cuts his own pomander ball. These are tied with bright ribbons, topped with a tiny bell, to drive away evil spirits, and a sprig of rosemary.

How To Make a Pomander Ball

First, obtain good cloves, long-stemmed, firm, and unbroken. One pound will do for ten to twelve oranges. Second, use good apples, oranges, crab apples, limes (these make very fragrant pomanders), lemons, or kumquats. Oranges and apples are the most satisfactory, except for providing variety in shape and odor. Third, you will need one-half pound of mixed ground spices, (cinnamon in the greater amount, cloves, a teaspoon of powdered ginger, and whole nutmeg grated fresh) and two ounces of orris root (crush this in a mortar or roll with a rolling pin).

Now you are ready to work. Check fruits for soft spots; if any are found, discard them. Hold a perfect fruit firmly, but do not squeeze it. I work over a large surface to prevent too much tension in one spot and I seldom find it advisable to use a darning needle or anything else to puncture holes. Indeed, it seems to me this slows up the process and has a tendency to enlarge the opening for the clove which may make it loosen before the skin shrinks to hold it tight. Insert the cloves closely with heads touching. Try to finish one ball in a day's time, before the skin starts to shrink and harden, which makes insertion of the rest of the cloves difficult. If small splits occur in the skin, do not worry about it but go ahead and finish. If the splits are large, they may be sewed together.

To complete the pomander ball, put the spice mixture in a large open bowl, add fruits with the cloves in them and turn them in the spices until each is well coated. This fills in the spaces which the cloves do not completely cover. Leave the balls in this mixture, stirring once each day until they begin to lose the weight of the juice. Do not close tightly until well dried. Balls prepared in this manner do not shrink to any extent in drying, but if not rolled in spices they often shrivel to the size of a crab apple. The scent lasts for years; the scent is stronger when the ball is just made and not completely dry, but moisture in the atmosphere will intensify the odor again.

To hang the pomander ball, thread a large-eyed needle with a narrow velvet or composition ribbon and run it through the fruit about an inch from the top. Another bow can be tied into this and the ribbon will not pull away as the fruit shrinks. This method works better than tying ribbons around the outside of the pomander. Pomanders appear these days in elaborate dress. A thin veil of net may be put around each, ending in a frill at the top where it is tied with silk or velvet ribbons and decorated with tiny apples, oranges, or other artificial fruits or flowers.

Tie pomanders in groups of different sizes, perhaps combining oranges, limes, and crab apples. I hang cascades of six or more balls from ceiling beams in our long living room for Christmas decoration.

To renew a pomander ball, wash off dust and accumulated spices with hot water. Put a drop or two of clove oil on it, roll in the spice bath and leave there for a few days. Then retie with fresh ribbons.

Pomander Christmas Tree

It has been my custom for several years to decorate a red cedar Christmas tree with spices and their products. Toward the end of November I make about twenty-five pomander balls for the tree. They are fresh, fragrant, and heavy as the juices have not then dried out, so they are placed on sturdy branches and tied with glittering red

ribbons. Other decorations include sprigs of rosemary
and holly, cinnamon sticks tied with red bows, and nutmegs tied in clusters. Ginger and spice cookies, frosted
and decorated with colored sugars and candy pearls are
also a part of this decoration. Small brass bells are tied
to the end of each tree branch. Red Christmas balls, red
and gold icicles, the odor of spices, and the drying pomander balls combine to make this tree the very essence of
Christmas.

19. Christmas at Caprilands–
Legends and Recipes

> Now Christmas is come
> Let's beat up the drum,
>   And call all our neighbors together,
> And when they appear,
>   Let us make them such cheer
> As will keep out the wind and the weather.
>   —Washington Irving

The joyous busy time of bringing in Christmas trees comes early for us at Caprilands for we start our festivities on St. Nicholas' day, the sixth of December. This means a trip to the pastureland of a generous neighbor who not only allows us to cut a number of trees, but joins us in the fun.

The grove which now furnishes us with greens is a natural bird sanctuary, sheltered on a sloping hillside and filled with light and sun. The thick cedars grow there as though planted by some celestial artist, or a Druid priest transported from the Old World to recreate an enchanted wood in the New World. These tall trees are like pillars with the branches reaching up, growing thick and close to the slim, strong trunks. Blue berries are fruits, abundant in some years and decorative. Their seed furnishes a source for new trees, and there are always many young seedlings growing beside the parent trees.

JUNIPER—PLANT OF SANCTUARY

Close by the dignified cedars, great circles of frosty junipers toss their unruly branches about, forming a dense

207

Photograph by Herman F. Marshall

Door swag at Caprilands, made with artemisia as the background, with teasel heads, tansy, pinecones and tinkling bells.

thicket of needles so sharp that only a hunted creature would try to penetrate them. This is *Juniperus communis,* known in legend and history as the plant of sanctuary, for it furnished a hiding place for small animals that are the prey of dogs and hunters. It is said that the strong odor of the plant covers the scent of the animal seeking sanctuary, and the pursuer circles round in vain trying to locate its prey.

This native of our neglected pastures is also a familiar and venerated evergreen in Europe. It thrives in Sweden, Finland, Lapland, in England, also in the countries along the Mediterranean. In all these places legends and superstitions have grown up around it.

Even earlier, juniper was esteemed as one of the plants that protected the Holy Family when they were pursued by Herod's soldiers. As the hunted travelers passed, the spiny branches opened and folded them under the protecting needles. These became soft and downy underneath, providing a comfortable bed, but still sharp and spearlike on the outside. Thus the soldiers were repelled by the impenetrable mass of green and went on their way.

An older Biblical story calls the juniper the "plant of sanctuary," for, when Elijah was pursued by King Ahab, he was sheltered by the spiny branches. Thus the juniper early earned a reputation as a plant of succor, an asylum for the hunted.

As we decorate our house we recall some of the early uses of these herbal trees. The Greeks venerated the juniper as the tree of the furies. They burned the berries at funerals to keep away demons, and the green roots were used as an incense burned in tribute to the ruler of hell. In Italy, stables were protected from evil and thunderbolts by sprigs of its green, and in England, Sweden, and other Scandinavian countries, juniper branches were strewn over the floors for antiseptic purposes and to impart a refreshing sweet odor.

The smoke of juniper needles and the burning wood were recommended to drive away "All infection and corruption of the aire which bringeth the plague and such like contageous disease." The odor of the burning boughs was thought to promote sleep, and their use in Queen Elizabeth's chambers made this resinous fragrance popular throughout Britain.

French hospitals also used juniper berries with rosemary to purify the air and to prevent contagion. In that fine Norwegian novel *Kristin Lavransdatter*, we read of the constant burning of juniper and its berries during the black plague. At this time every hearth smoked with the heavy incense of the woods.

Not the least of the virtues of this magic tree is its reputed efficacy in driving away witches. To insure protection against them, plant a tree near your door as these creatures of the dark world are bound by all their laws to count every last needle before entering. If they are in error, they must start counting again, and, in so doing, they become weary and go away in despair.

The Story of Mistletoe

Mistletoe was the "all-heal" of the ancients and it was regarded by the Druids as the soul of their sacred tree, the oak. The ceremony of the cutting of the mistletoe was wonderful. Priests and their acolytes dressed in white robes, the golden sickle flashed in the sun, and the branches of the pearly plant fell into a woven cloth held to prevent its being defiled by touching the ground. White bullocks bore away the sacred load to the Druid temples where it was meted out for many miraculous cures.

In Sweden, mistletoe is called "thunder-besom" as it is associated with lightning and fire. There, those afflicted with epilepsy once carried a knife which had a handle of oak mistletoe to cut the spell of the disease. In Brittany, they call the mistletoe, *"herbe de la croix,"* believing that the crucifix was made from its wood when the clinging plant was once a tree. For this offense it was degraded to a parasite.

A Norse legend tells a happier story of mistletoe. Balder, the son Frigga, the goddess of love, was a handsome young god proud of his beauty and secure in his realm. He was envied by less fortunate dieties, but particularly by Loki, an evil spirit who used his cunning to find a way to strike Balder fatally.

Since Balder was protected against all injuries that came from the elements: water, air, fire, and earth, there was only one thing which could wound him, the mistletoe, which grew detached from the elements. Loki fashioned an arrow from the sacred twig and gave it to the blind god Helder, who in play directed it at Balder. The arrow pierced the handsome fellow who fell to the ground mortally wounded.

Frigga's grief was so great that her tears engulfed the mistletoe and were changed into pearl-like berries. The gods could not long endure the absence of the goddess of love and beauty, who was inconsolable and spent her days in weeping. A meeting of the powers was held and it was decided to restore Balder to life. Frigga's joy was as great as her grief, and she decreed that ever after mistletoe should be a symbol of peace, that it should be hung high in the air and whoever passed under it should receive a kiss from the goddess. Hence our custom of hanging a branch over doorways and exchanging a kiss of peace and friendship with those who enter.

How To Make Kissing Balls

A kissing ball was one of the early decorations of Europe, particularly of England. It preceded the Christmas tree, of more recent origin. This decoration was suspended from candelabras and later from chandeliers, making a most attractive display.

To make a kissing ball, form a sphere of small chicken wire or hardware cloth. Fill this with sphagnum moss in the natural lengths, not shredded. Moisten thoroughly and fill with sprigs of rosemary, gray and green santolina, and other fragrant herbs. Fill the lower section with sprigs of mistletoe, tie the whole ball with a big red bow, and hang from an arch for all to pass under.

If rosemary is not available in sufficient quantity, boxwood may be substituted for the basic green, and the rosemary, thymes, and other fragrant herbs used in lesser quantity. Greens may also be forced into a large apple— this keeps them fresh for a short period. These balls hanging in the air, dry out more quickly than other decorations. Therefore, they need frequent soaking to keep them fresh.

For balls which will last through the holiday season— December sixth to January sixth—I use dried materials. These may be inserted into a sphere of very fine chicken wire filled with moist but not wet sphagnum, or into a ball of Oasis or styrofoam.

Cut small sprigs of the best and whitest 'Silver King' artemisia. Fill the ball completely until it is covered. Now take dry holly and mistletoe (I save it from the previous year), spray with silver or gold, and while it is wet, sprinkle glitter liberally over it. Insert these sprigs in the ball or attach leaves to the frame with thin wire. Hang the gilded mistletoe from the lower part of the sphere and your guests will receive their Christmas kisses under a truly golden bough. Mistletoe was that golden bough, sung by Virgil, which enabled Aeneas to make the usually fatal journey to the dark regions under the earth and effect his return without harm.

Another glistening decoration can be made with the holly leaves that fall from the branches as they dry. Spray these with gold, sprinkle with glitter, and cover the ball with the leaves which have been pierced with the wire and wound up to make a stem. These leaves are brittle and must be handled carefully, but once in place they last indefinitely. They are beautiful shimmering in the air of a candle-lit room.

St. Nicholas Day at Caprilands

Wassaile the trees that they may beare
You many a plum and many a peare
For more or less fruit they will bring,
As you do give them wassailing.
                            —Robert Herrick

Each year at Caprilands we try to lengthen the Christmas season. It is such a happy time that I am always reluctant to remove the Christmas greens and glitter. Now we extend their time to January sixth, Twelfth-night, thus celebrating the feast of the lights and the coming of the Magi as the end of our Christmas cycle. However, even this extension did not seem quite enough, so we turned back to one of the earliest of the European celebrations for our inspiration, St. Nicholas Day, the sixth of December.

St. Nicholas was a rich and famous bishop in the early days of the Christian Church, and he became a most beloved saint. As patron saint of children, especially school boys, of poor maidens, sailors, travelers, and merchants; as a protector against thieves and robbers; and, as patron saint of Russia and seaport towns of Italy, his name was constantly used in prayers of Christian people.

Although he gave his name to Czars, for his many generous acts he was called the saint of the people and was invoked by the peaceable citizen, the laborer, and the merchant.

Nicholas was born in Panthere, a city in Lycia, Asia Minor. His parents were Christians of illustrious birth and great wealth. He was an extraordinary child, virtuous from birth, and so religious that his parents dedicated him at an early age to the church. Soon after his ordination his father and mother died of a plague and left him their vast fortune, which he used in charitable works. It is as a giver of gifts that St. Nicholas is best remembered, especially at Christmas.

St. Nicholas in his role of patron saint of mariners was revered in Holland, where he was represented as a bishop in rich ecclesiastical regalia. He rode, tall and straight, on his white horse carrying bags of gold as gifts for the deserving, while behind him trudged his servant, "Black Peter," laden with switches for the children who had misbehaved.

In recent ceremonies in one of the ports of Holland, a

ship brings in a St. Nicholas in full regalia. He is driven with great pomp to the city hall where he speaks to the people, praising them for the good that they have done and reprimanding them for their errors. After the ceremony there is holiday fare to be tasted, and a real celebration follows. Christmas comes as a religious holiday, a true *Holy Day*, and is not confused with gift-giving.

It is an odd turn of history that transforms this dignified, ascetic bishop into our "fat and jolly good Saint Nick" and that translates the name St. Nicholas into "Santa Claus." His memory is preserved, however, in the giving of gifts, the love of children, and in the red robes and long white beard of Santa Claus. In his New World guise, good St. Nicholas is with us every Christmas.

CHRISTMAS RECIPES FROM CAPRILANDS

Christmas parties are many at Caprilands. The foods and customs are suggested by St. Nicholas Day and also St. Lucy's Day, December thirteenth, the time of the feast of the lights for which many good dishes are baked and much steaming glogg is served. Some of these recipes indicate a preference for chocolate, though it was not known in the time of St. Nicholas. Cocoa beans were first brought out of the New World from Mexico to Europe by the Spanish conquerors, and thus the chocolate was touched by the genius of French, Dutch, and Viennese cooks.

THE WASSAIL BOWL FOR CHRISTMAS CHEER

The steaming wassail bowl is the focal point of all our Christmas parties. Its fragrance fills the house and even penetrates to the outside air. It is handsome, too, as it stands in state on a bed of green moss in the center of a large round tray, with plants of rosemary for background and a circle of holly with frosty artemisia around it. On Christmas Day it holds our own Caprilands' version of Swedish glogg.

1 quart port wine	¼ cup chopped almonds
½ cup raisins	½ cup candied fruit peel
4 small peces ginger root or candied ginger	4 four-inch pieces stick cinnamon
6 cardamom seeds, shelled, and crushed	12 cloves

Mix all above together and simmer 1 hour.

2 quarts port wine	1 quart 100-proof brandy
2 quarts cider	

Mix the 2 quarts of wine and the cider and heat until warm, taking care that mixture does not get hot enough to steam. Add to the first simmered wine mixture. Warm the brandy and pour 1 jigger or 2 ounces into each mug. Heat 1 cup of the brandy to boiling to float on top of the bowl and for lighting. Bring the glogg in flaming. Ladle this over the warmed brandy in the mugs and hand them around at once. Serves 24 in 8-ounce mugs.

Hint: If any Christmas glogg is left over, make a glogg salad. This is a rare circumstance so don't plan on it. For each 2 cups of glogg add two cups of cooked cranberries or raisins and 2 envelopes of gelatin dissolved in a little cold water, to stiffen the mixture. This makes a pretty salad to decorate a cold meat platter at Christmas.

LAMB'S-WOOL WASSAIL BOWL

This is the wassail of Robert Herrick and Washington Irving. Irving wrote that it "was sometimes composed of ale instead of wine—with nutmeg, sugar, toast, ginger and roasted crabs [crab apples]. In this way the nut-browned beverage is still prepared in some old families and around the hearths of some substantial farmers at Christmas."

In his "Twelfth Night" Herrick sang:

> Next crowne the bowles full
> With gentle Lamb's Wool,
> And sugar and nutmeg and ginger,
> With store of ale, too;
> And thus ye must doe,
> To make the Wassaile a swinger.

BISHOP'S WINE

This is Capriland's version of a wine cup proper for a bishop, but it is also suited to our customs and way of serving, and equally as agreeable to our non-ecclesiastical guests.

Pour 2 quarts of sweet cider into a metal container. We use a copper-lined, two-handled cooking pot that can be carried steaming hot to the table. Put in 4 sticks of cinnamon, 6 cloves, and 1 orange, quartered but unpeeled. Grate nutmeg over the top or sprinkle a good half-teaspoon of powdered nutmeg. Let simmer for 30 minutes, then stir in 2 quarts of port wine. Heat until steaming but not boiling. Serve in pottery mugs with a stick of cinnamon in each. We stir this in the pot with a very long piece of cinnamon bark instead of a spoon. Serves 12 in 8-ounce mugs.

CHEESE AND OLIVE LOGS

This Christmas canapé can be conveniently prepared well in advance of the busiest season of entertaining.

1 3-ounce package blue cheese	chopped chives or shallot or grated onion
1 6-ounce package cream cheese	1 tablespoon dried parsley
¼ cup butter, softened	½ cup brandy
¾ cup chopped stuffed olives, or 1 tablespoon	Toasted sesame seeds

Mash together the cheeses and butter. Work in the olives or herbs, and parsley. Add enough brandy to moisten. Form into a roll and roll in the sesame seeds. Wrap in waxed paper. Place briefly in a freezer for quick chilling; but do not freeze. Remove from refrigerator for 10 minutes or so before serving. This is difficult to slice if it is too cold. Makes about 25 slices.

CAPRILANDS CHRISTMAS SPREAD

This spread is the bright cherry-red of Christmas. It samples practically the whole harvest of herbs and delights youngsters as well as grown-ups. Make a lot of this for it keeps well in the refrigerator and just about forever if you put it in the freezer.

1 clove garlic, crushed
4 tablespoons olive oil
2 cups tomato puree (about) or 1-pound can Italian-type tomatoes with basil leaf
½ pound sharp cheddar cheese, grated
1 clove garlic, sliced
1 teaspoon dried basil, or 2 teaspoons chopped green basil

½ teaspoon oregano
2 tablespoons Capriland's Herb Mustard
2 sprigs rosemary, chopped
Dash of grated nutmeg
¼ teaspoon freshly ground black pepper
1 teaspoon fennel or caraway seeds
1 teaspoon sugar
Salt to taste

Sauté garlic in olive oil. Stir in all the other ingredients and heat until well blended. Then beat until smooth. Serve hot on crackers, or serve cold as a thick dip. Or place a jar of it in the center of a ring of crackers and let guests help themselves. As a spread this serves 35 to 40; as a dip it serves 25 to 30.

Hint: In winter we enjoy this heated and served on fingers of crisp toast with strips of bacon, the plates garnished with fresh basil from window box or greenhouse.

CAPRILANDS PETITE PÂTÉ

An easy recipe and very popular here as a change from a cream-based canapé.

½ pound liverwurst
½ pound country sausage
2 eggs, beaten
¼ cup sherry
3 shallots, chopped
2 cloves garlic, crushed

½ cup sliced fresh mushrooms
Butter
Salt and pepper to taste
6 to 8 strips bacon
3 bay leaves
Flour and water for paste

Mash and mix liverwurst and sausage wth eggs, sherry, shallots, and garlic. Sauté mushrooms in a little butter. Add to liverwurst mixture, and whip until blended. Turn into three small earthenware pots or "Marmites," lined with the strips of bacon. Put a bay leaf on top of each. Seal with a thick flour and water paste but remove this and the bay leaf when serving. Bake at 350° for one hour. (Sausage must be well cooked.) Serves 25 to 35.

BISHOP'S BREAD

For St. Nicholas Day or any Christmas festival; a delicious dessert bread with the texture of fruit cake and the rich taste of Dutch chocolate. Like the French *pain d'épice*, we prefer it without butter.

1 cup sifted all-purpose flour	3 cardamom seeds, crushed
1 teaspoon soda	¾ cup chopped almonds or walnuts
⅔ cup granulated sugar	
6 eggs, separated	1 6-ounce package chocolate bits
¾ cup raisins	
½ cup chopped citron or dried fruits	

Sift together flour, soda, and sugar. Whip egg whites stiff. Beat yolks, combine yolks with the dry mixture, and add all other ingredients. Then fold in whites and turn batter into a buttered and floured 4½"x8" bread pan. Bake in a slow oven, about 300°, for 1 hour. Cool and *let stand over night* for best cutting. This makes one large loaf, as indicated, but you can bake it in two smaller pans. Slice thin and cut the larger slices in half for this is very rich. Serves about 35.

PAIN d'ÈPICE-SPICE BREAD

Most popular of all our Christmas breads is this traditional French one, the recipe for which was sent to us by a correspondent in Philadelphia. This "spice bread" has the advantage of keeping almost indefinitely if wrapped in foil and stored in a cool dry place or in a refrigerator. It has the rich, spicy odors associated with Christmas, but it is not heavy or overly rich for it contains no eggs, milk, or shortening, depending upon honey for smoothness and candied fruits for moisture.

1 teaspoon anise seed	1½ teaspoons baking soda
¾ cup boiling water	½ teaspoon salt
½ cup chopped fruits and peels	1 teaspoon powdered cinnamon
½ cup strained honey	1 teaspoon freshly grated nutmeg
2¼ cups sifted all-purpose flour	½ teaspoon powdered cloves
½ cup granulated sugar	

Soak anise seed in the boiling water for 5 minutes. Combine fruit, honey, and sugar. Stir the anise water while it is still warm into the honey mixture. Stir until all is well mixed and sugar dissolved. Sift together the dry ingredients and spices. Combine with the honey mixture and stir until smooth. Turn into a greased loaf pan. Bake in a slow oven, not above 350°, for 1 hour. Let stand a day so it will be easy to slice very thin. It will yield about 30 pieces.

Hint: Serve this as a cake or spread lightly with softened sweet butter. This is also excellent for a sweet sandwich with a cream cheese filling.

CARDAMOM BREAD

2 cups milk	4 eggs, beaten light
2 cakes compressed yeast	10 cardamom seeds, crushed
1 teaspoon salt	
1 cup granulated sugar	8 cups sifted all-purpose flour
4 tablespoons butter	

Scald milk and cool to lukewarm. Crumble yeast into a large, warmed bowl. Stir in the milk, salt, sugar, and butter. Blend in the eggs and add the cardamom seeds. Gradually stir in the flour and mix thoroughly. Knead well. Then place dough in a greased bowl in a warm place and cover with a cloth. Let rise until double in bulk. Shape into 2 loaves and bake in a 375° oven for 45 minutes.

Hints: It is not necessary to shell cardamom seeds. You can crush them with a rolling pin or pulverize them in a mortar. The shells flick off easily or disappear in the dough. You can make buns instead of loaves from this dough. It will make about 20 buns. Bake these on a greased cooky sheet in a 400° oven for 25 to 30 minutes. For St. Lucy's Day spread loaves or buns with confectioners' sugar moistened with sherry or milk to a spreading consistency and decorate with a sun motif of yellow fruits or candied fruit peel with a sprinkling of colored sugar.

CHRISTMAS CONFETTI CASSEROLE

2 cups rice	½ cup chopped parsley
6 cups water	1 teaspoon salt
3 medium-sized onions, sliced	½ teaspoon freshly ground black pepper
1 cup chopped celery	½ cup cubed pineapple
½ pound butter	4 pimientos, chopped
1 teaspoon basil	½ cup sliced stuffed olives
½ teaspoon dried marjoram or 1 teaspoon chopped fresh marjoram	¼ cup chopped candied ginger
	½ cup blanched slivered almonds

Cook the rice in the water until tender. Wash in cool water, then drain. Prepare the sauce. Cook the onions and celery in the butter until soft. Add the basil, marjoram, half the parsley, and the salt and pepper. Then stir in the pineapple, pimientos, and olives. Pour the sauce over the rice, and fluff with a fork until the rice is well coated. Correct the seasoning as needed. Put in a fireproof casserole. Spread the ginger and almonds over the rice, and sprinkle on the rest of the parsley. Serves 8 to 12.

Hint: For an all-in-one-meal, add 2 cups chopped cooked chicken or flaked white tuna fish to the sauce. Add chives from the window box; dried parsley also may be used.

WINE SALAD MOLD

Excellent to have on hand for the homecoming family and for refrigerator-raiders at any time. This keeps well and is pretty and Christmasy in appearance.

2 cups cranberries	2 cups port wine
1 cup granulated sugar	2 envelopes unflavored
1 cup water	gelatin in cold water to
Juice of 2 lemons	soften
1 teaspoon grated lemon rind	½ cup chopped dates
	1 cup raisins
6 cardamom seeds, shelled and crushed	1 cup chopped walnuts or mixed nuts
2 tablespoons sesame seeds	1 3-ounce package cream cheese
2 packages lime gelatin	½ cup mayonnaise
1 cup hot water	

Cook cranberries and sugar in the water. Add lemon juice, lemon rind, and the seeds. Dissolve lime gelatin in hot water and add to port wine. Add gelatin, dissolved, to the wine mixture. Stir in cooked cranberries, raisins, dates, nuts, cream cheese, and mayonnaise. Pour mixture into 2 one-quart, star-shaped molds. This wine jelly is good without dressing. As a salad, this serves 8 to 12; as a side dish 16 to 24.

Hint: Or use an open center mold and fill with whipped cream flavored with crème de menthe.

CHEESE TEA BISCUITS

½ cup sifted flour
4 teaspoons baking
   powder
Pinch of salt
⅛ pound butter
½ cup grated sharp ched-
   dar cheese

1 egg
¾ cup milk
2 teaspoons chopped
   green (or dried) sage or
   rosemary
Butter
Sesame seeds

Sift together flour, baking powder, and salt. Cut the ⅛ pound butter and cheese into the mixture. Stir in egg and milk. Mix well. Add the sage or rosemary. Roll out the dough about ¼-inch thick. Cut into 2-inch rounds. Dot with butter and sprinkle with sesame seeds. Bake in 425° oven for 10 minutes. Makes 12 biscuits.

A Dictionary of
Fifty Selected Herbs

Each illustrated and described, including botanical, family, and common names, history, present-day uses, culture and propagation. Four large, important groups are not included here, but are found in the appropriate season—scented geraniums in winter, thymes in spring, mints in summer, and artemisias in autumn.

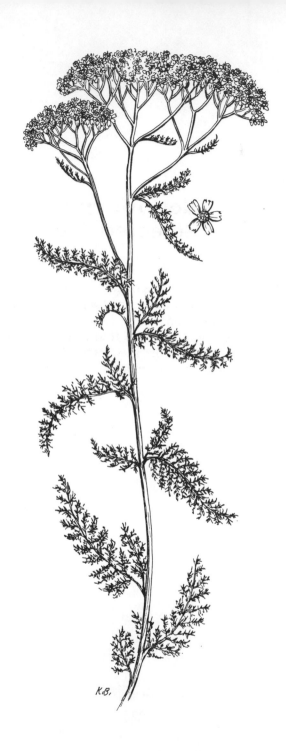

K.B.

ACHILLEA

Compositae

Thou pretty herb of Venus tree
Thy true name it is Yarrow
Now who my bosom friend must be,
Pray tell thou me to-morrow.
—J. O. Halliwell

Common yarrow (*Achillea millefolium*), according to legend, was used by Achilles to stop bleeding wounds of his soldiers, hence the name "military herb." Yarrow tea was once used in treating fevers, colds, and kidney disorders. The leaves were used fresh in salads and dried for snuff.

Description:
Hardy perennial, to 2 ft. Leaves gray-green, finely divided, giving name "milfoil" (thousand-leaved). Flowers grayish white or pale lavender in flattened cymes. *A. m. rosea* (red yarrow) has dark red or bright pink flowers. *A. filipendulina*, 4 to 5 ft., has large dark yellow flowers; its varieties range from pale cream to the golden yellow of 'Gold Plate.' *A. ptarmica* ('The Pearl' or sneezewort), 2 ft., has white flowers. The dwarf yarrows (*A. nana, A. tomentosa*, and *A. t. webbiana*) make good ground covers.

Uses:
Flower arrangements, fresh or dried. Ironclad garden perennials for late spring and summer color.

Culture:
Full sun and well-drained soil. Propagate by dividing roots, spring or fall; or transplant self-sown seedlings.

225

K.B.

ACONITUM

Ranunculaceae

Our land is from the rage of tigers freed,
Nor nourishes the lion's angry seed,
Nor pois'nous aconite is here produced,
Or grows unknown, or is, when known refused.
                    —John Dryden

The root of aconite (*Aconitum napellus*) has long been known as a source of poison once used on arrows to destroy wolves, hence the name "wolfbane." In the middle ages, this plant was known as monkshood, or helmet flower owing to the shape of the flower.

Description:
Hardy perennial, to 4 ft. Leaves divided two or three times into narrow segments. Flowers in blue spikes. Old roots last only a year and new plants are produced by young shoots from the parent. The 'Sparks' variety is considered best for late summer color in the garden. It sends spikes of dark blue to a height of 5 ft. *A. n. bicolor* has blue and white flowers. *A. fischeri*, 2 to 3 ft., has dark blue blooms. *A. f. wilsoni*, 6 to 7 ft., has mauve flowers.

Uses:
Outstanding for late summer and fall color, but dangerous to have around children. Medicinally it is to be used only by a physician.

Culture:
Partial shade with evenly moist, rich soil. Propagate by division of the roots in autumn. Spring-sown seeds reach maturity in two or three years.

227

AGRIMONIA

Rosaceae

If it be leyd under mann's heed,
He shal sleepyn as he were deed;
He shal never drede ne wakyn
Till fro under his heed it be takyn.
—Old English Medical Manuscript

Common agrimony (*Agrimonia eupatoria*), also known as church steeples and cocklebur, received its generic name from the Greek word *argemone,* applied to plants that were healing to the eyes. The specific name *eupatoria* refers to Mithridates Eupator, a famous king who concocted remedies. Agrimony was once used for jaundice and skin disorders, and with mugwort and vinegar as a back rub. It is still collected as a medicinal herb in England.

Description:
Hardy perennial, 1 to 3 ft. Leaves similar to those of a wild rose. Flowers yellow, small, and numerous, occurring close together on a slender spike from June to September. The plant is downy and gives off a pleasant odor. It grows wild in Scotland.

Uses:
The whole plant, dried, is ground to be made into a tea said to be excellent as a spring tonic. Historically, the yellow blossoms have served as a source of dye.

Culture:
Dry soil with full sun or light shade. Propagate by sowing seeds collected from a dried spike. Germinates easily and, once established, it self-sows.

229

AJUGA

Labiatae

> With hearts responsive
> And enfranchised eyes,
> We thank thee Lord,
> For those first tiny, prayerful folded hands
> That pierce the winter's crust . . .
> —John Oxenham

Bugleweed, blue bugle, or carpenter's herb (*Ajuga reptans*) was once a medicinal plant used for hemorrhage, and it is reputed to have a mild narcotic action similar to that of digitalis.

Description:
Hardy perennial, to 5 ins., astringent, bitter, and aromatic. Leaves occur in rosettes that form a ground cover. Flowers clear blue on short spikes in early spring. *A. r. alba* has white flowers and green foliage. *A. r. variegata* has blue flowers and green leaves variegated with creamy white.

Uses:
Invaluable as a ground cover. It will thrive where few other herbs will grow and may be used where grass is difficult to establish, as under trees and shrubs.

Culture:
Needs shade and well-drained soil. Multiplies rapidly by means of underground stolons. Solid beds of ajuga need to be thinned every year. Divide and transplant in spring or fall.

K·B·

ALLIUM

Liliaceae

Let onion atoms lurk within the bowl
And, half suspected, animate the whole.
—Sydney Smith

The shallot (*Allium cepa ascalonicum*) is considered the most delectable of all onions. At one time it was known as eschalot, brought back by the Crusaders from Ascalon, an ancient city in West Palestine, and introduced into England and the Continent by them.

⟨⟩ *Description:*
Perennial bulb, 6 ins., onion-like. Blooms rarely.

⟨⟩ *Uses:*
Cloves of the bulbs are used in sauces for meats, with steaks, in dressings, in vinegars, for salads, and in sauce for fish. Harvest when the bulblets have multiplied so that the thickened clump forms a mound that rises partially out of the ground, usually between the first and the middle of September. Dig, tie in bunches, and hang to cure in an airy place. When dry, store in a ventilated sack, preferably a real onion bag, removing one clove from each clump for next year's seed. Hang in a cool, but frost-free, dry place. If left in the ground over winter the bulbs frequently rot.

⟨⟩ *Culture:*
Full sun in well-drained, fertile soil. Plant the sets in early spring, covering to a depth of twice their length.

233

ALLIUM

Liliaceae

This is every cook's opinion,
No savory dish without an onion,
But lest your kissing should be spoiled
Your onions must be fully boiled.
                                        —Jonathan Swift

Top onion (*Allium cepa viviparum*) also known as perennial or Egyptian onion, is a practical onion to grow for use in early spring. It can also be a really handsome back border for the culinary garden. This plant was symbolic, to the Egyptians, of the Universe. Vast quantities of it were consumed by the workmen who built the pyramids, for Herodotus said it took nine tons of gold to pay for the "pungent onion."

Description:

Hardy perennial, 3 ft., with succulent hollow stems, ballooned toward the top, and crowned by a head of new plants. The weight of these increases until the whole stem falls to the ground, and there the bulbs take root and form another colony.

Uses:

Cut the spears of the young leaves as they appear in the spring for salads and to use with sorrel soup. Use the bulblets like small onions (they are very strong), or pickle as cocktail onions. Cut plants back after they have borne the top bulblets, and fresh green shoots will grow again.

Culture:

Full sun in well-cultivated, fertile garden soil.

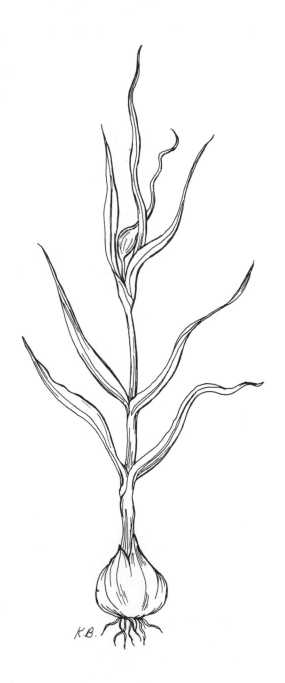

ALLIUM

Liliaceae

And, most dear actors, eat no onions nor garlic,
for we are to utter sweet breath.
—Shakespeare

Garlic (*Allium sativum*) has been important from ancient times, and is still a part of the Hebrew Talmudic rule which decrees that it be used in certain dishes. There is a legend that garlic came into the world on Satan's left foot, while onion came on his right. In the past, it was fed to fighting cocks and animals and to athletes to give them strength. Ramson or wild garlic received its name from ram, alluding to the strong smell.

🔖 *Description:*
Hardy perennial, 2 ft. I find that the giant garlic or rocambole (*A. scorodoprasum*) is much more interesting to grow. It is similar in appearance to the Egyptian onion, producing new plants at the top of very slender stems, to 3 ft. The bulbs are about ⅛ in. across, tightly interlaced, smelling strongly of garlic and useful in cheese mixtures or as a substitute for garlic.

🔖 *Uses:*
Harvest the bulbs of garlic after the tops die down and store for the winter in open mesh bags. This is such a common seasoning that its uses do not need to be outlined. In fact, I do not consider this a worthwhile garden plant, as it is so easily obtainable from the warm, sunny climates of Texas, California, and Louisiana where it is grown commercially.

237

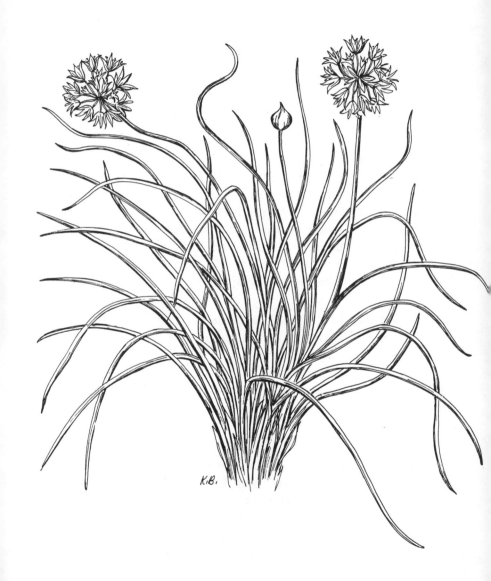

ALLIUM

Liliaceae

They are indeed a kind of leeks, hot and dry in the fourth
degree, and so under the domination of Mars . . . if they be
eaten raw they send up very hurtful vapours to the brain
causing troublesome sleep and spoiling the eyesight.
—Nicholas Culpeper

Chives (*Allium schoenoprasum*) is one of the most
familiar of all plants to the herb grower. The plants are
cultivated for the onion-flavored, edible leaves, as a border for the culinary garden, and for the heads of lilac-
colored flowers which may be used in arrangements.

    ℞ *Description:*
Hardy perennial to 1 ft., producing fountains of hollow,
cylindrical leaves. The variety 'Ruby Gem' has gray foliage and pink-ruby flowers; another variety, *A. tuberosum*,
often called garlic chives or Chinese chives, blooms naturally in July and August, but is forced by florists for early
spring flower shows. It has wider leaves than common
chives, and the white flowers grow in attractive starlike
clusters on long slender stems, very fragrant.

    ℞ *Uses:*
Cut the leaves for soups and salads from early spring on;
use in cream cheese mixtures, with mashed potatoes, in
hamburger, or with eggs in omelettes. Chives can be
frozen fresh, or dried for winter seasoning.

    ℞ *Culture:*
Sunny, well-drained garden loam. Sow seeds in spring or
fall. Divide established clumps every third or fourth year.

239

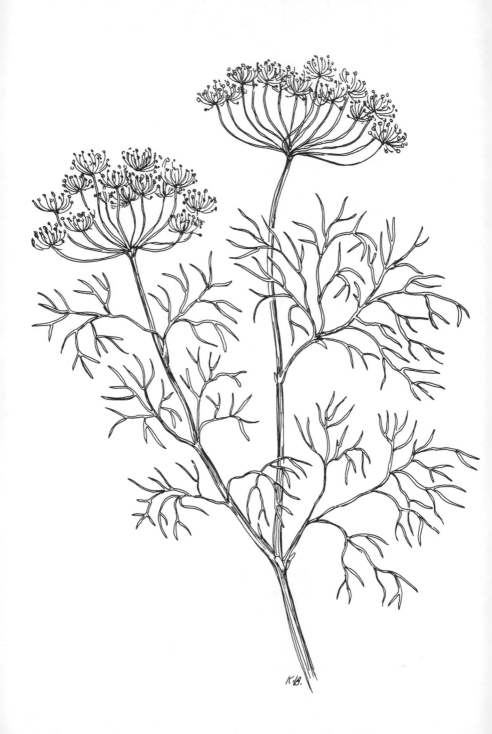

ANETHUM

Umbelliferae

Therewith her Vervain and her Dill
That hindereth witches of their will.
—Michael Drayton

Dill (*Anethum graveolens*) received its name from the old Norse word *dilla*, to lull, referring to the soothing properties of the plant. It has been used by magicians to cast spells and employed as a charm against such spells.

Description:
Hardy annual sometimes classed as a biennial, 2 to 2½ ft., native of Mediterranean shores and southern Russia. It grows in the grain fields of Spain, Portugal, and Italy. The plant is upright, branching out from a single stalk with the feathery leaves, known as "dill weed." Flowers in flat terminal umbels, numerous and yellow, followed by "dill seed" in midsummer. The seeds are pungent tasting and retain their potency for three years or more.

Uses:
Harvest dill weed (the leaves) early in summer, then chop fine and dry in a basket, turning often. Sprinkle on fish, salad, and soups during winter. Harvest the seeds as soon as the head is ripe, otherwise they will drop off and be lost. Large umbels of green dill are used to flavor cucumber pickles.

Culture:
Rich, sandy, well-drained soil in full sun. Propagate by sowing seeds in the spring. If all seed heads are not harvested, dill may self-sow.

241

K.B.

ANGELICA
Umbelliferae

Contagious aire ingendring pestilence,
Infects not those who in their mouth have Tae'en
Angelica, that happy Counterbane.
Sent down from heaven by some Celestial scout
As well the name and nature both avow't.
                                        —DuBartas

Angelica (*Angelica archangelica*) was once used in pagan ceremonies in Iceland. Later it was adapted by Christians for use at the springtime festival of the Annunciation. The plant blooms in some parts of the world on May 8, the Day of St. Michael the Archangel, and hence it was considered a charm against evil spirits. Medicinally, it was used against contagion and for purifying the blood.

℞ *Description:*
Hardy biennial, grown as a perennial if the flower stalks are not allowed to develop and set seed. If allowed to bloom and seed, the old plant dies, but its place is taken in the spring by self-sown seedlings. Grows 4 to 7 ft. tall. Leaves celery-like, divided into three-part leaflets, strongly aromatic of gin and juniper. Flowers greenish white in spectacular umbels.

℞ *Uses:*
Seeds in making a liqueur, in vermouth and chartreuse, and as a flavoring for wines; also in perfumes. The candied stems are a traditional French decoration for Christmas cakes and buns; also made into jams and jellies.

℞ *Culture:*
Rich, moist soil and partial shade in a cool part of the garden. Propagate by sowing seeds immediately after they ripen on the plant, that is, in the fall.

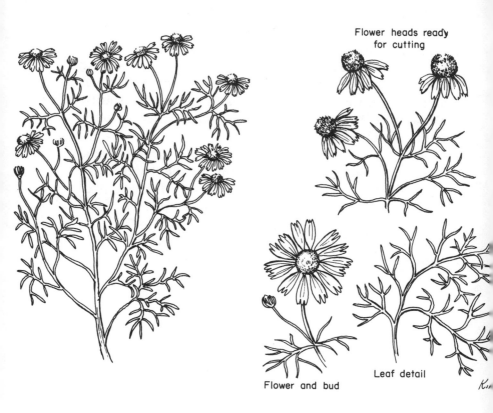

Flower heads ready
for cutting

Flower and bud

Leaf detail

ANTHEMIS

Compositae

For though the camomile, the more it is trodden
on, the faster it grows, yet youth, the more
it is wasted, the sooner it wears.
—Shakespeare

English camomile (*Anthemis nobilis*) also known as
ground apple, was once considered the plants' physician,
as some gardeners believed that planting this herb among
drooping and sickly plants would revive them. The
Spanish call it *manzanilla,* and use it to flavor one of their
lightest and driest sherries. Most of camomile's history
relates to its use as a tea in relieving nervousness, for
neuralgia, pains in the head, and nervous colic. It is also
the tea given to Peter Rabbit after his famous bout with
Mr. McGregor. Early herbals recommend it for sleepless-
ness and as a sure cure for nightmares. Camomile lawns
were once possible in the moist climate of England, but
our climate is too rugged to grow them in this capacity.

🍃 *Description:*
A creeping perennial, about 1 in. high, except to 12 ins.
while in bloom. Foliage very fine and fernlike. The flowers are white daisies with yellow centers.

🍃 *Uses:*
The dried flower heads are brewed for the tea.

🍃 *Culture:*
Sun to partial shade in moist, well-drained soil. Sow seeds
in spring or fall, or purchase plants. Once established,
camomiles will self-sow.

KB.

ANTHRISCUS

Umbelliferae

Sweete Spanish Chervile, ought never to be wanting in our sallets—for it is exceeding wholesome and charming to the spirits. . . . this . . . is used in tarts and serves alone for divers sauces.

—John Evelyn

Chervil (*Anthriscus cerefolium*), also called beaked parsley and French parsley, is the gourmet's parsley. True chervil is often confused with sweet cicely which is sometimes called "sweet chervil." Therefore, when early writers speak of chervil, they mean sweet cicely or sweet chervil (*Myrrhis odorata*), not the plant discussed here.

⌘ Description:
Annual, 1 to 2 ft. Leaves alternate, fernlike, and spreading. The plant resembles Italian parsley, though more delicate, and turns reddish in the fall. Small white flowers in compound umbels.

⌘ Uses:
Attractive in garden. Use leaves in salads and soups, with oysters, and as a garnish. The curled variety is best to grow as it has the flavor of anise.

⌘ Culture:
Moist, well-drained soil in partial shade. Sow seeds early in spring for an early summer crop; sow again in late summer for a fall harvest and one in early spring. Self-sows year after year.

K.B.

BORAGO

Boraginaceae

Here is sweet water and borage for blending,
Comfort and courage to drink at your will.
—Nora Hopper

Borage (*Borago officinalis*) gained great popularity from the belief that a tea brewed from it gave courage as well as flavor to the person who drank it. The French used the tea in treating feverish catarrhs. Gerard said, "A sirup concocted of the floures quieteth the lunatick person and leaves eaten raw do engender good blood."

Description:
Hardy annual, 1 to 3 ft. Leaves oval, 6 to 8 ins. long, blue-green, and covered with fine hairs. These occur first in a basal rosette, then a succulent, prickly stem rises and branches out. Flowers star-shaped, heavenly blue and pink or lavender.

Uses:
Pick young leaves and use in salads for their cool cucumber flavor. Float the flowers in cups of wine, using claret, fruit juice, gin, and sugar. To candy the flowers, cut fresh, dip in beaten egg whites, then in sugar, and dry.

Culture:
Sunny location with well-drained, moist soil. Sow seeds in late fall or early spring where they are to grow. Cut back frequently to keep borage in good condition. If some old plants are dug out of the bed in midsummer, self-sown seedlings will fill the gaps and provide a fresh crop for autumn.

249

K.B.

CARUM

Umbelliferae

Nay, you shall see my orchard, where, in an
arbour we will eat a last year's pippin of
my own grafting, with a dish of caraways.
—Shakespeare

Caraway(*Carum carvi*)seeds are reputed to strengthen
vision and to confer the gift of memory on all who eat
them. They were once thought to prevent the theft of any
object that contained them. Lovers were given the seeds
as a cure for fickleness, and pigeons were fed them to prevent their straying.

Description:
Hardy biennial, 1 to 3 ft. Furrowed stems with finely cut
leaves resembling the carrot's. Umbels of white flowers
in June of the second year.

Uses:
Caraway oil is extracted from the leaves and seeds. Young
leaves are sometimes used in soup; seeds, in applesauce,
apple pie, cookies, cakes and breads; the oil, in perfume,
soap, and in making a liqueur called kümmel; also to dis-
guise the taste of medicines and to stimulate digestion.
The thick, tapering roots, similar to parsnips but smaller,
are considered a delicacy for the table. Harvest the brown
crescent-shaped seeds before they fall to the ground and
before the birds begin to eat them, usually in August.

Culture:
Full sun and average, well-drained garden soil. Sow seeds
in September for an early spring crop of leaves and seeds
the following summer.

251

K.B.

CHENOPODIUM

Chenopodiaceae

Ambrosia was my mother's favorite, hence it is mine.
It was her favorite because she loved its pure spicy
fragrance. . . . This ever-present and ever-welcome scent
which pervaded the entire garden if leaf or flower
of the loved ambrosia be crushed, is curious and
characteristic, a true "ambrosiack odor" to use Ben
Jonson's words.

—Alice Morse Earle

Ambrosia (*Chenopodium botrys*) is known also as
Jerusalem oak and feather geranium.

🏵 *Description:*

Hardy annual, 2 ft., decorative and fragrant. Self-sown
seedlings appear in May with leaves like those of a small
oak tree. They are red on the back, dark green and marked like an oak on the top. As the plant grows, feathery
branches develop and the leaf-size diminishes. Sprays of
greenish flowers develop until, at maturity, the entire
plant looks like a lime-green plume.

🏵 *Uses:*

When branches have filled out to the seed stage, cut and
place in vases to dry naturally, without water. If kept out
of the sun, they will dry to a beautiful shade of green, welcome for fall and winter arrangements. Sprigs of ambrosia can be used in gin drinks as a flavoring.

🏵 *Culture:*

Full sun in sandy garden soil. Broadcast seeds over well-
prepared soil in fall or spring. Seedlings generally need
thinning; extras can be transplanted while they are still
small. Allow 12 ins. between seedlings. The most difficult
thing about ambrosia is that persons who do not know it
in the seedling stage mistake it for a weed.

CHRYSANTHEMUM

Compositae

Then balm and mint help to make up
My chaplet and for trial
Costmary that so likes the cup
And next it pennyroyal.
                            —Michael Drayton

Costmary (*Chrysanthemum balsamita* var. *tanace-toides*), also called alehost, is a native of the Orient now naturalized in our country. The French dedicated this herb to the Virgin Mary, but most of its associations have been with Mary Magdalene. Literature may refer to the plant as either St. Mary's herb or sweet Mary. The common name, "Bible leaf," came from Colonial times when it went to church as a marker for the Bible or prayerbook, but most of the pungent leaves were chewed on instead, during the endless sermons, as the minty flavor was supposed to keep the listener awake.

Description:
Hardy perennial, 2 to 3 ft., stiff stems with erect branches, short, and slightly downy. Leaves 6 to 8 ins. long with toothed margins. Flowers small, button-like, pale yellow, resembling tansy.

Uses:
Leaf as a bookmark; fresh or dry for tea and iced drinks. Place in closets and drawers, along with lavender, for a sweet odor.

Culture:
Thrives in well-drained soil and full sun, but will grow in semishade. Propagate by root division in spring or fall. Divide plants every third year.

255

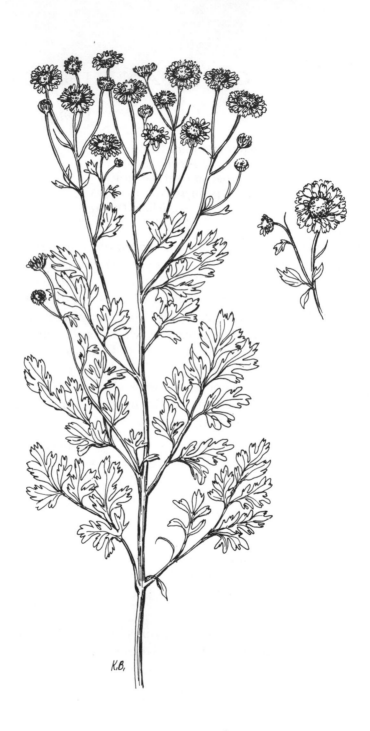

K.B.

CHRYSANTHEMUM

Compositae

There's many feet on this moor tonight,
And they fall so light as they turn and pass,
So light and true that they shake no dew,
From the featherfew and the hungry grass.
—Nora Hopper

Feverfew *(Chrysanthemum parthenium)* was named for its use in the treatment of fevers, but the showy white daisy flowers gave it a happier common name, "bride's button." In the past this plant was located close to dwellings because it was reputed to purify the atmosphere and to ward off disease. It was employed in the treatment of hysteria, nervousness, and lowness of spirits. A tincture made from feverfew warded off insects, and a wash of it was used to relieve the pain of insect bites.

Description:
Hardy perennial, 2 to 3 ft. Leaves light green with strong daisy-like odor. The inch-wide white daisies entirely cover the plants in June. If plants are cut back afterwards to maintain a neat appearance there will be some recurrent bloom later.

Uses:
In the perennial flower border and as a cut flower.

Culture:
Sun to partial shade in moist, well-drained soil. Sow seeds or set out plants in the early spring. Divide established plants every fall or spring, replanting only the strongest divisions.

257

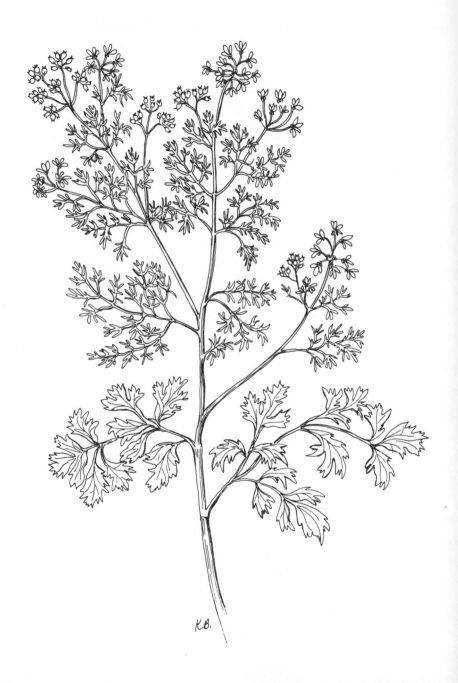

K.B.

CORIANDRUM

Umbelliferae

And the manna was as coriander seed, and the
colour thereof as the colour of bdellium.
Numbers 11:7

Coriander (*Coriandrum sativum*) is one of the earliest
known spices: found in Egyptian tombs and used as a
meat preservative in Rome. It came to England with the
Romans and was cultivated in monastery gardens during the Middle Ages. Coriander was brought to America
with the first colonists. It was used medicinally by the
Egyptians and by Hippocrates. In *The Thousand and One
Nights* coriander was used as an aphrodisiac and associated with fennel to summon devils.

Description:
Annual, 2 ft. Leaves finely cut like parsley. Delicate
flowers in umbels, rosy lavender, appearing in late June.

Uses:
Harvest seeds as early as possible, otherwise they will
bend the weak stems to the ground and be lost. Use
in curry, in chopped meat, stews, sausage, gingerbread,
cookies, and candies. The seed is very fragrant as well
as flavorful and is often used in potpourri.

Culture:
Full sun in well-drained, moist, and fertile soil. Sow
seeds in early spring where they are to grow, and thin out
the seedlings while they are still small. If not harvested
promptly, the seeds will self-sow and spring up all around
the parent plants.

259

K.B.

FOENICULUM

Umbelliferae

Above the lowly plants it towers,
The fennel with its yellow flowers,
And in an earlier age than ours
Was gifted with the wondrous powers
Lost vision to restore.
—Henry Wadsworth Longfellow

Fennel (*Foeniculum vulgare*) was esteemed in ancient times as the herb to strengthen sight; and seeds, leaves, and roots were used for those "that are grown fat," wrote William Coles, "to . . . cause them to grow more gaunt and lank."

Description:
Perennial sometimes grown as an annual, 4 to 5 ft. The stems are blue-green, smooth and glossy, flattened at base. Leaves bright green and feathery. Yellow flowers in umbels. Florence fennel (*F. vulgare* var. *dulce*), also called finocchio, has an enlarged leaf base which is cooked as a vegetable. The young stems of Sicilian fennel (*F. vulgare* var. *piperitum*) can be blanched and eaten like celery. Fennel varieties with bronze or copper foliage are preferred in the West because of their color, hardiness, perennial habits, and good flavor.

Uses:
Tender leaves and stems in relishes, salads, and as a garnish. Use leaves for flavoring in fish sauces, soups, and stews; ripe seeds to flavor puddings, spiced beets, sauerkraut, spaghetti, soups, breads, cakes, candy, and alcoholic beverages.

Culture:
Full sun in average garden soil. Propagate by sowing seeds in the spring after the soil is warm.

261

GALIUM

Rubiaceae

Sleep, sweet little babe, on the bed I have spread thee;
Sleep, fond little life, on the straw scattered o'er,
'Mid the petals of roses, and pansies I've laid thee,
In crib of white lilies; blue bells on the floor.
—Old Latin Hymn

Our Lady's bedstraw (*Galium verum*) is an herb said to have been present in the manger hay in Bethlehem where it made a bed for the Christ Child. In the reign of Henry VIII it was used as a hair dye. In Gerard's day it was an ointment and a foot bath.

Description:
Hardy perennial, 2 ft. Dainty foliage creeps along the ground in spring; later, as the yellow, fragrant blossoms develop in June, the plant grows taller until July, when the stems become stiff and dry. The small, slender leaves form whorls about the stems.

Uses:

As a filler in flower arrangements.

Culture:
Full sun to partial shade in average garden soil, even in unmanageable problem areas provided they are well-drained. Obtain plants and, after they become established and have multiplied, divide the roots in spring using the young offshoots. Water well and deeply until the roots take hold. This is a spreading plant and can crowd out weeds. If used as a ground cover, it may be cut back sharply and often to keep low, or allowed to grow until finished blooming, then cut back. Young plants of bedstraw bloom all through July and sometimes in the fall. This plant has become naturalized in the Berkshire Mountains of New England.

263

K.B.

HYSSOPUS

Labiatae

Purge me with hyssop, and I shall be clean:
wash me, and I shall be whiter than snow.
—Psalm 51:7

Hyssop (*Hyssopus officinalis*) was once considered a Bible plant, but recent research has proven that it was a native of Europe and not known in Palestine. Hyssop was once a remedy for quinsy and was used in treatments of colds and lung diseases. A decoction of it was supposed to remove bruises, and the oil was used in perfumes and liqueurs.

Description:
Hardy perennial, 1 to 1½ ft. Plant bears a slight resemblance to boxwood. Leaves narrow, small and pointed, dark green on woody stems. Flowers dark blue, pink, or white in spikes.

Uses:
Sometimes employed as a hedge, but some old plants die out annually and have to be replaced with strong seedlings. The flowers are excellent for cutting. Hyssop's culinary uses are largely in the past as its flavor and odor do not generally please contemporary tastes.

Culture:
Full sun, well-drained garden soil, rather alkaline. Seeds sown in well-prepared, moist soil in the spring germinate readily, becoming sturdy seedlings that transplant easily. If used as a hedge, plant a double row of seeds. Keep the main part of the hedge trimmed, but allow plants on the ends or in an out-of-the-way place to bloom so that self-sown seedlings can replace plants that die out.

K.B.

LAMIUM

Labiatae

It makes the heart merry,
Drives away melancholy,
Quickens the spirits.
—Nicholas Culpeper

Lamiums have an interesting past as medicinal herbs, and today they make outstanding ground cover plants. *Lamium album,* the white dead nettle or white archangel, resembles the stinging nettle, but does not have its irritating disadvantages. In the past the flowers were baked in sugar, and a water distilled of them was said to make the heart merry, to give good color, and to make the vital spirits livelier. Tincture of the astringent plant was applied with cotton to stop bleeding. It was used also as a blood purifier and for eczema. *L. maculatum,* once called "cobbler's bench," has heart-shaped leaves marked with silver and spikes of white or light purple flowers. It is one of the most decorative of all ground covers, long-blooming, and the foliage stays attractive even after the first freezes of autumn. A prolific but not rampant ground cover.

Description:
Both species mentioned are hardy perennials.

Uses:
As showy ground cover plants where the attractive foliage sets off white or purple flowers depending on the variety.

Culture:
Partial sun to shade in good soil. Propagate by removing portions of the creeping stems which have rooted into the moist earth in spring or fall.

267

K.B.

LAURUS

Lauraceae

And when from Daphne's tree he plucks more Baies
His shepherd pipe may chant more heavenly lays.
—William Browne

Bay (*Laurus nobilis*) on its native shores of the Mediterranean grows to a majestic tree 60 ft. tall. The leaves, berries, and oil all have narcotic properties. Oil of bay is used for sprains, and the leaves were once used for a tea. Other plants called laurel, as our native *Kalmia latifolia*, cannot be used as bay. There are only two plants whose leaves are used as bay, *Laurus nobilis* and *Magnolia glauca*. Native laurels are poisonous and should not be used at all.

   Description:
Tender perennial, 3 to 6 ft. when cultivated in a pot or large tub. Elegant, smooth-barked tree, evergreen leaves thick, smooth, and dark in color. Flowers small, in clusters, seldom appearing in the North.

   Uses:
As an ornamental pot-grown tree for the garden in warm weather, for house or greenhouse during cold seasons. Use leaves for seasoning in stews, in casseroles, and pâtés.

   Culture:
See Chapter 2. Propagate by rooting cuttings in moist sand and peat moss; provide shade and a moist atmosphere. Rooting many take six months or more. Suckers and cuttings from them root more quickly.

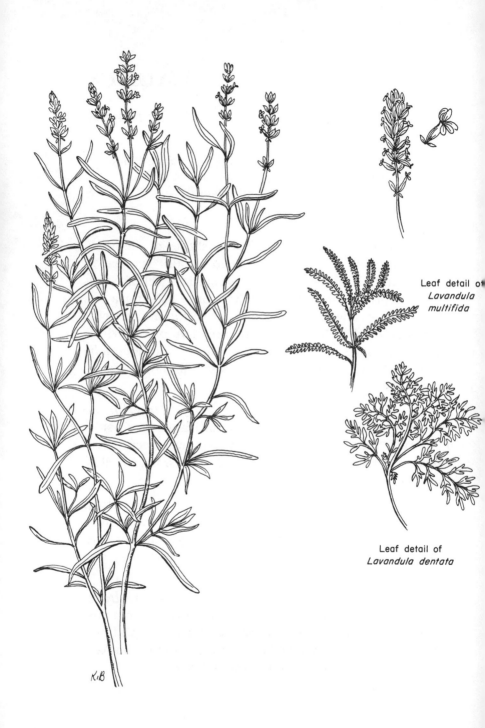

Leaf detail of *Lavandula multifida*

Leaf detail of *Lavandula dentata*

K.B

LAVANDULA

Labiatae

Lavender is of especial good use for all griefes
and paines of the head and brain.
—John Parkinson

Lavender (*Lavandula officinalis*) came to England
with the Romans and found its happiest home there. It
was used by the Greeks and Romans much as we use it
today: for its clean sweet scent in washing water, soaps,
pomades, and perfuming sheets. It was a strewing herb
in medieval times and a medicine believed to cure 43
ills of the flesh and spirit. Lavender has always been
used to attract the bees and it produces an epicure's
honey.

Description:
Hardy perennial, 1 to 3 ft. A woody semishrub that is
many-branched with narrow leaves, 1 to 2 ins. long, gray-
green and velvety. Flowers small and lavender, in whorls
of 6 to 10 on long-stemmed slender spikes. There are
small species and varieties that make fine ornamental
border plants; larger ones can be used for unclipped
hedges. Some tender kinds that grow well indoors are
discussed in Chapter 2.

Uses:
Dried leaves and flowers in potpourri. Oil of lavender is
used in soaps and perfumes.

Culture:
Sunny, well-drained, alkaline soil. To grow from seeds,
see the last part of Chapter 5. Lavender can also be
propagated from slips with the heel attached, in moist
sand; July is a good time to do this.

271

K.B.

LEVISTICUM

Umbelliferae

An herb of the sun, under the sign Taurus,
if Saturn offend the throat . . . this is your
cure.
> —Nicholas Culpeper

Lovage *(Levisticum officinale)* is a native of the Balkan countries, Greece, and other Mediterranean parts. It is one of the oldest salad herbs and was a favorite in colonial gardens. The English use it chiefly for confectionary: coating the seeds with sugar. Lovage was an ancient cure for ague; also for intestinal disorders.

℞ *Description:*
Hardy perennial, 3 to 5 ft. A vigorous, coarse plant. Leaves dark green resembling celery in appearance, odor, and taste. Flowers small, greenish, in small umbels; not decorative. The plant turns yellow and unattractive in late summer.

℞ *Uses:*
Harvest tender leaves for soups, stews, potato salad, salad greens, sauces. Blanch stems and eat as celery. The seeds, whole or ground, make cordials and may be used in meat pies, salads, and candies. Oil from the roots flavors some tobacco blends.

℞ *Culture:*
Partial shade in fertile, deep, and evenly moist soil. May be propagated by division in spring, or from seeds, if they are sown in autumn immediately after they have ripened. Cover them lightly, and germination should occur the following spring.

273

K.B.

LINUM

Linaceae

If flax is put in the shoes it
preserves from poverty.
—Old Proverb

Flax (*Linum usitatissimum* and *L. perenne*), the
source of linen and native to all Mediterranean countries,
is a crop about which many legends have grown up. Both
species have been used for linen, but the first mentioned
is more important. The fresh herb was applied for rheumatic pains, colds, and coughs. Flax seed as a poultice
softened hard swellings. If a baby did not thrive he was
laid upon the ground in a flax field, flax seeds were sprinkled over him, and it was believed that he would recover
as the seeds sprouted.

Description:
L. usitatissimum is an annual, 1 to 2 ft. It has slender
blue-green leaves on willowy stems and bright blue flowers. *L. perenne* is a hardy perennial, to 2 ft. The blue
flowers open with the sun, wither by noon. The blooms
appear in June and July, but young plants frequently have
another blossoming period in fall.

Uses:
For color in the herb garden.

Culture:
Both species like full sun. *L. usitatissimum* needs a rich,
moist soil. *L. perenne* does better in a well-drained akla-
line soil, and best perpetuates itself by reseeding in a soil
made porous by gravel and rocks. Sow flax seeds in the
spring where the plants are to grow.

275

K.B.

LIPPIA

Verbenaceae

It grows along the old cathedral wall,
Where volcano shadows fall,
Herba Luisa of sweetest smell
Makes a tea as well.

—A. G. S.

Lemon verbena *(Lippia citriodora)*, native to Central and South America, was long thought to be an herb of colonial gardens. Actually, it was one of the later arrivals in North America. Some say that the Spanish conquistadors took it back to Spain, and from there the plant spread through the south of Europe. In Latin America the lemon verbena is called *herba luisa,* and it is used for healing.

℞ *Description:*
Tender perennial, to 6 ft. as a tubbed plant. Leaves yellow-green indoors, glossy and darker outdoors. Flowers white and insignificant, borne infrequently.

℞ *Uses:*
Dry the leaves for potpourri and to steep for tea. Fresh leaves may be used to garnish salads, to make some jellies and desserts. The lemon verbena oil of commerce comes from another plant called lemon grass *(Cymbopogon citratus)*.

℞ *Culture:*
See Chapter 2.

277

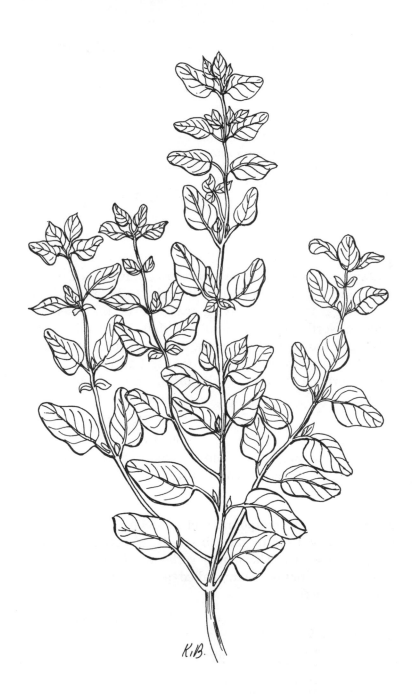

K.B.

MAJORANA

Labiatae

And though sweet Marjoram will your garden paint
With no gay colors, yet preserve the plant,
Whose fragrance will invite your kind regard,
When her known virtues have her worth declared;
On Simonis' shore fair Venus raised the plant,
Which from the Goddess touch derived her scent.
—René Rapin

Sweet marjoram (*Majorana hortensis*, sometimes listed as *Origanum majorana*) was used by the Greeks as a medicine for narcotic poisoning, convulsions, and dropsy. Because of its sweetness it was used also as a polish for furniture and as a strewing herb.

Description:
Tender perennial, grown as an annual in the North, to 1 ft. Leaves gray-green, rounded, and velvety. Flowers in white clusters like the blossoms of hops.

Uses:
Plants attractive in a border. Use fresh or dried leaves in soups, in stuffings for pork or lamb, and with eggs. The leaves may be used also in potpourri, and in English country places they are brewed into tea. Harvest the fresh leaves any time. Cut frequently to prevent blossoming. Wash well and hang up to dry overnight, then finish the drying process in a basket. Remove leaves when dry, crush, and store.

Culture:
Full sun in well-drained, alkaline soil. Sow seeds in carefully pulverized soil in the spring. Cover lightly with shredded sphagnum moss and keep moist. Germination may be slow. After transplanting seedlings, water well, and keep shaded until the roots take hold. Cuttings root easily. For culture indoors, see Chapter 2.

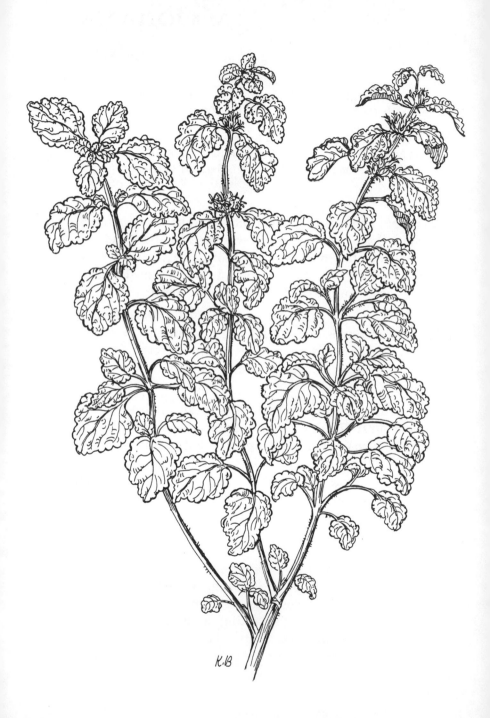

K.B

MARRUBIUM

Labiatae

Horehound is one of the five plants stated by the Mishna to be the "bitter herbs" which the Jews were ordered to take for the feast of the Passover.

—Richard Folkard

Horehound (*Marrubium vulgare*) has been used as a medicine since early Roman times. The Egyptians called it the seed of Horus, bull's blood, and eye of the star. It is an ancient antidote for vegetable poisons, and recommended by Gerard, "To those who have drunk poyson or have been bitten of serpents."

Description:
Perennial, only half-hardy in severely cold climates, to 2 ft. Leaves wrinkled and almost white, forming rosettes in early growth. In summer the plant branches out and puts on a burlike blossom. For best appearance keep the blooms cut off, although in this treatment you lose the self-sown seedlings that are useful in making living, autumn wreaths.

Uses:
As flavoring for famous horehound candy; as a tea to treat coughs and as a syrup for children's coughs and colds. The strange musky odor disappears upon drying.

Culture:
Full sun and sandy, dry soil. Except in mild climates, treat as a biennial, sowing a few seeds each year. Horehound can also be propagated by making cuttings in the spring or summer, or by dividing large plants in the spring. Interesting to try potted on a sunny cool window sill, or in a home greenhouse for the winter.

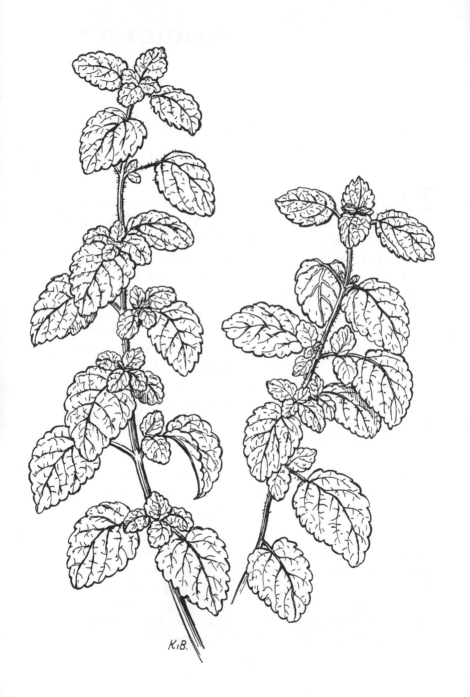

K.B.

MELISSA

Labiatae

The several chairs of order look you scour
With juice of balm and every precious flower.
—Shakespeare

Lemon balm (*Melissa officinalis*) came from the mountainous regions of southern Europe. Linnaeus named it *melissa*, the Greek word for bee, owing to the bees' attraction to the plant. Lemon balm was an ingredient of the famous Carmelite water, and in the past has been used along with honey as a potion to assure longevity.

Description:

Hardy perennial, 1 to 2 ft., with branches growing on a square stem. Leaves broadly heart-shaped, toothed, 1 to 3 ins. long. Flowers inconspicuous, white or yellowish, off and on from June to October.

Uses:

Makes an excellent mild tea. Good also for punch, for claret cup, fruit desserts, and as a garnish for fish. The oil is distilled and used in perfumery and also as a furniture polish. The dry leaves are used in potpourri.

Culture:

Grows freely in any soil, but best in a well-drained location. Needs sun half a day, but will grow in shade. When plants are in a flower border, they need to be cut back to keep the foliage a good color as it has a tendency to turn yellow after flowering. Propagate by transplanting self-sown seedlings, or by sowing seeds (germination is slow).

283

K.B.

MONARDA

Labiatae

Speak not, whisper not,
Here bloweth thyme and bergamot,
Softly on thee every hour
Secret herbs their spices shower.
                    —Walter de la Mare

Beebalm (*Monarda didyma*), known also as bergamot and oswego tea, is one of the few native American herbs used in the garden.

℞ *Description:*
Hardy perennial, to 3 ft. Leaves 4 to 6 ins. long, dark green. Flowers in dense terminal clusters with reddish bracts, the color magenta, pink, purple, red, or white, depending on the variety.

℞ *Uses:*
Outstanding in the perennial border. The fragrant plants emit the characteristic odor of bergamot, similar to that of citrus. Use the leaves to make a tea, in potpourri, to flavor apple jelly, in fruit salads, and wine cups. Bergamot oil comes from a tropical tree, not from this plant, though the odors are similar. Bergamot flowers are excellent cut; long-lasting and effective in colonial arrangements.

℞ *Culture:*
Sun to partial shade in rich, evenly moist soil. Cut back after bloom as the foliage is sometimes unattractive in late summer. Propagate by division in spring or fall.

MYRRHIS

Umbelliferae

Very good for old people who are dull
and without courage.
—Old Saying

Sweet cicely (*Myrrhis odorata*) has been known by
many common names including myrrh flower, sweet chervil, anise fern, and shepherd's needle. In history it has
been useful in treating coughs and as a gentle stimulant
and tonic for young girls. A decoction of the roots in wine
was taken for bites of vipers and mad dogs. An ointment
eased skin eruptions and the pains of gout.

Description:
Hardy perennial, 2 to 3 ft. The long thick root sends up
branching stems of fragrant, anise-scented leaves that
resemble the fronds of a delicate fern at maturity. These
are downy on the undersides and marked with white
spots. The white flowers which appear in late May and
early June are followed by seeds an inch long and dark
brown when ripe.

Uses:
The spicy seeds fresh and green in herb mixtures as a
spice. Use the leaves in salads or as a filling in pastries.
The roots may be eaten like fennel, raw or boiled.

Culture:
Shady, moist soil. To grow from seeds, plant in autumn
while the seeds are still fresh. Transplant to permanent
positions in the spring, allowing plenty of space for the
mature plants. An excellent plant for the shady flower
garden.

287

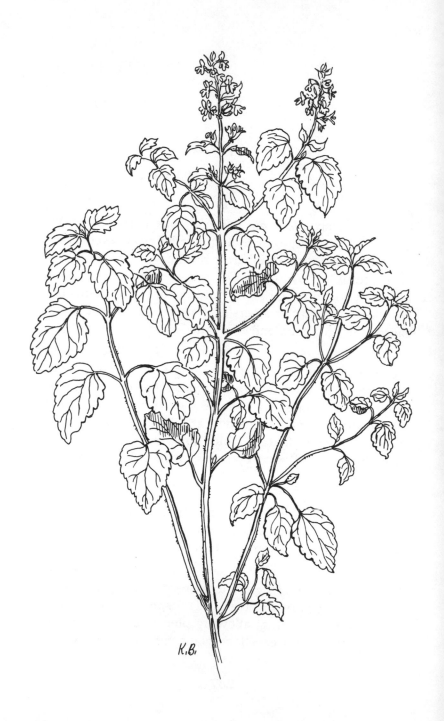

K.B.

NEPETA

Labiatae

If you set it, the cats will eat it,
If you sow it, the cats won't know it.
—Old Rhyme

Catnip (*Nepeta cataria*), known variously as catnip, catmint, and catnep, is a native of Europe, common in England, and an escapee from American gardens until now it is considered wild.

🕮 *Description:*
Hardy perennial, 2 to 3 ft. Sturdy stems, straight and similar to other mints, square and set with leaves 2 to 3 ins. long, downy, heart-shaped, green above, gray below. Flowers pale purplish in dense clusters on spikes. The plant is attractive to bees, almost irresistible to cats, and disliked by rats. Other species recommended for the garden include *N. mussini, N.* 'Six Hills Giant,' *N. grandiflora, N. macrantha* (blue flowers in spring), *N. nuda* and *N. reticulata.*

🕮 *Uses:*
Cats usually like dried leaves and blossoms better than fresh. A tea brewed from dried leaves may be used to soothe the nerves. All the nepetas are decorative, and they are remarkable in dry weather, continuing to bloom until fall if cut back after the first flowering.

🕮 *Culture:*
Sun or partial shade in sandy or rich soil. Catnip self-sows after it has become established. Propagate also by division of roots in spring or fall.

289

K.B.

OCIMUM

Labiatae

Madonna, wherefore hast thou sent to me
   Sweet basil and mignonette?
Embleming love and health, which never yet
   In the same wreath might be.
         —Percy Bysshe Shelley

Sweet basil (*Ocimum basilicum*) is the most commonly grown basil although there are many others in cultivation. All have a clovelike flavor and spicy odor, some more
pungent than others.

Description:
Annual, to 2 ft. Leaves 1 to 2 ins. long, shining dark
green and pointed. The flowers are white or purplish in
spikes. *O. crispum* from Japan is called lettuceleaf basil;
it is excellent in salads. *O. basilicum* 'Bush' forms a large
bush with lemon odor and taste; its variety *minimum* has
tiny leaves and, if spaced 4 ins. apart in a row, each plant
will grow like a small shrub. 'Dark Opal' has reddish-
purple foliage, striking in plantings with gray-foliaged
plants, and white or pink flowers.

Uses:
Leaves in salads, vinegars, spaghetti, soups, with meat,
game, fish, and tomato dishes. Excellent also in flower
arrangements. Harvest before the plants blossom; cut off
flower buds to keep plants producing all summer. Always
leave two leaves or a circle of leaves toward the base of
each branch; new tops will grow in a week.

Culture:
Sun to partial shade in average, but moist garden soil.
After the weather has warmed in the spring, sow seeds
where the plants are to grow.

K.B.

ORIGANUM

Labiatae

Where the bee can suck no honey, she leaves her
sting behind; and where the bear cannot find
origanum to heal his grief, he blasteth all other
leaves with his breath.
> —Beaumont and Fletcher

Oregano (*Origanum vulgare*), also called wild marjoram, comes from the early name "organy," because of
its use in hot bags as an application for rheumatic swellings. Gerard says, "Organy is very good against the wam-
bling of the stomacke."

𝔔 *Description:*
Hardy perennial, 2 ft. Leaves dull, gray-green, oval, with
stems often purple. Flowers pink, white, purple or lilac.
The most flavorsome oregano is a small-leaved, almost
trailing plant with white flowers. It is easily overrun by
the coarser types and needs to be kept separate and wintered inside.

𝔔 *Uses:*
Leaves, fresh or dried, in spaghetti sauce, sparingly in
salads, on tomatoes, in herb seasoning mixtures. Use
flowers fresh in summer arrangements or dried in winter
wreaths and bouquets.

𝔔 *Culture:*
Full sun and average garden soil, on the dry side and
always well-drained. Propagate by division of established
plants in the spring, by rooting cuttings, or by sowing
seeds. The seeds usually produce considerable variation.

K.B.

PETROSELINUM

Umbelliferae

At Sparta's Palace twenty beauteous mayds,
The pride of Greece, fresh garlands crowned their heads
With hyacinths and twining parsley drest,
Graced joyful Menelaus' marriage feast.
                                        —Theocritus

Parsley (*Petroselinum crispum*) is one of the first
plants used in wreath making. Chaplets of it were worn
at Roman and Greek banquets to absorb the fumes of the
wine and thus prevent inebriation. Parsley was eaten
after dining to remove the odor of garlic and onions, prov-
ing that our twentieth-century exploitation of chlorophyll
as a breath-sweetener is nothing new.

Description:
Curly parsley is a hardy biennial usually cultivated as an
annual. It has bright green, tightly curled leaves and
makes an excellent border for the culinary garden. Italian
parsley, also a hardy biennial cultivated as an annual, has
large plain leaves reminiscent of a fern which may be cut
in quantity for salad greens, or cooked as a vegetable.

Uses:
Cut all through the season, using generously in salads,
soups, casseroles, and omelettes with other vegetables.

Culture:
Full sun or partial shade in humusy, moist soil. To grow
from seeds, broadcast or plant in shallow drills in well-
prepared soil. Sow in midsummer for autumn cutting
and to have small plants to bring inside for winter window boxes; for an early summer crop, sow seeds in earliest spring.

295

PIMPINELLA

Umbelliferae

... for ye pay tithe of mint, and anise, and cummin ...
—Matthew 23:23

Anise (*Pimpinella anisum*) was used as a spice in Roman times and was the chief flavoring of the *mustacae*, cakes made of meal and filled with anise, cumin, and other flavorings. This was eaten to prevent indigestion and may be a forerunner of our wedding cake. The seed of anise was thought to avert the evil eye, and in Biblical lands it was used in payment of taxes. The oil has been used as mouse bait.

Description:
Annual, 1 to 1½ ft. Leaves finely cut, gray-green. Flowers white, small, in an umbel about 2 ins. across. The seeds are light-colored, crescent-shaped, with a small piece of stem that clings to them after harvesting.

Uses:
Watch plants carefully after flowers form to insure harvesting the seeds before they ripen and fall to the ground. When the seeds are fully formed, cut heads into a paper bag. Use as flavoring for cakes, cookies, candies, applesauce, stews, liqueurs, and wines, and use to impart fragrance to soaps, perfumes, and potpourri. Use fresh anise leaves in salads as a garnish.

Culture:
Sunny, well-drained soil enriched by the addition of compost. Sow the seeds very early in spring.

K.B.

ROSMARINUS

Labiatae

Young men and maids do ready stand
With sweet Rosemary in their hands—
A perfect token of your virgin's life.
       —Old Ballad (Roxburghe Collection)

Rosemary (*Rosmarinus officinalis*) is the herb of memory which it is said to restore, and it also brings good luck, prevents witchcraft, disinfects the air, and has been used traditionally at weddings and funerals.

☙ Description:
Tender perennial, 3 to 6 ft. There are many variations, but all are considered forms of common rosemary. The needle-like leaves vary in color from gray-green to dark green; some are shiny, broad, or very narrow. All are thick and without stems, gray or white on the undersides. The blossoms may be white-rose, pale lavender, pale or dark blue.

☙ Uses:
Green or dried, sparingly on chicken, in gravy with lamb, in soups, stuffings, sauces, dressings, in jelly, and as a tea. Rosemary oil is used in medicine, perfumes, hair preparations, bath soaps, and mouth washes.

☙ Culture:
Full sun to partial shade with evenly moist, well-drained, and alkaline soil. Provide liquid fertilizer several times during the active growing season. Root cuttings in sand or vermiculite using 4- to 6-inch pieces of new wood or healthy end tips. Seeds are not difficult, but are usually slow to germinate and require three years to bloom.

299

RUMEX

Polygonaceae

Sorrel sharpens the appetite, assuages heat,
cools the liver and strengthens the heart; ...
in the making of sallets imparts a grateful
quickness to the rest as supplying the want of
oranges and lemons. Together with salt, it gives
both the name and the relish to sallets from the
vapidity, which renders not plants and herbs only,
but men themselves pleasant and agreeable.
                                        —John Evelyn

French sorrel (*Rumex scutatus*) is a native of southern
France, Switzerland, and Germany. Historically its uses
have been largely culinary, although it is alleged to "cool
any inflamation and heat of the blood—a cordial to the
heart." It was thought to be a source of iron and was once
called "cuckoo's meate" because the bird was supposed to
clear its singing voice by eating it.

℞ *Description:*
Hardy perennial, 2 ft. Resembles the related and common
dock of the fields. Leaves succulent, long and shield-
shaped, light green in color, sometimes veined with red.
Flowers like dock but smaller, softer in appearance, and
a warm red-brown color.

℞ *Uses:*
In sorrel soup, sparingly in salads, as a sauce for beef, or
cooked with beet tops, spinach, or cabbage. Cut early in
the spring and freeze some leaves for use later in the year.
If allowed to blossom, use the flowering heads in dried
arrangements. Cut to ground after harvest to encourage
new growth for a fall crop.

℞ *Culture:*
Sun to partial shade in rich, well-drained soil. Buy a plant,
then allow it to multiply. Difficult to obtain seeds of the
true variety. Broadleaf garden sorrel is a good substitute.

301

RUTA

Rutaceae

Then sprinkled she the juice of rue,
That groweth underneath the yew,
With nine drops of the midnight dew
From lunarie distilling.
                    —Michael Drayton

Rue (*Ruta graveolens*), also called sweet rue and herb of grace, was once used to treat many diseases. It was said to bestow second sight, to preserve vision, and was used against old age and stiffening joints. Holy water was sprinkled with sprigs of rue, hence the name "herb of grace." Arrows supposedly found their mark after being dipped in the juice of rue, and rue is still used in Lithuania as a courting herb to announce engagements.

꧁ *Description:*
Hardy perennial, 3 ft. Leaves alternate, blue-green, musky smelling, much divided and notched on erect, stout woody stems. Yellow flowers that resemble a cluster of stars are followed by red-brown seed pods that look hand carved.

꧁ *Uses:*
As an ornamental plant toward the back of the border where it will have little opportunity to cause skin irritations, for which it is known, but where the foliage, flowers, and seed heads can be enjoyed. The dried seed heads are excellent for use in wreaths and swags.

꧁ *Culture:*
Full sun to partial shade in average garden soil, preferably dry, stony, and alkaline. Propagate by dividing old plants in late spring or, after blooming, by rooting cuttings or sowing seeds.

SALVIA

Labiatae

Sage is singularly good for the head and the brain; it quick-
eneth the senses and the memory; strengtheneth the sinews;
restoreth health to those that hath the palsy; and takes away
shaky trembling of the members.

—John Gerard

Common sage (*Salvia officinalis*), in history, has been
the herb of health and of the aged. An old French couplet
expresses these virtues well, "Sage helps the nerves and
by its powerful might Palsy is cured and fever put to
flight." The Chinese once used it in preference to their
own teas, and employed it medicinally for headaches.
The fresh leaves were once used to strenghten the gums
and to whiten teeth; also it was used as a wash to darken
gray hair.

Description:
Hardy perennial, 3 ft. Leaves oblong, gray and pebbly, on
stiff stems that become woody and gnarled with age.
Flowers blue in whorls with lipped corollas that tempt the
bees and hummingbirds.

Uses:
Cut leaves of common sage at any time for cheese sand-
wiches, soufflés, and stuffings. Use dried in sausages,
with cheese, pork, poultry, as stuffing seasoning in turkey,
and as a tea.

Culture:
Sunny site with moist, well-drained garden soil. Seeds of
common sage sown in early spring will produce fine plants
for cutting by fall. Propagate in spring or early fall by
dividing old plants.

305

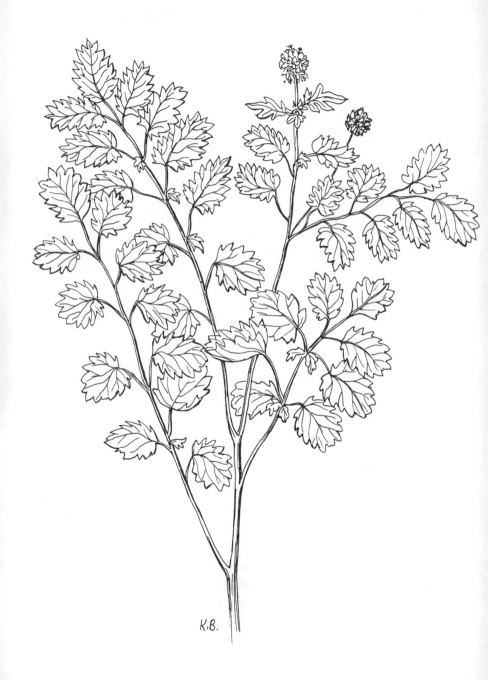

K.B.

SANGUISORBA

Rosaceae

But those which perfume the Aire most delightfully, not passed by as the rest, but being Trodden upon and Crushed, are Three: That is, Burnet, Wilde-Time, and Water-Mints. Therefore, you are to set whole Allies of them, to have the Pleasure, when you walke or tread.

—Francis Bacon

Salad burnet (*Sanguisorba minor*), of Mediterranean origin, then naturalized in England and Asia, came to America with the Pilgrims. As a cordial, it was used to promote perspiration, and infused in wine and beer it became a cure for gout.

Description:
Hardy perennial, 1 to 2 ft., evergreen. Leaves bear a similarity to those of the wild rose and remain nearly flat on the ground until flowering time. Flowers deep, but pale crimson in a round head.

Uses:
Fresh leaves smell of cucumber and may be cut while tender for salads, vinegars, cream cheese, drinks, seasoning green butters, and as a garnish. They do not dry well. Keep some plants close to the house, sheltered in a coldframe or in a cool greenhouse, to provide winter greens.

Culture:
Sun with well-drained, alkaline soil. Sow seeds in late fall, early spring, and summer to have tender salad greens all year. Difficult to transplant except as a small seedling. This is one of the most decorative of herbs, worthy of space in most gardens.

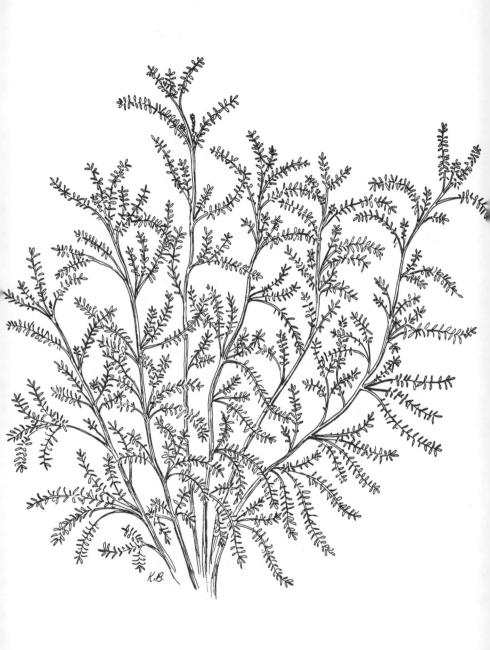

SANTOLINA

Compositae

White Satten groweth pretty well, so doth Lavender-Cotton.
—John Josselyn

Lavender-cotton (*Santolina chamaecyparissus*) is one of the most ornamental of all herbs. It is a native of southern Europe and North Africa.

℞ *Description:*
Hardy perennial, 1 to 2 ft. Leaves very fine, yet sturdy; gray to white at certain seasons, but blue-gray while young. Flowers, few, globular and yellow, best trimmed off for neatness. *S. viridis* is a vigorous green santolina with a strong odor and interesting bright yellow flowers.

℞ *Uses:*
For borders, especially in the knot garden, and as accent plants when grown in clumps.

℞ *Culture:*
Full sun and average garden soil, dry or moist but perfectly drained. Propagate by rooting cuttings in sand or vermiculite. Transplant rooted cuttings into small pots until they make balls of roots, then move into the garden. Cut tops back to make plants bush out. Santolina is hardy in central and southern New England, considered half-hardy in the Berkshires, and must be covered in any area if it is to look presentable in the spring. Trim carefully in the fall as santolinas do not die to the ground but come out along the old wood.

309

SATUREJA

Labiatae

Mercury-claims dominion over this herb.
Keep it dry by you all the year, if you
love yourself and your ease.
       —Nicholas Culpeper

Summer savory (*Satureja hortensis*) is a Mediterranean native. Virgil grew savory for his bees, and the Romans used its hot peppery flavor before Eastern spices were widely known. Vinegar flavored with savory was used as a dressing and sauce.

৯ *Description:*
Annual, 1 to 1½ ft. Leaves narrow, dark green, on stout stems that become branched and treelike in late summer, turning reddish and purple in fall. Flowers pale lavender or pure white, sometimes with a pink cast, covering the plant like drops of dew in July.

৯ *Uses:*
Cut two or three times during the drying season, preferably before the blossoms form. Leave some to mature, but harvest for good green color from non-blooming plants. Hang to dry in a warm, dry place. Pull leaves off —a long task—make sure they are chip dry and store in bottles. Use in cooking green beans, for all bean dishes, in stuffings, with rice, in soups, gravies, and sauces.

৯ *Culture:*
Sunny location in well-drained garden loam. Sow seeds in early spring, allowing about four weeks for germination. Broadcast in a wide, well-prepared row. Mulch with salt hay to prevent weeds and to keep leaves clean for cutting.

K.B

SATUREJA

Labiatae

Sound savorie, and brazil, hartie-hale,
Fat Colwortes and comforting Perseline,
Cold Lettuce and refreshing Rosmarine.
—Lady Northcote

Winter savory (*Satureja montana*) is a native of the mountainous regions of southern Europe.

℞ *Description:*

Hardy perennial, 6 to 12 ins. Leaves narrow on branches that form a low, spreading growth. Flowers either white or blue. This is a good border plant, but at its best when planted in a wall garden. *S. m. pygmaea* is dwarf, about 4 ins. tall, and highly to be recommended.

℞ *Uses:*

Harvest as for summer savory. Use in cooking green beans, other bean dishes, in stuffings, with rice, in soups, gravies, and bouquet garni. Winter savory, too, with basil is a substitute for salt and pepper in salt-free diets. Used occasionally in salad dressings. Winter savory was once a proper dressing for trout. The leaves can be made into a peppery-tasting tea.

℞ *Culture:*

Sunny, perfectly drained soil, on the lean side. Propagate by hilling up an established plant with humusy, moist soil. New plants will be ready to separate in four to six weeks.

313

K.B.

STACHYS

Labiatae

Lamb's-car (*Stachys olympica*, or sometimes *S. lanata*), a native of the Caucasus, and bishop's wort (*S. grandiflora* syn. *betonica*) from Europe and Asia Minor were once classified with the betonys. The whole plants were collected for a flavorful tea, said to have all the good qualities of China tea plus virtues of its own. Betony was once thought to sanctify those who carried it.

Description:
Hardy perennials, *S. olympica* to 1 ft., *S. grandiflora* to 3 ft. *S. olympica* leaves are long-stemmed and linear, heavily covered by white "lamb's" hairs that give the plant a beautiful silvery appearance. Flowers purple, in spikes. *S. grandiflora* leaves are rough, covered with short hairs, and filled with oil that gives off an odor at a touch. Most of the elongated heart-shaped leaves spring from the root, large and on long stalks. The flower stems rise 1 to 3 ft. with pairs of leaves set on opposite sides of the stems. Flowers purplish red, in whorls on the spikes, in July and August.

Uses:
For flower arrangements and as showy border plants.

Culture:
Sunny with moist, well-drained soil. Propagate by division of established plants in spring or fall.

315

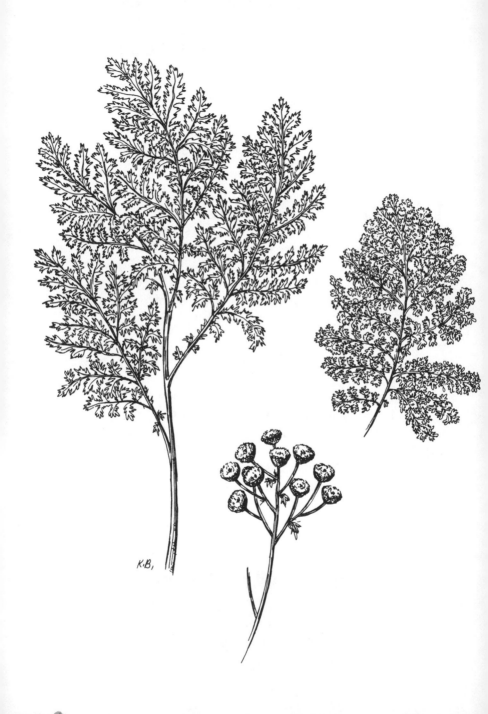

K.B.

TANACETUM

Compositae

On Easter Sunday be the pudding seen
To which the Tansy lends her sober green.
        —*The Oxford Sausage*

Tansy (*Tanacetum vulgare*) has been called such names as bitter buttons, *herbe St. Marc,* and *Chrysanthemum vulgare.* It was once used as a bitter tea to bring out measles, also in tansy cakes for Easter festivities in England, and in New England coffins as a preservative—or as a symbol of immortality from its ancient use by Greeks and Romans at burials. It was believed effective for keeping away ants and flies, and the large leaves were kept in many colonial pantries for this purpose.

℞ Description:
Hardy perennial, 3 ft. Attractive plant with coarse fernlike leaves. Flowers like yellow buttons in clusters. The variety *crispum,* or fernleaf tansy, is smaller and better for cultivated gardens.

℞ Uses:
Dry the flowers as everlastings for fall and winter arrangements, wreaths, and swags.

℞ Culture:
Sun to partial shade in almost any soil provided it is not wet for long periods. The chief problem with this plant is keeping it from becoming a weed, but if you should want to propagate it, do so by dividing well-established plants. Tansy is best when planted against a fence that will give it some protection from high winds and rains.

317

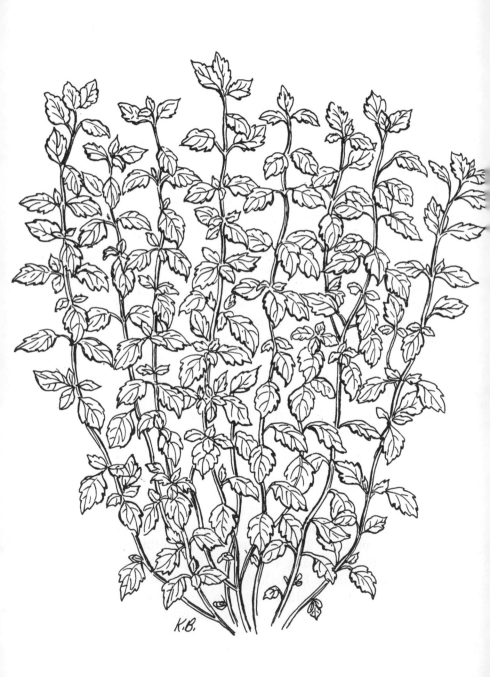

K.B.

TEUCRIUM

Labiatae

I like also little heaps in the Nature of the Mole Hills (such are in wilde Heaths) to be set some with Wilde-Time; Some with pincks; some with Germander, that gives a good flower to the eye.

—Francis Bacon

Germander (*Teucrium lucidum*) provided the basis of an ancient treatment for gout. Emperor Charles V is the most famous person to have been cured by this remedy. He took a decoction of the herb for sixty days in succession. It is native of the Greek islands.

Description:
Hardy perennial, 1 to 1½ ft. This plant lends itself to clipping as a small hedge and resembles boxwood. The leaves are small, stiff, and glossy dark green, the edges toothed. Flowers magenta, but best kept cut off so that the plants will stay bushy and full as a hedge. *T. chamaedrys* is hardier, almost a creeping plant, with leaves that turn reddish in fall or when the soil is dry. It makes a good ground cover for dry places and has rosy flowers.

Uses:
As small hedge for the perennial border or herb garden.

Culture:
Sun in well-drained, moist garden loam. Propagate by rooting cuttings early in the growing season. Cover with salt hay in the wintertime.

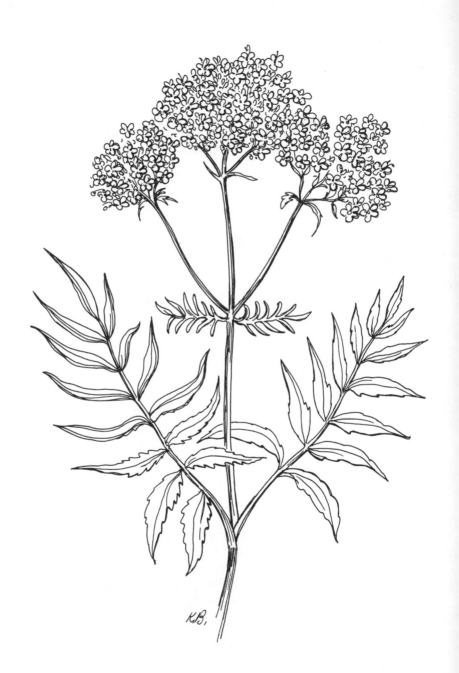

K.B.

VALERIANA

Valerianaceae

Then springen herbes grete and smale,
The licoris and the setewale.
　　　　　　　—Chaucer

Garden heliotrope (*Valeriana officinalis*), also called phu, all-heal, setewale, and capon's tail, is a fragrant medicinal herb. While the carrion odor of the root is unpleasant to humans, it is relished by cats, dogs, and rats (it has been used as a ratbait). The root has been used as a drug to promote sleep, to quieten and soothe nerves, to cure insomnia, to treat epilepsy and in heart medicines for palpitations. Asiatic variations of *V. officinalis* were used as spices and perfumes.

🏵 *Description:*
Hardy perennial, 3 to 5 ft. Leaves lance-shaped in pairs. Flowers pale pink in flattened cluster, or cyme, at intervals during the summer, starting in June. They are sweet, smelling of heliotrope.

🏵 *Uses:*
As an attractive flowering herb for the back of the border.

🏵 *Culture:*
Sun or shade in rich, moist garden soil. Propagate by removing sideshoots of old plants. Set firmly and deeply so that animals will not catch the odor of the root and dig it up.

321

K·B·

VIOLA

Violaceae

Reform the errours of the Spring;
Make that the tulips may have share
Of sweetness, seeing they are fair;
And Roses of their Thorns disarm:
    But most procure
That Violets may a longer Age endure.
—Andrew Marvell

Violets (*Viola* species) of all types are important plants for the herb garden. The heart's-ease violas were used as a love-charm in Shakespeare's day, as a symbol of the Trinity in monastery gardens, as a medicine for eczema, and the flowers were cordials for the heart. The roots and seeds were used as purgatives.

℞ *Description:*

V. odorata is the sweet English violet. *V. tricolor* is the heart's-ease or Johnny-jump-up, ever a favorite of poets and herbalists.

℞ *Uses:*

Attractive border and ground cover. Candy the flowers for use on tops of cakes. Use them fresh in punch, in flower arrangements, and in miniature winter plantings where they will provide bloom out of season. Violets appeared in many food and drink recipes of the past, some of which have been revived. Violets appear in the May wine along with strawberries, and there is a violet jelly, a violet sherbet, and I have heard of violet fritters.

℞ *Culture:*

Partial to full shade in humusy, moist soil. Propagate by dividing well-established clumps after they finish blooming. Guard violets closely or they will become troublesome weeds. *V. tricolor* or Johnny-jump-up is a self-sowing annual.

323

EARLY AMERICAN HERBS

From *New-England's Rarities discovered*

This list was prepared in 1672 by John Josselyn; his
spelling and punctuation have been retained here.

Spearmint,
Rew, will hardly grow
Fetherfew prospereth exceedingly;
Southernwood, is no Plant for this Country, Nor
Rosemary. Nor
Bayes.
White-Satten groweth pretty well, so doth
Lavender-Cotten, But
Lavender is not for this Climate.
Penny Royal
Smalledge.
Ground Ivey, or Ale Hoof.
Gilly Flowers will continue two Years.
Fennel must be taken up, and kept in a Warm Cellar all
Winter
Horseleek prospereth notably
Holly hocks
Enula Canpana, in two years time the Roots rot.
Comferie, with White Flowers.
Coriander, and
Dill, and
Annis thrive exceedingly, but Annis Seed, as also the
    seed of
Fennel seldom come to maturity; the Seed of Annis is
    commonly eaten with a Fly.
Clary never lasts but one Summer, the Roots rot with
    the Frost.
Sparagus thrives exceedingly, so does
Garden Sorrel, but Patience and
Sweet Bryer or Eglantine
Bloodwort but Sorrily, but
Patience and
English Roses very pleasantly.
Celandine, by the West Country now called Kenning Wort,
    grows but slowly.

Muschater, as well as in England
Dittander or Pepperwort flourisheth notably and so doth
Tansie

Many of these plants struggled in cold New England on their arrival, but later adapted themselves and became the staples of the herb garden, notably rue, southernwood, lavender; rosemary thrives inside. We learned that it was necessary to protect plants here that were perfectly hardy in the milder winters of the British Isles.

FLOWERS FOR THE HERB GARDEN

Agastache
Alyssum, sweet
Astilbe
Bachelor's-button (*Centaurea*)
Balsam (*Impatiens*)
Baptisia
Bergamot (*Monarda*)
Bleeding-heart (*Dicentra*)
Borage
Bouncing Bet (*Saponaria*)
Bugle (*Ajuga*)
Calendula
California poppy (*Eschscholtzia*)
Candytuft (*Iberis*)
Canterbury Bells (*Campanula*)
Carnation (*Dianthus*)
Christmas rose (*Helleborus*)
Cobbler's bench (*Lamium*)
Cockscomb (*Celosia*)
Coreopsis
Cyclamen (hardy perennial
   types)
Dahlia
Daphne
Draba
Dropwort (*Filipendula*)
Edelweiss (*Leontopodium*)
Feverfew (*Chrysanthemum
   parthenium*)
Flax (*Linum*)
Flowering Tobacco (*Nicotiana*)
Forget-me-not (*Myosotis*)
Foxglove (*Digitalis*)
Fritillaria
Gas Plant or Fraxinella
   (*Dictamnus*)

Globe amaranth (*Gomphrena*)
Heliotrope
Hollyhock
Honesty (*Lunaria*)
Iris
Jacob's ladder (*Polemonium*)
Larkspur
Leopard's-bane (*Doronicum*)
Lily, Madonna
Lily-of-the-Valley (*Convallaria*)
Lobelia
Love-in-a-Mist (*Nigella*)
Love-lies-Bleeding
   (*Amaranthus*)
Lungwort (*Pulmonaria*)
Lupine
Marguerite Daisy
   (*Chrysanthemum frutescens*)
Marigold (*Tagetes pumila*,
   lemon-scented)
Michaelmas Daisy (*Aster*)
Mignonette
Monkshood (*Aconitum*)
Morning-glory (*Ipomoea*)
Nasturtium
Oxalis
Painted Daisy (*Pyrethrum*)
Pansy
Pasque Flower (*Anemone
   pulsatilla*)
Peony
Pinks (*Dianthus*)
Plumbago
Plume Poppy (*Bocconia*)
Poppy Mallow (*Callirhoe*)
Ranunculus

Rock Cress *(Aubrietia)*
Rose Moss *(Portulaca)*
Rudbeckia
Saint John's-wort *(Hypericum)*
Scarlet Pimpernel *(Anagallis)*
Snow-on-the-Mountain
  (Euphorbia marginata)
Star-of-Bethlehem
  (Ornithogalum umbellatum)
Statice

Strawflower *(Helichrysum)*
Sunflower *(Helianthus)*
Sun rose *(Helianthemum)*
Thermopsis
Toadflax *(Linaria)*
Verbena
Viper's Bugloss *(Echium)*
Wallflower *(Cheiranthus)*
Wishbone Flower *(Torenia)*
Yarrow *(Achillea)*

HERBS FOR A MEDITATION GARDEN

(Also suitable for the Biblical and Saints' Garden)

Apple *(Malus pumila)*
Archangel *(Lamium galeobdolon)*
Basil *(Ocimum basilicum)*
Bishop's-weed or Goutweed *(Aegopodium podagraria)*
Boxwood *(Buxus sempervirens)*
Bryony, Black *(Tamus communis)*
Camomile *(Anthemis nobilis)*
Candlemas Bells or Snowdrops *(Galanthus)*
Canterbury Bells *(Campanula medium)*
Cedar *(Juniperus* species)
Christmas Rose *(Helleborus niger)*
Chrysanthemum (white pompon hybrids)
Cockscomb *(Celosia)*
Cowslip *(Primula veris)*
Crocus *(Crocus vernus)*
Crown Imperial *(Fritillaria imperialis)*
Daffodil *(Narcissus)*
Daisy, English *(Bellis perennis)*
Dandelion *(Taraxacum officinale)*
Fennel *(Foeniculum vulgare)*
Fern, Maidenhair *(Adiantum capillus-vernis)*
Fern, Royal or St. Christopher's *(Osmunda regalis)*
Fig *(Ficus carica)*
Flax *(Linum* species)
Foxglove or Our Lady's Gloves *(Digitalis purpurea)*
Fuchsia or Our Lady's Eardrops *(Fuchsia)*
Garlic *(Allium sativum)*
Ground Ivy *(Nepeta hederacea)*
Herba Benedicta or Wood Avens *(Geum)*
Herba Sancta Mariae *(Mentha)*
Herb Robert *(Geranium robertianum)*
Herba Trinite *(Viola tricolor)*
Holly *(Ilex aquifolium)*
Holy Ghost Plant *(Angelica)*
Hop *(Humulus lupulus)*
Houseleek *(Sempervivum tectorum)*
Iris *(Iris germanica)*

327

Ivy, English *(Hedera helix)*
Juniper *(Juniperus* species and varieties)
Ladders to Heaven or Lily-of-the-Valley *(Convallaria majalis)*
Laurel *(Laurus nobilis)*
Leek *(Allium porrum)*
Lilies of the Field *(Anemone coronaria)*
Lily, Madonna *(Lilium candidum)*
Lotus, Egyptian *(Nymphaea caerulea)*
Love-in-a-Mist *(Nigella damascena)*
Lungwort *(Pulmonaria officinalis)*
Lychnis, Scarlet *(Lychnis chalcedonica)*
Marigold *(Calendula officinalis)*
Meadowsweet *(Spiraea ulmaria)*
Michaelmas Daisy *(Aster)*
Monkshood *(Aconitum)*
Mugwort or St. John's Plant *(Artemisia vulgaris)*
Mullein, Great, or Lady's Candlestick *(Verbascum thapsis)*
Mustard *(Brassica oleracea ramosa)*
Myrrh *(Myrrhis odorata)*
Myrtle *(Myrtus communis)*
Nettle *(Urtica dioica)*
Oleander *(Nerium oleander)*
Olive *(Olea europaea)*
Ossier *(Salix caprea)*
Our Lady's Bedstraw *(Galium)*
Our Lady's Candlesticks *(Primula)*
Our Lady's Cushion *(Armeria* or thrift)
Our Lady's Hands *(Lamium maculatum)*
Our Lady's Mantle *(Alchemilla)*
Our Lady's Seal or Solomon's Seal *(Polygonatum multiflorum)*
Our Lady's Slippers *(Impatiens balsamina* and *Lotus corniculatus)*
Our Lady's Smock *(Cardamine pratensis)*
Palm, Date *(Phoenix dactylifera)*
Papyrus *(Cyperus papyrus)*
Parsley *(Petroselinum crispum)*
Pasque Flower *(Anemone pulsatilla)*
Passion Flower *(Passiflora coerulea)*
Peony *(Paeonia officinalis)*
Pig Nut *(Arachis hypogea)*
Pine *(Pinus sylvestris)*
Poppy *(Papaver sylvestris)*
Portulaca or Our Lady's Purse *(Portulaca oleracea)*
Quaking Grass *(Briza media)*
Ragwort *(Senecio jacobaea)*
Reed *(Arunda donax)*
Ribands or Our Lady's Ribbon Grass *(Phalaris)*
Rose *(Rosa,* many species and varieties)
Rosemary *(Rosmarinus officinalis)*
Rushes *(Juncus effusus)*
St. Barnaby's Thistle *(Centaurea solstitalis)*
St. Bridget's Anemone *(Anemone coronaria)*
St. George's Beard *(Sempervivum tectorum)*

St. James'-wort (*Senecio jacobaea*)
St. John's-wort (*Hypericum*)
Santa Maria (*Button Chrysanthemums*)
Shamrock or Wood Sorrel (*Oxalis acetosella*)
Silver Weed (*Potentilla anserina*)
Star of Bethlehem (*Ornithogalum umbellatum*)
Strawberry, Barren (*Potentilla sterilis*)
Strawberry, Wild (*Fragaria vesca*)
Sunflower (*Helianthus annus*)
Tansy (*Tanacetum vulgare*)
Teasel or Our Lady's Basin (*Dipsacus sylvestris*)
Vervain (*Verbena officinalis*)
Violet (*Viola odorata*)
Virgin's Bower (*Clematis vitalba*)
Woundwort (*Stachys germanica* or *S. olympica*)

SOME HERBAL TREES

Almond
Apple
Ash (*Fraxinus* species)
Birch
Cherry
Chestnut, Horse and Sweet
Citrus
Dogwood, American
Elm, Common and Slippery
   (*Ulmus fulva*)
Eucalyptus
Golden Arbor-vitae
Hawthorne

Holly
Jasmine
Juniper
Linden
Mountain-ash (*Sorbus* species)
Myrtle
Peach
Quince
Sassafras
Sourwood
Walnut
Willow

SHRUBS FOR THE HERB GARDEN

Barberry
Bayberry
Boxwood
Broom (*Cytisus*)
Carolina Allspice (*Calycanthus*)
Chaste Tree (*Vitex*
   agnus-castus)
Daphne
Eglantine or Sweet Briar
   (*Rosa eglanteria*)

Elder
Fringe Tree (*Chionanthus*)
Hydrangea
Lilac
Mountain Laurel
Medlar Tree (*Mespilus*)
Senna (*Cassia* species)
Spicebush
Viburnum
Witch Hazel

HERBS TO GROW AS HEDGES

Germander
Hyssop (keep clipped)
Rue (keep clipped)
Sage

Santolina chamaecyparissus
Thyme, Narrowleaf French
   (low)

Herbs for Ground Covers

Ajuga (bugle)
Camomile
Geranium, True *(Geranium lancastriense)*
Ground Ivy *(Nepeta hederacea)*
Pennyroyal

Periwinkle *(Vinca minor)*
Strawberry
Thyme
Woodruff, Sweet
Yarrow (creeping types)

Herbs for Low Borders

Allium senescens glaucum
Artemisia 'Silver Mound'
Cerastium (snow-in-summer)
Chives
Germander
Ivy, English
Lamb's-ears *(Stachys olympica)*
Nepeta mussini

Parsley
Pelargonium 'Apple' and 'Old Spice'
Santolina chamaecyparissus
Savory, Winter
Strawberry
Thyme

Herbs for Secondary Borders

Artemisia frigida and *A. pontica*
Hyssop
Lady's Mantle *(Alchemilla)*
Lavender
Mint, Orange
Pelargonium graveolens (rose geraniums)

Rue
Sage *(Salvia officinalis)*
Santolina, green and *Santolina tomentosum*

Herbs for Tall Accent

Artemisia abrotanum
Artemisia absinthium
Artemisia ludoviciana
Artemisia 'Silver King'
Artemisia vulgaris

Elecampane *(Inula helenium)*
Nepeta reticulata
Tansy
Teasel

Herbs to Cut for Fresh Bouquets

Agrimony
Allium
Alyssum
Artemisia
Bachelor's-button
Balm, Lemon
Basil
Bedstraw
Beebalm
Calendula

Camomile
Dill
Foxglove
Fraxinella
Geraniums, Scented
Helianthus
Hyssop
Lady's Mantle
Lamb's-ear
Lavender

Lily-of-the-Valley
Lunaria
Mint
Monarda
Nasturtium
Nepeta
Nigella
Oregano
Perilla
Pinks
Potentilla
Rosemary
Rudbeckia

Rue
Sage
Savory
Sweet Cicely
Sweet Rocket
Tansy
Tarragon
Valerian
Veronica
Woad
Woodruff, Sweet
Wormwood, Roman
Yarrow

Herbs With Fragrant Foliage

Agastache
Balm, Lemon
Basil
Borage
Burnet
Camomile
Lavender
Marjoram
Mint (orange, apple, spearmint,
    peppermint, and pineapple)
Monarda
Myrtle
Oregano

Pelargoniums, scented types
Pennyroyal
Rosemary
Sage, Pineapple
Southernwood (lemon and
    camphor)
Strawberry
Sweet Cicely
Tarragon (when dried)
Thymes (especially lemon,
    nutmeg, and 'Caprilands')
Verbena, Lemon
Woodruff, Sweet

Herbs for the Gray Garden

Achillea or Yarrow (creeping types)
Ajuga, variegated
Allium senescens glaucum
Anthemis kelwayi
Artemisia pontica, A. frigida, A. stelleriana, 'Silver Mound,' 'Silver
    King,' mugwort, and southernwood
Cerastium tomentosum
Chives 'Ruby Gem'
Geranium 'Nutmeg' and 'Southernwood'
Lavandula vera and *L. spica*
Nepeta hederacea variegata (variegated ground ivy)
Rosemary, gray-leaved variety
Rue
Sage (*Salvia officinalis* and its variety 'Tricolor')
Santolina chamaecyparissus and *S. tomentosa*
Thyme (*Thymus britannicus,* wooly, *T. glabrescens* and
    T. lanicaulis)

HERBS FOR THE BEES

Agastache
Balm, Lemon
Bergamot (*Monarda didyma*)
Borage
Dropwort (*Filipendula
  hexapetala*)
Hyssop
Lamium

Lavender
Melilot (*Melilotus* species)
Mint (*Mentha* species)
Nepetas
Rosemary
Sage (*Salvia* species)
Sweet Cicely (*Myrrhis odorata*)
Thyme

HERBS BOILED AS VEGETABLES

Borage
Chervil
Chicory
Fennel
Good-King-Henry
  (*Chenopodium
  bonus-henricus*)
Kale

Leeks
Lovage
Mustard
Orach (*Atriplex hortensis*)
Parsley
Rampion (*Phyteuma* species)
Sorrel

HERB SEEDS FOR SEASONING

Anise
Caraway
Coriander
Cumin
Dill

Fennel
Lovage
Mustard
Poppy
Sesame

HERBS FOR SUN-FILTERED SHADE

Ajuga (Bugle)
Angelica
Arenaria
Balm, Lemon
Bay, Sweet
Camphor Tree
Chervil
Cimicifuga (snakeroot)
Comfrey (*Symphytum* species)
Costmary
Ginger
Good-King-Henry
Ground Ivy
Lamium
Lily-of-the-Valley

Lovage
Lungwort
Mint
Myrtle
Oregano
Parsley
Periwinkle
Savory, Winter
Southernwood
Sweet Cicely
Verbena, Lemon
Violet
Woodruff, Sweet
Wormwood, Roman

HERBS FOR MOIST SOIL

Angelica
Lovage

Mint
Woodruff, Sweet

HERBS FOR DRY SOIL

Allium
Artemisia
Lavender

Nepeta
Santolina
Thyme

HERBAL TREES FOR TUBS

Bay, Southern *(Magnolia virginiana)*
Bay, Sweet *(Laurus nobilis)*
Camphor Tree
Citrus (Lemon and Orange)
Geranium, Lemon
Jasmine
Lavandula dentata and *L. heterophylla*

Leptospermum
Myrtle
Olive, Sweet *(Osmanthus fragrans)*
Rosemary
Sage, Pineapple
Verbena, Lemon

acorus — AK or us
abrotanum — ab ro TAY num
abrotanifolium —
    ab row tan if FOH lee um
absinthium — ab SINTH ee um
achillea — ak il LEE uh
aconitum — ak oh NYE tum
agrimonia —
    ag rim MOH nee uh
ajuga — aj YEW guh
alba — AL buh
albiflora — al bif FLOH ruh
albula — AL bew luh
album — AL bum
alchemilla — al kem MILL uh
allium — AL lee um
alyssum — al LISS um
amaranthus —
    am ah RANTH us
amomum — am MOW mum
angelica — an JELL ik uh
anethum — an NEETH um
angustifolius —
    an gus tif FOH lee us
anisum — an NIZE um
annua — ANN yew uh
anthemis — ANTH em iss
anthriscus — an THRIZ kus
archangelica —
    ark an JELL ik uh
argenteus — ar JEN tee us
artemisia — art em MIZ ee uh
arvensis — ar VEN siss
ascalonicum —
    as kah LON ik um
asperula — ass PEAR yew luh
aureus — AW ree us
azoricus — az ZOHR ik us
balsamita — ball SAM it uh
baptisia — bap TIZ ee uh
barona — ba ROH nuh
basilicum — ba SILL ik um
benzoin — BEN zoin
blandfordianum —
    bland ford ee AY num

blossfeldiana —
    bloss feld ee AY nuh
borage — BOH raj
boraginaceae —
    boh raj ih NAY see ee
borago — boh RAY go
borealis — bor ee AY liss
boswellia — boz WELL ee uh
botrys — BOT tris
brigida — BRIH gid duh
caeruleum — see REW lee um
calamintha —
    kal uh MINTH uh
calamus — KAL a mus
calendula — kal END yew luh
camphora — KAMP for uh
capitatum — kap it TAY tum
cardamom — KAR dam om
cardamomum —
    kar da MO mum
carteri — KAR ter eye
carum — KAY rum
carvi — KAR vy
caryophyllata —
    ka ree oh fill LAY tuh
cataria — ka TARE ee uh
caudatus — kau DAY tus
centaurea — sen TAW ree uh
centaureus — sen TAW ree us
cepa — SEE pa
cerefolium —
    sir eh FOH lee um
cernuum — SER new um
chaenostoma —
    kee NOSS tom uh
chamaecyparissus —
    kam ee sip ar ISS us
chamaedrys — kam MEE driss
chenopodiaceae —
    ken o po di A see ee
chenopodium —
    kee noh POH dee um
chinensis — chin NEN sis
chrysanthemum —
    kriss ANTH em um

cimicinus — sim ee SIGH nuss
cinnamonium —
  sin am MOH nee um
cissus — SIS sus
citrata — sit RAY tah
citratus — sit RAY tus
citriodora — sit ree oh DOH ruh
citronella — sit row NELL uh
coccineus — kok SIN ee us
commiphora —
  kom MIFF oh ruh
communis — kom MEW niss
compositae — kom POZ i tee
conglomerata —
  kon glom er RAY tuh
coriandrum —
  koh ree AN drum
crispum — KRIS pum
cyaneum — sigh AY nee um
cyanus — sigh AN us
cymbopogon —
  sim boh POH gon
cytisus — SIT iss us
damascena — dam ass SEE nuh
daphne — DAFF nee
delphinium — del FIN ee um
dentata — den TAY tuh
denticulatum —
  den tik yew LAY tum
dictamnus — dik TAM nus
didyma — DID e muh
dipterix — DIP ter iks
domesticum —
  dom MESS tik um
dracunculus —
  dray KUNK yew lus
dulce — DUL see
echinatum — ek in NAY tum
elettaria — el et TAY ree uh
eugenia — yew JEEN ee uh
euonymus — yew ON ih mus
eupatoria —
  yew pat TOH ree uh
fastigiatum — fas tij ji A tum
filifolia — fill eh FOH lee uh
filicifolium —
  fil iss if FOH lee um
filipendulina —
  fill eh pen dew LIE nuh
fischeri — FISH er eye
fistulosum — fiss tew LOH sum
flavum — FLAY vum

florentina — floh ren TEE nuh
foeniculum — fee NIK yew lum
fluminensis — floo min EN siss
fragrans — FRAY granz
fragrantissimus —
  fray gran TISS eh mus
frigida — FRIJ ih duh
galeobdolon —
  gay lee OB doh lon
galium — GAY lee um
gentilis — JEN till iss
germanica — jer MAN ih kuh
giganteum — jye GAN tee um
glabra — GLAY bruh
glacealis — glay see A lis
glaucum — GLAW kum
globosa — globe OH suh
glutinosum —
  glew tin NOH sum
gomphrena — gom FREE nuh
grandiflora —
  gran dif FLOH ruh
graveolens — grav VEE ol enz
grossularioides —
  gross yew lar ee OI deez
gymnocarpa — jim no KAR pa
heliotropium —
  he lee oh TROH pee um
hortensis — hor TEN sis
hyssopus — HISS op us
ilex — EYE lex
iris — EYE riss
isatis — EYE sa tiss
japonicus — jap PON ih kus
juniper — JEW nip er
kalmia — KAL mee uh
karataviense —
  kar uh TAV ee en see
labiatae — lay bee AY tee ee
lactiflora — lack teh FLOH ruh
lamium — LAY mee um
lanata — lan NAY tuh
lanicaulis — lan ee KAW liss
lanuginosus —
  lan new jin NOH sus
latiflora — lat if FLOH ruh
laurus — LAW rus
lavandula — la VAN dew la
levisticum — lev VIST ik um
liliaceae — lil ee AY see ee
limoneum — lim MOH nee um
linum — LYE num

lippia — LIP ee uh
logeei — low GEE ee
longifolia — lon jif FOH lee ah
lucidum — LEW sid um
ludoviciana —
lew doh vih see AY nah
maculatum —
mak yew LAY tum
majorana — maj or RAY nuh
majus — MAY jus
maritima — ma RIT ih mah
marrubium — mar ROO bee um
marschallianus —
mar shall ee A nus
matricaria —
mat rik KAY ree uh
melissa — meh LISS uh
mezereum — meh ZEER ee um
microphyllus —
mye kroh FILL us
millefolium —
mil ef FOH lee um
minor — MYE nor
monarda — mon NARD uh
montana — mon TAY nah
multifida — mull TIF eye duh
mussini — mus SEEN ee
myrrha — MER uh
myrrhis — MER iss
myrtus — MERT us
nana — NAY nuh
napellus — nap PELL us
neapolitanum —
nee a pol ih TAY num
nepeta — NEP eh tah
nervosum — ner VOH sum
niliaca — nye lee A kuh
nobilis — NOH bil iss
nuda — NEW duh
nummularius —
num yew LAR ee us
ocimum — OSS i mum
odorata — oh dor RAY tah
odoratissimum —
oh doh rah TISS ih mum
officinalis — off iss in NAY liss
olympica — oh LIM pic kuh
onites — oh NYE teez
origanum — or RIG an um
parthenium —
par THEEN ee um

pelargonium —
pel are GOH nee um
peltatum — pel TAY tum
perenne — per REN ee
perilla — per ILL uh
petroselinum —
pet row sell EYE num
pimpinella — pim pin NELL uh
pinnata — pin NAY tuh
pinnatifida —
pin na TIFF ih duh
piperita — pie per EE tuh
pontica — PONT ik uh
porrum — POR rum
prostratum — pross TRAY tum
ptarmica — TAR mik uh
pulchellum — pull CHELL um
pulegium — pool EE jee um
pumila — PEW mil uh
punctata — punk TAY tuh
purpurascens —
pur pur RASS senz
quercifolium —
queer ci FOH lee um
ramosum — ram MOH sum
ranunculaceae —
ruh nun kew LAY see ee
reptans — REPP tanz
requieni — reck qwee EN eye
reticulata — ret ik yew LAY tuh
rhombifolia —
rom bif FOH lee uh
rosa — ROH zuh
rosaceae — roh ZAY see ee
roseum — ROH zee um
rosmarinus —
rose muh RYE nus
rotundifolia —
roh tun dif FOH lee uh
rugosa — roo GOH suh
rumex — ROO mex
ruta — ROO tah
rutilans — ROO tih lanz
salvia — SAL vee uh
sanctum — SANK tum
sanguisorba —
san gwis SORB uh
santolina — san toh LYE nuh
sativum — sat TYE vum
sativus — sat TYE vus
satureja — sat tour EE uh

scabrum — SKAY brum
schmidtiana —
   schmitt ee AY nuh
schoenoprasum —
   skee noh PRAY sum
scoparius — skoh PAY ree us
scorodoprasum —
   skor roh doh PRAY sum
scutatus — skew TAY tus
senescens — sen ES senz
serpyllum — ser PILL lum
sinensis — sin NEN siss
sinuata — sin you A tuh
spica — SPY ka
spicata — spy KAY tuh
stachys — STAY kiss
stelleriana — stell er ee A nuh
stoechas — STEE kuss
striata — stry A tuh
styrax — STY racks
sylvestris — sil VESS triss
tagetes — ta JEE teez
tanacetum — tan uh SEE tum
teucrium — TEW kree um
thea — THEE uh
thermopsis — ther MOP sis
thymus — TIE mus
tinctoria — tink TOH ree uh

tomentosum —
   toh men TOH sum
tradescantia —
   trad es KANT ee uh
tricolor — TRY color
tridentata — try den TAY tuh
tuberosum — too ber ROH sum
umbelliferae —
   um bel LIF fer ee
usitatissimum —
   yew sit ah TISS im um
valeriana — val eer ee AY nuh
variegata — vay ree ee GAY tuh
vera — VER ruh
verbenaceae —
   ver be NAY see ee
veronica — ver RON ik uh
verum — VEHR um
vetiveria — vet ih VEER ee uh
vinca — VIN kuh
viola — VYE oh lah
viridis — VIHR id iss
viviparum — vye VIP ar um
vulgare — vul GAIR ee
vulgaris — vul GAY riss
webbiana — web ee A nuh
wilsoni — WILL son eye
zeylanicum — zee LAN ik um
zizanioides — zi zan ih OI deez

337

Index

[*Italic numbers refer to illustrations*]

Achillea filipendulina, 134, 225
  f. 'Gold Plate,' 225
  main discussion of, 224-225
  millefolium, 224-225
  m. rosea, 225
  nana, 225
  ptarmica, 225
  'The Pearl,' 225
  tomentosa, 225
  t. webbiana, 225
Aconite, 227
Aconitum fischeri, 227
  f. wilsoni, 227
  main discussion of, 226-227
  napellus, 227
  n. bicolor, 227
  n. 'Sparks,' 227
Acorus calamus, 182
Advent wreath, 196, *197,* 198
African baby's-breath, 19, 22, 150
  culture indoors, 22
  under fluorescent light, 19
Agastache, 10
Agrimonia eupatoria, main discussion of, 228-229
Agrimony, 7, 228-229
Ajuga reptans, 230-231
  r. alba, 231
  r. variegata, 231
Alchemilla vulgaris, 91-92
Alcohol rub, rose-scented, 42
Alehost, 255
Alkaline soil for herbs, 56
"All-heal," 210

Allium cepa ascalonicum, 232-233
  c. viviparum, 234-235
  ornamental kinds, 115
  sativum, 236-237
  schoenoprasum, 238-239
  s. 'Ruby Gem,' 239
  scorodoprasum, 237
  senescens, 57
  tuberosum, 239
Allspice, 182
Alyssum, basket-of-gold, 80
  muralis, 65
Amaranth, 194
Amaranthus caudatus, 126
Amaryllis, 20
Ambergris, 185
Ambrosia, 61, 126-127, 165, 198, 252-253
  main discussion of, 253
  sowing seeds, 61
Amomum cardamon, 23, 150
Anchovy spread with tarragon, 83
Anderson, Dr. Edgar, 104
Anethum graveolens, main discussion of, 240-241
Angelica, 7, 56, 62, 127, 242-243
  archangelica, 242-243
  main discussion of, 243
  propagation, 62
  tea, 48
  toleration of lime in soil, 56
Angel cake with rose geranium jelly, 41

Anise, 7, 103, 139, 173, 181, 296-297
  bread recipe, 139
  main discussion of, 297
  tea, 48
  with roast pork, 173
Anthemis nobilis, 48, 129, 244-245
  main discussion of, 245
Anthriscus cerefolium, main discussion of, 246-247
Apple mint, 7
Armillary dial, 4
Artemisia, 10-11, 62, 99, *122,* 127-128, 168, *195*
  abrotanum, 31, *155,* 160
  a. camphorata, 128, 162
  a. limoneum, 162
  absinthium, 38, 57, 128, 154, *155*-157
  annua, 153
  borealis, 160
  camphor-scented, *59,* 160, 162-163
  Christmas trees, 127, 165-166
  dracunculus sativus, 152, *155,* 164
  frigida, 57, 156
  giant, 17
  glacialis, 160
  harvesting, 127-128
  herba alba, 158
  in door swag, *208*
  judaica, 158
  lactiflora, 153
  laxa, 160
  lemon-scented, 160, 162
  ludoviciana, 57, 163
  l. albula, 127, 145, *155,* 163
  maritima, 159
  pontica, 145, 156, 159
  propagation, 62
  purshiana, 163-164

  schmidtiana nana, 158, 163-164
  'Silver King,' 7, *59,* 127, 146, *155,* 163, 165-166
  'Silver Mound,' 10, *57, 65, 93,* 146, 158, 163-164
  stelleriana, 156, 159-160
  swags, 166-167
  tangerine-scented, *65,* 145, 160, 163
  tridentata, 163-164
  vulgaris, 152-*155*
  wreath, everlasting, of, 198-199
Artemisias, 55, 150, 152-167
  decorative types, 163-164
Artichoke, Jerusalem, 17
Asperula odorata, 78-79
Attar of roses, 186-187

Baby's-breath, 166
  African, 19, 22, 150
Bachelor's-button, 20, 60, 128, 181
  sowing seeds, 60
Baptisia, 6, 128
Barbecue, herb garden for, 6-9
Basil, 6-7, 9, 11, 19-22, 60-61, *81,* 120, 123, 128, 168, 176, 181, *290*-291
  container for, 21
  culture indoors, 22
  'Dark Opal,' 19, 22, 291
  harvesting, 123
  in container garden, 22
  in home greenhouse, 20
  lettuceleaf, 291
  sowing seeds, 60-61
  under fluorescent light, 19
  when to cut, 120
Basket-of-gold alyssum, 80
Bay, sweet, 11, 19, 25-26, *59,* 151, 181, *195, 268*-269

culture indoors, 25-26
main discussion of, 269
under fluorescent light, 19
Bean, green, casserole, 140
Bedstraw, 57, 124
  pressing, 124
Beebalm, 6-7
Beer and caraway spread, 171
Begonia, wax, 20
Benches for herb garden, 17
"Benjamin," 185
Benzoin, 185-186
Bergamot, 93, 112, 285
  main discussion of, 285
  wild, 17
Betony, 315
Bible leaf, 146, 255
Biblical garden, 9
Birdbath, 4
Biscuits, cheese tea, 222
  rose geranium tea, 41
Bishop's bread, 218
Bishop's wine, 216
Bishop's-wort, 315
Borage, 9, 20, 22, 81, 97, 137,
    248-249
  culture indoors, 22
  feeding, 97
  in home greenhouse, 20
  in June wine recipe, 137
  main discussion of, 249
Borago officinalis, main dis-
    cussion of, 248-249
Boswellia carteri, 183
Boxes, for herbs, 20-21
Boxwood, 2, 6
  dwarf, 6
Bread, anise, 139
Bride's button, 257
Brigham, Dorcas, 36
Broccoli casserole, 86
Broom, 6, 129
Broomcorn, 129
Bugleweed, 231
Burnet, salad, 7, 9, 11, 22, 62,
    84, 306-307

in container garden, 22
in spring-green spread, 84
main discussion of, 307
sowing seeds, 62
Butterfly garden, 4, 5-7, 93,
    104
Butternut tree, 93

Cabbage, Chinese, 9
Cake, angel, with rose gera-
    nium jelly, 41
  rose geranium pudding, 41
  sponge, with geranium fla-
    vor, 41
Calamintha, 112
Calamus root, 182
Calendula, 7, 20, 60-61, 81,
    92-94, 118, 146, 181
  officinalis, 20, 48, 146
  sowing seeds, 60-61
  tea, 48
Camomile, 7, 80, 129
  English, 245
  tea, 48
Camphor tree, 22, 150
  culture indoors, 22-23
Canapes, pickles and peanut,
    83
Caprilands cheese rolls, 171
  Chile bean pot, 173
  Christmas dip, 217
  favorite green salad, 142
  herb dressing, 143
  petite pâté, 217
  potpourri, 188
  tea, 48
Captain Paul House, 153, 167
Caraway, 58, 60, 123, 251
  harvesting, 123
  main discussion of, 251
  sowing seeds, 58, 60
Cardamom, 19, 23, 150, 175,
    195
  bread, 219
  culture indoors, 23
  under fluorescent light, 19

Carpenter's herb, 231
Carum carvi, main discussion
    of, 250-251
Casserole, Caprilands sweet
    potato, 174
    green bean, 140
Catnip, 20, 23, *59*, 62, *81*,
    129, *288*-289
    culture indoors, 23
    in home greenhouse, 20
    main discussion of, 289
    sowing seeds, 62
    tea, 49
Cedar, 178
Centaurea, 20, 128
    cyanus, 20, 128
    gymnocarpa, 20
Chaenostoma fastigiatum, 22,
    150
Chard, Swiss, 9
Cheese and olive logs, 216
Cheese rolls, 171
    sauce, 140
    tea biscuits, 222
Chenopodium botrys. main
    discussion of, 252-253
Chervil, 7, 11, 60, 120, 122,
    247
    how to dry, 122
    sowing seeds, 60
    when to cut, 120
Chicory, 9
Chile bean pot, 173
Chinese cabbage, 9
    in Caprilands salad, 142
Chinese chives, 239
Chives, 6-9, 11, 16-17, 19, 21-
    23, 60, 62, *81*, 123,
    239
    culture indoors, 23
    garlic, 7, 9, 22, 239
    harvesting leaves, 123
    in container garden, 22
    in culinary box, 21-22
    sowing seeds, 60, 62
    under fluorescent light, 19

Christmas confetti casserole,
    220
    legends and recipes, 207-
    222
Chrysanthemum, 20, 48, 129,
    146, 254-256-257
    balsamita, 146
    b. tanacetoides, 254-255
    parthenium, 20, 48, 129,
    256-257
Cineraria, 20
Cinnamomum camphora, 22,
    150
    zeylanicum, 182
Cinnamon bark/sticks, 182,
    195
Cissus rhombifolia, 40
Civet, 185
Claret bowl, the, 137
Clary sage, 6
Clematis virginiana, 55
Cloves, 182
Cobbler's bench, 267
Coleus, 20
Comfrey, *122*
Commiphora myrrha, 183
Cookies, brown autumn, 175
    rose, jelly-filled, 143
    sugared rose, 144
Coriander, 7, 58, 60, 123,
    175, 181, 258-259
    harvesting, 123
    sowing seeds, 58, 60
Coriandrum sativum, main
    discussion of, 258-
    259
Corn, Indian, 166
Costmary, 7, 124, 146, 255
    main discussion of, 255
    pressing leaves, 124
    tea, 48
Coumarin, 80
Cranesbill, 13
Crocus, 80, 84
    sativus, 84
Cumin, harvesting, 123

Curtin, L. M. S., 111, 158
Cyclamen, 20
Cytisus scoparius, 129

Daffodil, 181, 194
Delphinium, 129-130, 181
    drying flowers, 129-130
Dill, 9, 23, 61, *81*, 97, 123,
        141, 166, *240-241*
    butter sauce, 141
    culture indoors, 23
    feeding, 97
    harvesting, 123
    sowing seeds, 61
    sticks (recipe), 84
Dipterix odorata, 186
Dittany of Crete, 23, 150
    culture indoors, 23
Dock, for arrangements, 130
Dooryard garden, 7, *8*, 9
    at Caprilands, 55, 57
Dressing, Caprilands herb,
        143
Drying herbs, 120-134
Drying shed at Caprilands,
        122
Dry soil, herbs for, 333
Dusty miller, 20

Early American herbs, 325-
        326
Egyptian onion, 235
Elder, 166
Elettaria cardamomum, 23
English ivy, 40, 196
    small-leaved, 196
Entryway garden at Capri-
        lands, *59*
Eugenia caryophyllata, 182
*Euonymus japonicus micro-
        phyllus*, 196
Euphorbia marginata, 146

Feather geranium, 253
Feeding herbs, 97
Fennel, 20, 62, *81*, 123, 260-
        261

bronze, 9
    harvesting, 123
    in home greenhouse, 20
    main discussion of, 261
    sowing seeds, 62
Fertilizing herbs, 97
Feverfew, 20, 257
    main discussion, 257
Finocchio, 261
Fixatives to hold flower fra-
        grances, 185
Flax, 130, 274-275
    main discussion of, 275
"Flea-away," 109
Flowers for the herb garden,
        326-327
Fluorescent lights, 19
Foeniculum vulgare, 260-261
    v. dulce, 261
    v. piperitum, 261
Forsythia, 181
Fragrance, capturing, 179
Fragrant foilage, herbs with,
        331
    leaves, 181
    petals, 181
    seeds, 181
Fraise des bois, 7, 52
Frankincense, 182-183
Freesia, 20
Furniture for the herb gar-
        den, 17

Galium verum, 262-263
Garlic, 6, 236-237
    giant, 237
Garlic chives, 7, 9, 22, 239
Geranium, 'Apple,' 22, 27,
        30, 35, 39, 94
    'Apricot,' 36
    'Attar of Roses,' 30-31
    'Camphor Rose,' 33
    climbing, 36
    'Cocoanut,' 34
    fernleaf, 32
    filbert-scented, 36

fingerbowl, 31
'Gooseberry-leaved,' 31
ivy, 'Sunset,' 39
lemon, 22, 27, 29, *30*, 31, 94, 181
'Lime-scented,' 34
'Little Leaf Rose,' 33
'Nutmeg,' 22, 27, 32, 35, 39-40
oakleaf, 27, 35-36
'Old Spice,' 35, 40
peppermint, 22, 27, 29-*30*, 39, 94, 181
perennial, 13
'Pheasant's Foot,' 32
pressing leaves, 124
'Rober's Lemon Rose,' 29, 33, 39
rose, 21-22, 27, 31, 39, 40, 94, 181
 in culinary box, 21-22
 jelly, 40
 sugar, 40
skelton-leaf rose, 32
'Southernwood-leaved,' 29
strawberry, *30*
'Sunset' ivy, 39
trailing, 13, 39
'Variegated   Mint-scented Rose,' 33
variegated rose, 33
zonal, 181
Geraniums, feeding window boxes of, 97
 for hanging baskets, 39
 garden of, 13, *14*, 15
 in home greenhouse, 19
 in window boxes, 37
 scented, 19, 27-42, *38*
Germander, 2, 6, 11, 15, 53, 62, *93*, 148, 150, 193, *318*-319
 main discussion of, 319
 propagation, 62
 winter protection, 148, 150
Gingerbread for canapes, 171

fruit, with coriander, 172
 Pain d'Epice, 218-219
Globe amaranth, 130, 196
Gnaphalium   obtusifolium, 166, 198
Goldes, 93-94
Gomphrena globosa, 130, 196
Grape ivy, 40
Gray garden, herbs for, 331-332
Green bean casserole, 140
Greenhouse, home, 19-20
 list of herbs for, 20
Green sauce for meat, 141

Harvesting herbs, 120-134
Harvest party, 168-176
Heart's-ease, 323
Heather, *98*
Hedge rose, 166
Hedges, herbs to grow as, 329-330
Helianthemum, 17
Helichrysum, 132
Heliotrope, fragrant, 150
 garden, *320*-321
Heliotropium   arborescens, 150
Helmet flower, 227
Henbane, 194
Herbal trees, 329
 for tubs, 333
Herb and cheese topping, 87
Herb and honey salad dressing, 143
Herb garden, mulching the, 96-97
Herb names, how to pronounce, 334-337
Herb seeds for seasoning, 332
Herb show, plans for, 114-119
Herb Society of America, 116
Herbs, as house plants, 18-26
 feeding, 97
 for a meditation garden,

327-329
for drying, 9-11
for dry soil, 333
for low borders, 330
for moist soil, 332
for secondary borders, 330
for sun-filtered shade, 332
for tall accent, 330
for the gray garden, 331-332
pest control, 99
planting a garden of, 54-63
to cut for fresh bouquets, 330-331
to grow as hedges, 329-330
weeding, 98-99
when to water, 95-96
with fragrant foliage, 331
Hoc sirpillum, 66
Hollyhock, 17
Holly tea, 48
Horehound, 23, 53, 62, 123, 193-194, 196, *280-281*
culture indoors, 23
harvesting, 123
main discussion of, 281
sowing seeds, 62
Horsemint, 112
Hyssop, 6-7, 10-11, 60, 62, 146, 264-265
main discussion of, 265
sowing seeds, 60, 62
Hyssopus officinalis, 264-265

Ilex paraguariensis, 48
Indian corn, 166
Iris florentina, 185
germanica, 185
Japanese, 130
Isatis tinctoria, 134

Japanese iris, 130
Jelly, rose geranium, 40
Jelly-filled rose cookies, 143
Jerusalem artichoke, 17
Jerusalem oak, 253

Johnny-jump-up, 6, 80, 83, 146, 323
Juniper, *93,* 178, 196, 207-210
plant of sanctuary, the legends, 207-210
pyramidal, 178
Savin, 196
Juniperus communis, 209

Kale, in Caprilands salad, 142
Kalmia latifolia, 269
Kissing ball, how to make, 211-212
Kitchen garden at Caprilands, *81*
Knot garden, 15

Lady's mantle, 6, 13, *91-92*
Lamb's-ears, 11, 124, 130, 145, 193-194, *314-315*
main discussion of, 315
pressing leaves, 124
wassail bowl, 215
Lamium album, 267
maculatum, 266-267
Larkspur, 136
Larson, Esther, garden of, *98,* 153
Laurus nobilis, 151, 194, *268-269*
main discussion of, 269
Lavandula, 23-24
dentata, 24, 150
heterophylla, 24
multifida, 24, 150
officinalis, 23, 270-271
spica, from seeds, 63
stoechas, 24, 150
vera, from seeds, 63
Lavender, 6, 11, 13, 15, 19, 23-24, 53, 56, *59-60,* 62-63, *93-94,* 131, 146, 149-150, 181, 193-194, 196, 270-271

culture indoors, 23-24
fernleaf, 24, 150
French, 150
fringed, 150
main discussion of, 271
need for lime in soil, 56
potpourri, 189
sowing seeds, 60, 62-63
under fluorescent light, 19
winter protection, 149-150
Lavender-cotton, 146, *308-309*
Lemon balm, 6, 9, 11, 19-20, 22, 24, 34, 62, 123, 137-138, 150, 181, 282-283
  culture indoors, 24
  harvesting, 123
  in container garden, 22
  in home greenhouse, 20
  in punch recipe, 137-138
  main discussion of, 283
  sowing seeds, 62
  tea, 48
  under fluorescent light, 19
Lemon verbena, 6-7, 11, 19-20, 22, 24, *38*, 97, 122, 150, 276-277
  culture indoors, 24
  feeding, 97
  how to dry leaves, 122
  in container garden, 22
  in home greenhouse, 20
  jar, 189
  tea, 48
  under fluorescent light, 19
Lettuce, in Caprilands salad, 142
  oakleaf, 9
Levisticum officinale, 272-273
Limonium sinuatum, 132
  vulgare, 132
Linum perenne, 275
  usitatissimum, 275
Lippia citriodora, 150, 276-

277
Logee, Ernest, 35
Logee's North Street Greenhouses, 34
Lovage, 6-7, 9, 56, 62, *81*, 122, 131, 272-273
  how to dry, 122
  main discussion of, 273
  sowing seeds, 62
  toleration of lime in soil, 56

Magnolia glauca, 269
Majorana hortensis, 151, 278-279
Manzanilla, 245
Marigold, 92, 118, 146
  lemon-scented, 138
  Scotch, 138
Marjoram, sweet, 6-7, 19-22, 26, 60-62, *81*, 120, 123, 151, 176, 181, 278-279
  culture indoors, 26
  harvesting, 123
  in culinary box, 21-22
  in home greenhouse, 20
  sowing seeds, 60-62
    under fluorescent light, 19
  when to cut, 120
Marrubium vulgare, 280-281
Mary garden, 9
Mary's gold, 92
Mary's mantle, 91
Maté, 46
May Day party, 78-89
Meditation garden, herbs for, 327-329
Melissa officinalis, 34, 282-283
  punch bowl, 137-138
Mentha arvensis, 106
  citrata, 106-*107*
  gentilis, 108
  in mythology, 104

niliaca, 108
piperita, 48, *107*-108
pulegium, *107*, 109, 150
requieni, 109
rotundifolia, *107*, 110
r. variegata, *107*, 110
spicata, 103, *107*, 111
s. longifolia, 111
sylvestris, 111
viridis, 111
Methoxychlor, 99
Michaelmas daisy, 170
Midsummer party, 135-144
Mignonette, 11
Milfoil, 225
Mint, 6, 13, 19-20, 24, 56, 62, *81*, 93-94, 101-113, 123, 146, 150, 168
apple, 7, 24, *107*, 110, *122*
culture indoors, 24
bergamot, 106
brandy, 108
Corsican, 24, 109
culture indoors, 24
curly, 24, *38*, 94, 108
culture indoors, 24
Egyptian, 108
golden apple, 108
harvesting, 123
history of, 102
horse, 112
in home greenhouse, 20
nomenclature, 104-106
orange, 7, 9, 11, 24, 94, 102, 106-*107*, 138
cooler (summer drink), 138
culture indoors, 24
recipe for punch, 106
pineapple, 7, 11, 21, 24, *107*, 110, 139
cooler (summer drink), 139
culture indoors, 24
in culinary box, 21
potpourri, 190

propagation, 62, 104
rust disease, 99
silver, 24
culture indoors, 24
soil for, 56
sowing seeds, 62
tea, 47, 49
under fluorescent light, 19
wooly, 24, 112
culture indoors, 24
Mistletoe, the story of, 210-211
Moist soil, herbs for, 332
Moldenke, Harold N., 157-158
Monarda, 112
didyma, 50, 284-285
main discussion of, 285
punctata, 112
spotted, 112
Monkshood, 227
Morning glory, 91
Mother-of-thyme, 69-70, 146
Mugwort, 136, 152-154, *155*, 166
sweet, 153
Mulching the herb garden, 96-97
Mullein, 17, 124, 131
pressing leaves, 124
Musk, 185
Myrrh, 122, 182-184
how to dry, 122
in potpourri, 182-184
Myrrhis odorata, 286-287
Myrtle, 80, 194, 196
Myrtus communis, 196

Nasturtium, 20, *81*
Nepeta cataria, 288-289
grandiflora, 289
macrantha, 289
mussini, 289
nuda, 289
reticulata, 289
'Six Hills Giant,' 289

Nettle, white dead, 267
Nutmegs, *195*

Oak, 194
Ocimum basilicum, 290-291
   b. 'Bush,' 291
   b. 'Dark Opal,' 291
   b. minimum, 291
   crispum, 291
Olive, 194
Onion, Egyptian (perennial or top), 6-7, 9, 11, *81, 93,* 235
Orach, red, 131
Orange blossoms, 194
Orange mint, 7, 9, 11, 181
Oregano, 1, 7, 17, 21, *81,* 123, 131, 165, 181, 198, 292-293
   harvesting, 123
   in culinary box, 21
   main discussion of, 293
Origanum dictamnus, 150
   majorana, 279
   vulgare, 66, 292-293
Orris root, 182, 185
Oswego tea, 50, 285
Our Lady's basin, 92
Our Lady's bedstrawn, 196, 263

Pain d'Epice, 218-219
Palm, 194
Pansy, 181
Parsley, 6-9, 11, 19-21, 25, 60-61, 122, 194, *294-295*
   beaked or French, 247
   culture indoors, 25
   curly, 21, 295
   from seed, 25
   how to dry, 122
   in culinary box, 21
   in home greenhouse, 20
   Italian curly, 7, 9, 11, *81,* 295

plainleaf, 9
sowing seeds, 60-61
under fluorescent light, 19
Patchouli, 184
Pears in port wine, 174-175
Pelargonium, 13, 22, 28, 29
   abrotanifolium, 29
   'Attar of Roses,' 31
   blandfordianum, 31
   capitatum, 29, 30, 31
   'Clorinda,' *30,* 31, 39
   'Concolor Lace,' 39
   crispum, 29, 31
   c. 'Gooseberry-leaved,' 31
   c. minor, 31
   c. 'Prince Rupert,' *30,* 32
   c. 'Prince Rupert Variegated,' 32
   denticulatum, 32
   domesticum, 31
   'Dr. Livingston,' *30,* 32
   echinatum, 31
   filicifolium, 32
   fragrans 'Nutmeg,' 32, 39, 40
   glutinosum, 32
   graveolens, 31, 33, 34, 39-40, 46
   g. camphoratum, 33
   g. 'Gray Lady Plymouth,' 33
   g. 'Lady Plymouth,' 33
   g. 'Little Gem,' 33
   g. minor, 33
   g. 'Rober's Lemon Rose,' 33, 39, 46
   g. 'Variegated Mint-scented Rose,' 33
   grossularioides 'Cocoanut,' 34
   'Joy Lucille,' 34, 40
   limoneum 'Lady Mary,' 34
   l. 'Lemon,' 34
   'Little Leaf Rose,' 33
   'Logee,' 35

logeei, 35
melissinum 'Lemon Balm,' 34, 40
'Mrs. Kingsley,' 34
nervosum 'Lime-scented,' 34
odoratissimum, 29-30
o. 'Apple,' 35, 39
'Old Scarlet Unique,' 35
'Old Spice,' 35, 40
peltatum, 13
'Prince of Orange,' 35
quercifolium, 31
q. 'Beauty,' 35, 40
q. 'Fair Ellen,' 35, 39
q. giganteum, 'Giant Oak,' 35
q. pinnatifidum 'Sharp-toothed Oak,' 35, 39
q. prostratum 'Prostrate Oak,' 35
q. 'Skelton's Unique,' 36, 39-40
q. 'Staghorn Oak,' *30*
q. 'Village Hill Hybrid,' 36, 39
'Rollison's Unique,' 36, 39-40
roseum, 29
'Roundleaf Rose Variegated,' 36
scabrum 'Apricot,' 36
scarborviae, 30
'Scarlet Unique,' 39
'Shottesham Pet,' 36, 39
'Shrubland Rose,' 36
'Skeleton Rose,' *30*
'Snowflake,' 36, 39
tomentosum, 22, 29, *30*, 34, 40
torento 'Ginger,' 37, 39
Pennyroyal, 7, 61-62, 103, *107*, 109, 124, 150, 178, 196
pressing, 124
sowing seeds, 61-62

Peppermint, 7, 9, 11, 24, *107*-108, 181
culture indoors, 24
Perilla, 1, *38*, 131
Periwinkle, 196
variegated, 40
Petroselinum crispum, 294-295
Pillow, scented, how to make, 192
Pimenta officinalis, 182
Pimpinella anisum, 296-297
Pine, 178
cones, 166, 198, *208*
Pineapple mint, 7, 11
Pineapple sage, 6-7
Pinks, 181
Plans for herb gardens, 3-17
Plants of the Bible, 157
Pogostemon cablin, 184
Pomander balls, how to make, 201-206
Christmas tree of, 205-206
Pomanders, *197*
history of, 202-204
Poplar, 194
Poppy, 194
Pork roast with anise, 173-174
Pot-herbs, see herbs boiled as vegetables, 332
Pot-marigold, 20, 118, 146
Potpourri, oils essential for, 186-187
recipes for, 188-192
when to make, 187
Pots, for herbs, 20-21
Propagation, herbs from seeds, 58
Punch, autumn red wine, 170
Punch bowl for St. Michael's Day, 170
Punch bowl, Melissa, 137-138
Punch, orange mint, 138
Punch, pineapple mint, 139

Recipes for autumn, 169-176
Red orach, 131
Rocambole, 237
Rosa chinensis, 166
  damascena, 187
  rugosa, 50
Rose geranium jar, 190
  pudding cake, 41
  sugar, 144
  tea, 46
  tea biscuits, 41
Rose hips, 122, 166
  tea of, 46, 50
Rose jar, 191
Rosemary, 7, 9, 11, 19, 21-
  22, 25, 59-60, 62, 81,
  93-95, 103, 122-124,
  150, 178, 181, 193-
  194, 195-196, 298-299
  culture indoors, 25
  how to dry, 122-123
  in culinary box, 21-22
  potted, 59
  pressing, 124
  propagation, 62
  prostrate, 6
  sowing seeds, 60, 62
  tea, 51
  under fluorescent light, 19
  when to water, 95
Rose oil, 182
Roses, 181
  old, 98
Rosmarinus officinalis, 150,
  298-299
Rotenone, 99
Ruddes, 93
Rue, 2, 6-7, 10-11, 60, 62, 93,
  132, 146, 150, 162,
  166, 193-194, 196,
  198, 302-303
  for accent, 10
  main discussion of, 303
  sowing seeds, 60, 62
Rumex scutatus, 300-301
Rust, of mint, cause, 99

Ruta graveolens, 302-303

Sachet, how to make, 192
Saffron buns, 84
  rice (recipe), 87
Sage, 2, 6-7, 9-10, 13, 15, 19-
  20, 22, 25, 59, 62, 81,
  93, 123, 146, 168,
  193, 196, 304-305
  culture indoors, 25
  harvesting leaves, 123
  in container garden, 22
  in home greenhouse, 20
  pineapple, 6-7, 25, 151,
  176
    culture indoors, 25
  silver, 159
  sowing seeds, 62
  tea, 51
  'Tricolor,' 25, 151, 194
  under fluorescent light, 19
  variegated, 13, 25, 194
Sagebrush, 164
Saint Fiacre, 2
  statue of, 4, 6, 92-93
Saint Francis, terra-cotta figure of, 11, 39
Saint John's herb, 136, 154
Saint John's-wort, 132, 198
Saint Michael's Day, 168
Saint Nicholas Day at Caprilands, 212-214
Saints Garden, 2, 54, 91
Salad burnet, 306-307
Salad, Caprilands favorite
  green, 142
Salad dressing, herb and
  honey, 143
Salmon puff, 141
Salt hay, 2, 148
Salvia, blue, 181
  officinalis, 51, 304-305
  o. 'Tricolor,' 151
  purpurascens, 194
  rutilans, 25, 151
Sandalwood, 184

Sanguisorba minor, 306-307
Santalum album, 184
Santolina, 2, 53, 56-57, 62,
    65, *93*, 145-146, 148,
    150, 193
  chamaecyparissus, 194,
    308-309
  gray, 6, 15, 194
  green, 6, 13, 15, 194
  need for lime in soil, 56
  propagation, 62
  viridis, 93, 309
  winter protection, 148, 150
Sassafras tea, 51
Satureja calamintha, 113
  hortensis, *310*-311
  montana, *312*-313
  m. pygmaea, 313
  nepeta, 112
Savory, *93*, 120, 123, 168
  harvesting, 123
  when to cut, 120
  summer, 6-7, 9, 60-61, *81*,
    310-311
    main discussion of, 311
    sowing seeds, 60-61
  winter, 6-7, 9, 11, 21, 26,
    62, *81*, 193, *312*-313
    culture indoors, 26
    in culinary box, 21
    main discussion of, 313
    sowing seeds, 62
Seeds, herbs from, 58
Sesame cookies, 88-89
Shallots, 132, 233
Shrubs for the herb garden,
    329
Snapdragon, 20
Sneezewort, 225
Snow-on-the-mountain, 146
Soil, how to prepare for plant-
    ing, 54
  pH for herbs, 56
Sorrel, 6, 11, 21, 85-86, 132
  French, 7, 9, *300*-301
  in culinary box, 21

soup (recipe), 85-86
Soup, summer squash, 139
Southernwood, 1, 6, *59*, *93*,
    152, *155*, 160, *161*-
    163
  camphor-scented, 13, 146,
    160, 162-163
  lemon-scented, 160, 162
  tangerine-scented, 145,
    160, 163
Spearmint, 7-9, 11, 24, *107*,
    111
  culture indoors, 24
Speedwell tea, 52
Spiced squares (recipe), 88
Spices for potpourri, 182
Spinach, in Caprilands salad,
    142
Sponge cake with geranium
    flavor, 41
Spring-green spread (recipe),
    84
Squash, summer, soup, 139
Stachys grandiflora, 315
  olympica, 130, 145, *314*-
    315
Stained-glass-window garden,
    15-16
Statice, 132, 194
Strawberry, 25, 181
  Alpine, 25
  'Baron Solemacher,' *181*
  culture indoors, 25
  French, 7
  runnerless, 25
  tea, 52
Strawflower, 132
Styrax benzoin, 186
Sugar frosting (recipe), 85
Sugar, rose geranium, 40, 144
Sugared rose cookies, 144
Sumac, 55, 57, 198
Summer squash soup, 139
Sweet alyssum, 146
Sweet bay, 151
Sweet cicely, 62, *286*-287

main discussion of, 287
sowing seeds, 62
Sweet pea, 20
Sweet potato casserole, 174
Sweet woodruff, 6, 56, 62, 78,
    79, 80, 82-83, 181,
    132-133, 196
  sowing seeds, 62
  toleration of lime in soil,
    56
Swiss chard, 9

Tagetes, 118, 138, 146
  pumila, 138
Tanacetum vulgare, *316*-317
  v. crispum, 317
Tansy, 7, 17, 55, 65, 133,
    150, 165, 194, 198,
    208, *316*-317
  fernleaf, 317
  in door swag, *208*
  tea, 52
Tarragon, 6-7, 9, 11, 21-22,
    62, *81*, 133-134, 152,
    155, 164, 181
  harvesting, 133-134
  in culinary box, 21-22
  propagation, 62
Tea, herb, 43-52
  holly, 2
  how to brew, 46
  wild thyme, 68
Teasel, 92, *122*, 134, 166, *208*
  in door swag, *208*
Teucrium chamaedrys, 319
  lucidum, 6, *318*-319
Thermopsis, 134
Thyme, 6-7, 15, 17, 21-22, 26,
    56, 57, *59*, 60-62, 64-
    77, *65*, *81*, 91, 93-94,
    98, 103, 122, 124,
    146-148, 168, 193,
    196
  'Caprilands,' 13, 72, 75
  caraway, 71
  creeping, 7, 11, 13, 53, 69

culinary, 9, 69
culture indoors, 26
golden, 10, 194
golden-edged, 26
golden lemon, 70
Greek, 66
how to dry, 122
how to plant, 75
in culinary box, 21-22
lemon, 11, 22, 70, 181, 194
  in container garden, 22
marjoram-leaved, 74
narrow-leaf French, 70,
    181, 194
need for lime in soil, 56
pressing, 124
Scandinavian, 71
'Silver Lemon,' 26, 70, 194
sowing seeds, 60-62, 76
tea, 68
trailing, 11
vinegar, 68
weeding, 77
winter care, 77, 148
wooly-stemmed, 70, 71
Thymum, 64
Thymus angustifolius, 69
  britannicus, 71
  chamaedrys, 71
  cimicinus, 71
  glaber, 71
  herba-barona, 71
  lanicaulis, 70, 71
  marschallianus, 71
  serpyllum, 67, 69, 70-74,
    76
    sowing seeds, 76
  s. albus, 72
  s. argenteus, 26, 70, 72
  s. aureus, 26, 70, 72
  s. 'Caprilands,' 72
  s. 'Clear Gold,' 73
  s. coccineus, 73
  s. c. Splendens, 73
  s. conglomerata, 73
  s. 'Golden Lemon,' 72

s. 'Gold-leaved,' 73
s. lanuginosus, 71, 73
s. l. 'Hall's Wooly,' 71, 73
s. micans, 74
s. 'Misty Green,' 74
s. nummularius, 74
s. 'Nutmeg,' 74
s. 'Pine-scented,' 74
s. roseus, 74
s. 'Silver Lemon,' 72
s. vulgaris, 70, 72, 74
vulgaris, 10, 53, 62, 67, 69-70, 75-76
   hedges of, 53
   sowing seeds, 62, 76
v. 'Broadleaf English,' 75
v. fragrantissimus, 26
v. 'Narrowleaf English,' 75
v. 'Narrowleaf French,' 75
zygis, 75
z. gracilis, 75
Tonka beans, 182, 185-186
Tonquin bean, 186
Top onion, 235
Tradescantia blossfeldiana, 40
   fluminensis striata, 39
Trees, herbal, 329
Tubs for herbs, 20-21

Valeriana officinalis, 320-321
Vegetables, herbs boiled as, 332
Venus' basin, 92
Verbena, lemon, 6-7, 11, 19-20, 22, 24, *38,* 97, 150, 181, 276-277
   culture indoors, 24
   in container garden, 22
   in home greenhouse, 20
   feeding, 97
   under fluorescent light, 19
Veronica officinalis, 52
Vervain, 136, 194
Vetiveria zizanoides, 184
Vetiver root, 184

Vinca major variegata, 40
   minor, 196
Vinegar, thyme, 68
Viola odorata, 323
   tricolor, 323
Violet, sweet, 80, 83, 181, 323

Wagonwheel garden of herbs, 11-13
Wandering Jew, 40
Wassail bowl, recipe, 214-215
Wassail bowl, lamb's-ear, recipe, 215
Wheel garden, 11 *12,* 13
Wine, Caprilands May, recipe, 82
Wine jelly, recipe, 83
Wine, June, 137
Wine salad mold, 221
Winter protection, 2, 147-151
Woad, 17, 134
Wolfbane, 227
Woodbine, 55
Wormwood, 7, *59,* 61-62, *65,* 128, 145, 152, 154, *155*-160, 166
   beach, 156, 159-160
   fringed, 156
   Roman, *65,* 145, 156, 159
   sowing seeds, 61-62
Wreath, Advent, 196, *197,* 198
   Caprilands herb and spice, *195,* 199-200
   everlasting, of artemisia, 198-199
   herb, how to make, 193-200
   living, how to make, 194
   making, history of, 193-194
Yarb patch, 15-16
Yarrow, 134, 166, 194, 198, 225
Yerbabuena, 111
Yew, 178